THE AMERICAN WAR IN VIET NAM

THE AMERICAN WAR IN VIET NAM

♦ CULTURAL MEMORIES AT THE TURN OF THE CENTURY

♦ SUSAN LYN EASTMAN

LEGACIES OF WAR · G. KURT PIEHLER, SERIES EDITOR

THE UNIVERSITY OF TENNESSEE PRESS / KNOXVILLE

The Legacies of War series presents a variety of works—from scholarly monographs to memoirs—that examine the impact of war on society, both in the United States and globally. The wide scope of the series might include war's effects on civilian populations, its lingering consequences for veterans, and the role of individual nations and the international community in confronting genocide and other injustices born of war.

Copyright © 2017 by The University of Tennessee Press / Knoxville.
All Rights Reserved. Manufactured in the United States of America.
First Edition.

LIBRARY OF CONGRESS CATALOGING-IN-PUBLICATION DATA
Names: Eastman, Susan Lyn, author.
Title: The American war in Viet Nam: cultural memories
at the turn of the century / Susan Lyn Eastman.
Description: Knoxville: The University of Tennessee Press, 2017. |
Series: Legacies of war | Includes bibliographical references and index.
Identifiers: LCCN 2016033833| ISBN 9781621902973 (hardcover) |
ISBN 9781621902997 (kindle)
Subjects: LCSH: Vietnam War, 1961–1975—Social aspects. | Vietnam War,
1961–1975—Influence. | Memory—Sociological aspects. | Collective memory. |
War and society.
Classification: LCC DS559.8.S6 E17 2017 | DDC 959.704/3—dc23
LC record available at https://lccn.loc.gov/2016033833

CONTENTS

ILLUSTRATIONS

FOREWORD

Why does the memory of some wars fade? Certainly the passing of a wartime generation can explain why conflicts such as the War of 1812, Spanish American War, Phillipine American War, and even the Korean War have fallen from the national consciousness. But time does not automatically lead to forgetfulness, and the American Civil War continues to evoke passions and even controversies even though the fighting ended over 150 years ago. Americans remember the American Revolution and continue to celebrate with parades, concerts, and fireworks, even if hatred of the former colonial oppressor has disappeared.

Many wars are forgotten despite the best efforts to preserve their memory. The generation that answered President Woodrow Wilson's call to "make the world safe for democracy" built thousands of monuments to commemorate the World War. They created a new national holiday, Armistice Day, to remember the "war to end all wars." This war spawned novels and poetry that have entered the literary canon. But America's entry in the Second World War in 1941 required a recasting of the commemoration of the World War into the First World War. In the aftermath of the Second World War, Armistice Day would be renamed Veterans Day and no longer just commemorate those who served in 1917-1918 but honor the servicemen and servicewomen who fought in all of America's wars. This reimagining of the First World War over time subsumed and ultimately fostered a fading of this conflict in the American collective memory.

The First World War and Vietnam War share many parallels. Both produced significant antiwar movements and deep divisions within society. Both spurred intense interest in commemoration through monuments as part of the process to heal those societal divisions. In the case of Vietnam, this conflict led to the revival of building war memorials that had largely fallen in abeyance after World War II. As Susan Lyn Eastman in the *American War in Viet Nam* shows convincingly, the United States's entry into major wars in Iraq and Afghanistan has not fostered the same forgetfulness that surrounded the First World War in the closing decades of the Twentieth Century. But like the First World War, memories of the Vietnam War have been recast and new ones fostered.

Vietnam still divides, and Americans profoundly disagree over the lessons that should be learned from it. In fact, Eastman argues that there is no one single memory of this war, but more accurately it should be viewed as a collected memory. Those who shape this memory through monuments, poetry, novels, motion pictures, and memoirs are diverse and include not just veterans but also their spouses, the children of the refugees that fled South Vietnam in 1975, and even former enemies. Literary works and memoirs by North Vietnamese and National Liberation Front adversaries have found an audience among Americans.

On a personal note, it has been gratifying as the series editor to see this work evolve from a dissertation proposal to a sophisticated interdisciplinary monograph that will interest anyone seeking to understand the impact of the Vietnam War on America's culture and society in the closing decades of the Twentieth Century and the opening years of the Twenty-First Century. This study illuminates not only the continuing hold of Vietnam on American collected memory but also how this conflict has shaped American's response to the continuing wars in Afghanistan and Iraq. As a teacher I am still haunted by the lecture I delivered on September 11, 2001, to my U.S. military history class while the attacks on the World Trade Center and Pentagon unfolded. In a class filled with ROTC cadets, I speculated on what these attacks meant for my students and how a possible war against Afghanistan might unfold, noting conflicts such as Vietnam. Sadly, fifteen years after invading Afghanistan the United States is engaged in a conflict that will likely surpass Vietnam as America's longest war.

G. KURT PIEHLER
Florida State University

PREFACE
• READING OF THE NAMES CEREMONY

THIRTIETH ANNIVERSARY
OF THE VIETNAM VETERANS MEMORIAL

As I approach the Vietnam Veterans Memorial, I hear murmuring echoes of voices reciting the names of the dead, but I cannot distinguish any names. These are women's voices and it feels appropriate . . . I am a woman here to read the names. Women endure great loss in war—they are wives, sisters, mothers, girlfriends, daughters. Later, I witness a sister among the readers; she paused to explain this when she read her brother's name. A daughter, too, fills our ranks. She is older. I feel a connection but do not speak to her because it is almost embarrassing to imply that because our fathers both served in the war we have something in common. We don't. My father is alive; hers is not. She has a label—a Gold Star Child. I can only argue for a label that semantics disputes: "Second-Generation." But we do have something in common; we are both affected by the war, and we are among the very few of our generation here today.

Walking down the east side of the memorial toward the stage at the apex, the memorial walkway feels wider, and the wall seems higher than the crush of the crowd I experienced on the Memorial Day weekend when I brought out-of-town guests to the Mall for their first visit. No, this time the wall overwhelms me as its height grows and I shrink. Today the apex feels like a chasm, as the critics once said. But that effect is appropriate. One should feel small, juxtaposed flesh against thousands of engraved names. The light is different today, the reflection does not layer over or appear behind the names, and the names are a clear grey, solidly etched into the black granite, not wavering liquid reflections as they appear at night.

Yellow ball caps identify the volunteers herding, arranging, and keeping time for other volunteers like myself who have come to participate—to read the names of the dead and missing for the Thirtieth Anniversary of the Vietnam Veterans Memorial. They are of the Vietnam Generation. The readers are, too. So are the observers waiting, listening in the seats arranged for the occasion and in anticipation of tomorrow's Veteran's Day ceremony at the Wall. I am thanked for "doing this," asked to take a seat among observers and other readers, asked to wait.

Now I wait in line. Three female friends of the Vietnam Generation and a man also of that age wait in front of me. A short line forms behind me; they are also men and women of the Vietnam Generation. I am distinctly younger among this group. But wait. I hear John Rambo's name being read and smile. Yes, John Rambo is on the Wall. Well, not really. His name is Arthur John Rambo. Tourists once made rubbings of his name. Do they still?

Repeatedly volunteers request that I read slowly because we are ahead of schedule. When the three female friends complete reading their lists of names, they form a circular hug—again, emotions surge inside me. But then a man reads, and now it is my turn. "Slowly," the volunteer requests, again. I walk slowly toward the stage . . . too slow, so I speed up to a normal walking pace.

At the podium I look up. I carefully enunciate the first name on my list of thirty. Robin—yes, a woman, I try to tell the audience as I say her name.[1] I pause between names. "Slowly, slowly"—the request echoes in my head. Between names, I look at those seated in front of the stage. This will help me slow down, I think. However, this gives me time to reflect. The Vietnam veteran among the audience watches me. Is he waiting for a name? Wondering about my age? My connection? I begin to think about each name, only 30 among the 58,307. Each died in a senseless war, each a senseless death; each had families and friends, each a potential life yet to live. Each loss significant. And I have only 30 to invoke, only 30 overwhelming names.

While my voice wavers among some names that begin to dance on the page as my eyes blur with tears, I breathe and calm myself, not wanting to swallow a single name, a single syllable, desiring that each should be heard clearly. I'm thinking again, between names. Yes, I am younger and my connection—my story—is that my generation, too, is affected by this war, these deaths, this memorial, these names, this loss. The war shaped my life and my identity. My father is a Vietnam veteran.

But now I am done, I've completed my list. As I walk off stage, my body trembles with the thought—that was only thirty names and now I am crying. My mother warned me. In the weeks leading up to the event, she asked me how many names I would read and declaratively questioned, "But aren't you sensitive?" I joked about this with friends in the days leading up to the ceremony, laughing about how I shrugged her off by saying, "But I'm not ten anymore, Ma."

When I eventually leave the site, I reflect on my tears: "I said I wouldn't cry, dammit!" My internal scolding mingles with Komunyakaa's "Facing It." He writes, "I said I wouldn't / dammit: No tears / I'm stone / I'm flesh" (3–5). I hear these lines with far greater clarity of emotion now. No longer the distant scholar of the poem. I, too, said I wouldn't cry, summoning my strength only to encounter the still "sensitive" self. I am not stone, I am flesh overwhelmed by the stone names that were once flesh and are now symbolically embodied flesh in a kind of objective-correlative transubstantiation of emotion brought on by the act of reading and feeling. And that was only thirty names. It was only thirty American names. Neither my reading nor this fittingly abstract memorial account for the deaths of so many others caused by the war, and it certainly does not account for the more than one million Vietnamese dead. It was, after all, only thirty names.

NOVEMBER 10, 2015
Washington, D.C.

ACKNOWLEDGMENTS

I am grateful to more people than I can name for their encouragement and patience through the challenges and successes of this endeavor. This book would not be possible without my family, my childhood experiences, and my father, Bruce Eastman. You are, to borrow the title of Tom Bissell's novel about his father, who also served in the war, "The Father of All Things." Without you it wouldn't have been possible. To my mother, Karen Eastman, whose loving support and constant understanding helped me survive so much more than just this process, thank you for seeing me as I am. My parents who, through my upbringing, helped ensure that neither I nor my life would be vapid. They gave me meaning. They showed me what it meant to work hard and to be disappointed and to keep pushing forward. Thank you for showing me how to persevere. My brothers, Matthew Eastman and Bryan Eastman, also played a significant role in shaping my childhood. I would also like to share my affection for "the girls" in my life, my sister Jennifer and her lovely daughters, Hannah and Hazel. I am grateful to Scott Henshaw for sharing the popular culture of our childhoods and being most intimately involved with the emotional challenges of the project. Thank you for understanding Michael Herr's "Vietnam. We've all been there" and our many years of "all Vietnam, all the time."

Many friends provided moral support along the way, particularly Tracy Pirkle, who continuously helps me cherish and connect with who I always was and continue to be and James Arnett who helped me conquer that last big hurdle.

This book began as a dissertation, and my committee, Dr. La Vinia Delois Jennings, Dr. Charles Maland, Dr. Benjamin Lee, and Dr. G. Kurt Piehler were all supportive and helpful. La Vinia tirelessly molded me into a sharper thinker and writer. Thank you for sharing your time with me and for believing in the import of the project. I would like to thank Dr. Maland for making a crucial impact on the possibility of this project when, during my master's thesis defense, he acknowledged and championed the personal significance the subject holds for me. I also appreciate Dr. Lee for enthusiastically joining the project and endorsing my approach. Finally, thank you Kurt for your generosity of spirit and for the conversations that always left me ready to write, for challenging me to consider if and when the war might be forgotten, and for guiding me through the process of professionalization.

Special recognition goes to Duery Felton, museum curator for the Vietnam Veterans Memorial Collection (VVMC) and Bob Sonderman, director of the National Parks Services Museum Resource Center, the facility that houses the VVMC. Mr. Felton was extremely helpful in preparing me to conduct archival research at the VVMC, and both he and Mr. Sonderman were generous with their time during my visits to the VVMC. Without their guidance and approval, I would not have been able to fully see the scope of objects that visitors leave at the Vietnam Veterans Memorial despite numerous visits to the memorial. That research was made possible by a faculty development grant provided by the Faculty Affairs Committee at Potomac State College of West Virginia University. In addition, the Office of Equity and Diversity at the University of Tennessee, Chattanooga graciously provided funding for indexing services.

I would also like to champion the poets who wrote such engaging poems and their presses who were generous with their permissions; thank you for reducing the stress and anxiety of the permissions process. My editor, Thomas Wells is perfect for helping first-time book authors through the publication process. He was always generously helpful and reasonable. So too was the staff at the University of Tennessee Press. The copyeditor Gene Adair was a careful, ethical reader.

I would also like to commend my students in my "Remembering the American War in Viet Nam" courses at the University of Tennessee–Knoxville who showed a sincere interest and revealed new modes of remembering the war. Here, I especially want to acknowledge Sarah Jones, who thanked me for providing "a way for [her] to understand [her] father better."

Finally, I want to recognize all who endure war as well as their families and those among them who share their memories.

A NOTE ON NOMENCLATURE

"Vietnam" is an American term used in the United States and elsewhere to signify an American "experience." However, as others have noted before, "Vietnam" is not a war, it is a country. Most Vietnamese words have one syllable; therefore, the name of the country is not "Vietnam," but Viet Nam, according to appropriate bifurcated rendering. Thus, what is commonly known in America as the "Vietnam War," and in Viet Nam as the "American War," is designated throughout this book as "the American War in Viet Nam." Moreover, Viet Nam has experienced and engaged in many wars. To term the American War in Viet Nam the "Vietnam War" privileges the American experience and ignores the very history of Viet Nam. The choice is not merely a matter of syntax; it is also political. This solution isn't perfect; it calls attention to only two countries involved in a far more complex war. However, recent suggestions to refer to the war as the "Second Indochina War" are not appealing because far too many audiences will not readily identify the "Second Indochina War" as the same war Americans once called "the Vietnam War." Still, because they are American place names, "Vietnam Veterans Memorial" and "Vietnam Women's Memorial," as well as "Vietnam veterans" and all other American titles of American memorials, groups, and organizations, in addition to the use of the name in quotations, maintain their original, fused American spelling.

THE AMERICAN WAR IN VIET NAM

INTRODUCTION
⋆ REMEMBRANCE BEYOND
THE BATTLEFIELD

The American War in Viet Nam (1959–75) was and remains a national crisis ripe for expressing both profound disillusionment *and* the emergence of American mythic identity and memory.[1] The war continues to disrupt the American myth of exceptionalism, which holds that American democracy is morally superior to other political systems and that powerful technology and indefatigable masculine capability back American foreign policy. More generally, the myth holds that the ideal American is self-reliant, capable of warding off foreign "evil," and inherently benevolent. The shattering of the myth of American exceptionalism during the war years is central to the battle over American remembrance of the war. As Americans confront the "War on Terror," they now encounter both attempts to reinstate the myth of American exceptionalism and memories of a collective disillusionment.

Myths of American exceptionalism depend on a powerful narrative of manifest destiny, patriotism, technological supremacy, masculine capability, democratic legitimacy, freedom, and dichotomies of good and evil. Americans learned from the Gulf of Tonkin controversy (1964) and Watergate scandals (1972–74) that they could no longer place implicit trust in their highest leaders.[2] The loss of the figurative national father stemmed from the acknowledgment that leaders are fallible, inept, self-serving, and at times dishonest.[3] Other important cultural shifts during the war era shattered myths of the exceptionalist American identity. These shifts include, but are not limited to, the civil rights movement of the 1960s, the second-wave feminist movement that began in the 1960s, the loss of pride in military service, and a felt impotence in the failure of an industrial and technological first-world superpower against an assumed third-world agrarian primitivism. These cultural shifts are key symbols of a personal and national identity compromised. Essentially they are a realization of lies, errors, inequalities, futile sacrifice, defeat, and ideals falling short of reality. In response to cultural shifts, memorial, literary, and cinematic subversions of disillusionment concerning American exceptionalism actively participate in cultural contestation over the memory of the American War in Viet Nam. Despite efforts at healing located in narratives and memorials of the American War in Viet Nam, the war continues to haunt American national memory, culture, politics, and military actions.

The texts addressed in the following chapters include a range of genres from memorials and poetry to cinematic and fictional narratives. With the exception of the Vietnam Veterans Memorial (1982), all representations of the war were published or produced since the Persian Gulf War (1990–1991) and through the "War on Terror" that began in response to the attacks on September 11, 2001 (9/11). Situating this exploration between these wars not only contemporizes the study but also imports twenty-first-century cultural, rhetorical, and political perspectives of understanding why the American War in Viet Nam continues to haunt the United States' politics and its military, government, soldiers, and civilians. Moreover, the choice of narratives aims to demonstrate that memories of the war are not solely American, nor Vietnamese, but that memories of the war find new transnational contexts in the twenty-first century via Vietnamese American and Philippine perspectives. Narrative representations of the war at the turn of the twenty-first century often simultaneously look to the prewar past and the postwar aftermath in order to demonstrate the flexibility of time, space, and place of memory.

MEMORY

This book considers several modes of memory. Imaginative memorial, literary, and cinematic representations of the American War in Viet Nam "always already" remember the war, culture, and society at the moment of their production. Yet these works also represent various means of remembering and memorializing the war and its aftereffects. The cultural relationship between memory and narrative found in memorial architecture, the time-based medium of narrative film as celluloid memorial, and the poem as memorial moment reveal the paradoxically time-bound and timeless nature of cultural memory. In addition, memorials, poetry, narrative remembrances, memorialization, and appropriation of the war have the potential to influence cultural memory, thereby affecting cultural, psychological, and political attitudes in the United States and around the world toward the prospect of war.

The focus on memories of the American War in Viet Nam establishes that a collected cultural memory—a culturally mediated gathering of contradictory memories—of the war and its aftermath in memorials, film, and literature published since 1990 demonstrates that the war cannot be simply relegated to the forgotten past. While some texts remember the war for the purpose of recuperation or reconciliation, other texts refuse the forgetfulness often required by recuperation and reconciliation.[4] Contending memories of the war expose the haunting nature and influence of the American War in Viet Nam on the "War on Terror."

TWENTY-FIRST CENTURY MEMORY

More than forty years after the 1975 fall of South Viet Nam's capital, Saigon, marked the undeniable end to the American War in Viet Nam, Americans summon the war for a variety of personal and political reasons in equally diverse ways as a test of faith, a barometer of truth and lies, a narrative of perseverance, and a legacy of error. For example, during the 2004 United States presidential election, Democratic presidential nominee John Kerry came under immediate Republican attack for invoking his service in the American War in Viet Nam to boost his credibility for the presidency. Specifically, a group called the Swift Boat Veterans for Truth responded to the Kerry campaign's focus on his service in the war, his receipt of Purple Heart medals for war wounds, his heroism during the war, and ultimately his courage to speak before Congress, asking for an end to the war in Viet Nam. Kerry's famous 1971 testimony before the U.S. Senate Foreign Relations Committee—wherein he asked, "How do you ask a man to die in Viet Nam? How do you ask a man to be the last man to die for a mistake?"—held particular relevance to his bid for the presidency during what many consider a misguided war in Iraq.[5]

However, John Kerry's service both in the military and against the war came under immediate fire. Questions of truth and authenticity pervaded as Swift Boat Veterans quickly swept in with allegations that Kerry's evocation of his wartime service was politically motivated and that all three of his Purple Heart medals resulted from superficial wounds "easily treated with band-aids" (3). They further claimed that Kerry incited the torture of American prisoners of war held in North Viet Nam when, in his allegedly "false" testimony before the Foreign Relations Committee, he spoke of American war crimes. Such assertions overshadowed incumbent President George W. Bush's service in and alleged desertion of the National Guard—the only military branch of service not deployed to Viet Nam during the war. Thus, Vietnam veteran John O'Neill and political science scholar Jerome Corsi alleged that John Kerry was "unfit for command," the phrase they used as the title of their book. United States citizens again engaged in a heated twenty-first-century debate over the war.

What does the 2004 presidential election reveal about America's cultural memory of the American War in Viet Nam? It suggests that the war continues to divide the country, that the war is not forgotten, and that the search for truth and authenticity stimulates memories of the war. American cultural memory of the American War in Viet Nam remains hotly contested. Historians and the public alike continue to debate who to blame for the loss of the war, which resulted in American withdrawal and the unification of Viet Nam under Communist control. Since the end of the war, the answer has varied from the antiwar movement and individuals such as Jane Fonda[6] to the veterans themselves, politicians, and the corruption in the southern Republic of Viet Nam (RVN). Because of the protracted ending and loss of the war, America's cultural memory of the war has experienced revolutions of healing, remembrance, and forgetfulness, in addition to revelations of ongoing psychological and political damage.

LITERARY AND CINEMATIC TRADITIONS • TWENTIETH-CENTURY REMEMBRANCE OF THE WAR

Representations of the war in cinematic and prose narratives evolved through several stages during the last forty years. Narratives of the 1970s tend to emphasize veteran guilt over fighting the war and civilian guilt over ignoring veterans. However, in 1979 Congress recognized posttraumatic stress disorder (PTSD), defined by the American Psychiatric Association as an anxiety disorder typified by avoidance, reexperiencing trauma, or hyperarousal.[7] With the recognition of PTSD, civilian concern for veterans began to replace guilt. Literary and cinematic traditions evolved in the early 1980s emphasizing recuperation—attempts to reestablish American masculinity or to "refight" the war: prisoner-of-war rescue narratives set in the 1980s provided a cathartic sense of redemption wherein private citizens accomplished rescue missions that the government could not carry out. In the late 1980s, narrative films emphasized realism and authenticity, yet war poetry of the decade responded to the national Vietnam Veterans Memorial (VVM) by meditating on the war's legacy and on American acts of memorialization.

THE "VIETNAM SYNDROME"

The 1980s were also a time in the United States when healing from the war became synonymous with revising memories of the war. Occurring within the specific historical context of the Reagan administration, the desire for recuperation and reconciliation, and thus healing, became a sought-after "cure" for the "Vietnam Syndrome"—a misnomer that categorizes antiwar sentiments as an "illness" in need of a "cure"—that has come to define the national postwar unwillingness to intervene militarily in the Third World.[8] According to literary and cultural critic Donald Pease, Ronald Reagan set forth a new understanding of the American War in Viet Nam, "renam[ing] the unwillingness to intervene in the Third-World a national pathology, the 'Vietnam Syndrome'" (558). Pease claimed that Reagan renamed American military reluctance because he was concerned with the "nation's loss of resolve" and thus hoped to reactivate "cold war certitudes" (558). Certainly, Reagan desired a "cure" for the "Vietnam Syndrome" and attempted to provide one in his 1980 Veterans of Foreign Wars convention campaign speech wherein he claimed that "for too long, we have lived with the 'Vietnam Syndrome' . . . [when the war] was, in truth, a noble cause. . . [And] we dishonor the [memory of the dead] when we give way to feelings of guilt as if we were doing something shameful" (Turner 63). Many United States citizens and Vietnam veterans hoped that the Vietnam Veterans Memorial would annul the "shame" and "guilt" associated with the war. However, as discussed in chapter 1, responses to and interactions with the memorial are too varied to symbolize collective national healing.

REMEMBERING THE WAR SINCE THE PERSIAN GULF WAR

The 1990s marked the post–Cold War era. Seemingly, Americans could then put Reagan's "Vietnam Syndrome" behind them. Yet in the 1990s the United States engaged in a war in the Middle East, the Persian Gulf War (1990–1991), wherein American troops pushed the Iraqi army out of Kuwait and back into

Iraq, a militaristic precursor to the twenty-first-century Iraq War. In addition to the guilt and isolationism of the 1970s, revision and so-called limited United States military incursions—Nicaragua, bombings in Libya, invasion of Grenada, and funding of revolutionaries in Afghanistan in their war against the Soviet Union—plagued the 1980s and the 1990s.

The Persian Gulf War conveyed sentiments of victory and righteousness for Americans toward U.S. military operations. Continued attempts to relegate the American War in Viet Nam to the forgotten past found what many hoped would be a "cure" for the "Vietnam Syndrome" in a new successful military intervention overseas—the Persian Gulf War. That war provided President George Herbert Walker Bush an opportunity to declare just days after the end of the war in 1991 that there would be "no more Vietnams" and that America had "finally kicked the Vietnam Syndrome" (qtd. in Turner 120). As literary scholar Lynda Boose aptly noted, the Persian Gulf War produced "the parades, the cheers, the public excitement over military hardware, and the popular sloganeering about a 'new pride in America.' . . . In short, a revivified militarism" (584). Postwar celebration in Anthony Swofford's Persian Gulf War memoir, *Jarhead: A Marine's Chronicle of the Persian Gulf War and Other Battles* (2003), and Sam Mendes's cinematic adaptation, *Jarhead* (2005), signifies the connection between the Persian Gulf War and the American War in Viet Nam. For example, on the bus ride back to his California Marine base, Swofford notes the cheering crowds lining the streets "to welcome home the heroes" (205). However, a specter from the American War in Viet Nam disrupts this moment when a Vietnam veteran boards the bus to congratulate the Marines. Swofford describes the man as "obviously on and off the streets for many years, in and out of VA hospitals" (250). "Somewhat drunk," with tears rolling down his face (250), Mendes's Vietnam veteran thanks the newly anointed Persian Gulf War veterans because they "did it clean . . . [and] made [America] proud" (*Jarhead*). Swofford reflects (and the film tries to depict) that the welcome-home parade "might help the Vietnam vet heal his wounds" (251).

The American War in Viet Nam haunts Swofford's memoir.. His father is a Vietnam veteran and Swofford is conceived during his father's R&R in Hawaii. Swofford grows up desiring to be a Marine and eventually serves in the Gulf War as a lance corporal in a Marine Corps scout/sniper platoon. Very early in the book Swofford emphasizes the fog of war. For example, about his time in the Gulf War, he writes that "my vision was blurred—by wind and sand and distance, by false signals, poor communication, bad coordinates, by stupidity and fear and ignorance, by valor and false pride. By the mirage" (2). As early as page 2 and throughout *Jarhead*, Swofford easily critiques the military, the war, the media, the bravado of war. Often, these moments center on the ghostly presence of the American War in Viet Nam. The basic training scenes echo the brutality of Stanley Kubrick's *Full Metal Jacket* (1987). The troops watch *Apocalypse Now* (1978), *Platoon* (1986), and *Full Metal Jacket* to prepare for war. Swofford engages in the debate about whether or not these films are antiwar as some suggest; however, he declares that these films are in fact "all pro-war, no matter what the supposed message . . . [because] the magic brutality of the films celebrates the terrible and despicable beauty of [the soldiers'] fighting skills" (64). Swofford exposes the futility and brutality of military service, of war, and on the second-to-last page of the book makes this as clear as possible for the reader when he writes, "Some wars are unavoidable and need well be fought, but this doesn't erase warfare's waste. Sorry, we must say to the mothers whose sons will die horribly. This will never end. Sorry" (255). Despite Swofford's rejection of the war, the memoir includes that sentimental, celebratory moment that Sam Mendes's cinematic adaptation *Jarhead* exemplifies.

Like Swofford's book and Mendes's version of *Jarhead*, the Persian Gulf War contradictorily subdued memories of the American War in Viet Nam as it simultaneously invoked and revised a collected cultural memory of the war. Several scholars have addressed the Persian Gulf War's influence on American memory of the war in Viet Nam. Pease and Kaplan's *Cultures of U.S. Imperialism* (1993), for example, includes several essays that contrast the war with the American War in Viet Nam, often emphasizing the Persian Gulf War's role in "finally kick[ing] the Vietnam Syndrome," as the first President Bush declared in 1991 at the end of the war. Still others, such as cultural critics Susan Jeffords and Lauren Rabinovitz, have conducted compelling studies on the media representation of the Persian Gulf War, arguing that the war was highly censored and sanitized in response to the media coverage of the war in Viet Nam.

Moreover, in the 1990s with fiftieth-anniversary celebrations of World War II battles, representations of World War II dominated the American cultural imagination. America could finally turn away from its losses and celebrate its successes during World War II and the Persian Gulf War. The few representations of the American War in Viet Nam during this time turned toward reconciliation based on the seemingly innocuous notion that everyone suffers in war, bolstering desires for reconciliation. At a time when new but subtle voices and perspectives on the war emerged, reconciliation surfaced with the inclusion of women's experiences and perspectives represented in the 1993 dedication of the Vietnam Women's Memorial (VWM). In addition, the appearance of Vietnamese literature in English translation contributed to reconciliation via recognition of mutual psychological distress.[9] Normalization of relations between the United States and Viet Nam in 1994 under President Bill Clinton, President George H. W. Bush's successor, lifted the trade embargo against Viet Nam and encouraged further diplomatic reconciliation.

Yet, limited military incursions and perceived peace would not last. With the September 11, 2001, attacks on the World Trade Center in New York City and the U.S. Pentagon, along with a possible attempt on the White House by a third hijacked passenger plane that crashed before reaching its suspected destination, a new "War on Terror" began. At the turn of the millennium, it seemed that the American War in Viet Nam might finally be relegated to the forgotten past as cultural representational production of the war slowed—with one glaring exception, Randall Wallace's *We Were Soldiers* (2002), a cinematic adaptation of Harold G. Moore and Joseph L. Galloway's memoir *We Were Soldiers Once . . . and Young* (1992). Although the publication and release of other memoirs, novels, and narrative films about the American War in Viet Nam occurred around the same time, audiences generally overlooked them in favor of the wider release of Wallace's film. Reconciliation and American memory of the war were consolidated most significantly in *We Were Soldiers*, a film that emphasizes the strength and suffering of American women and the People's Army of the Republic of Viet Nam (PAVN), also commonly referred to as the NVA (North Vietnamese Army) of North Viet Nam (more properly, the Democratic Republic of Viet Nam, or DRVN) as prominent narrative elements of reconciliation.

MEMORY AND MEMORIAL

Memory always negotiates a tenuous relationship with the past. Memory is not static; it is historically and culturally specific, meaning diverse things to people in different times, places, and cultures. Memory theorists raise important questions concerning the modes of memory that individuals, cultures, and nations implement and to what end. For example, Durkheimian theorist Maurice Halbwachs, the first to define "cultural memory," understands group identities as the primary structure for collective memory (Fentress and Wickham ix). In *Collective Cultural Memory* (1950), Halbwachs argues that individuals acquire memories through society—family, religion, and social class. He claims that all memories are therefore collective and are always in accordance with the predominant thoughts of a particular society. Halbwach's collective focus demands further questions: how, for example, can one explore collective memory without regarding the individual as submissively obeying an interiorized collective force? Considering Sigmund Freud's work on screen memories and his understanding of memories as composites mediated through representation, it is easier to understand the complex nature of memory as an entanglement of collective and individual memories. In addition, trauma theorist Cathy Caruth defines traumatic memory as belated and beyond the point or place of inception. Bleeding into and fermenting at the intersection of American memory and imagination, traumatic memory of the war exceeds individual soldiers, a singular generation, and specific countries.

Rejecting opposition between history and memory, cultural critic Marita Sturken contends that "cultural memory" rather than collective memory emerges at the intersection of history and memory. The concept of cultural memory engages other recent developments in memory theory put forth by critics James Young and Alison Landsberg. Writing within and against the tradition of memory theory, Landsberg labels memory in modern mass culture as "prosthetic" because the memories are not natural, organic, lived, or inherited, but derived from mediated representation. Landsberg defines prosthetic memory as an individual's "deeply felt memory of a past event through which he or she did not live" (2). Prosthetic memories share similarities with "post-memories," Marianne Hirsch's term for present and future remembrance of the Holocaust, because they provide for ongoing remembrance (3). Prosthetic memories can result from an engagement with a mediated representation of events not expressly experienced by those who form these prosthetic, rather than direct, memories. Inspired by Marcel Proust's description of the smell, texture, and taste of a piece of *petites madeleines* provoking childhood memories in *À la recereché du Temps Perdu*, translated as *Remembrance of Things Past* or *In Search of Lost Time* (1909–1922), Landsberg stresses that mediated representations or experiential sites—a film, a memorial, or a museum—arouse the senses of sight, sound, and touch. Exposure to these mediated representations holds the possibility for individuals to acquire prosthetic memories of an event or events being remembered or memorialized. Derived from mediated representation, prosthetic memory arises from a commingling of personal and historical memory, thereby making particular memories more widely available. Mediated representations of the American War in Viet Nam—memorials, poetry, prose narratives, and narrative films—rest at the center of the following chapters. Ultimately, collected cultural and prosthetic memories, because they reject unification of memory, refuse to relegate the American War in Viet Nam to the forgotten past.

While I adopt Landsberg's delineation of prosthetic memory as an inspiration, the term can be developed beyond her theory. The designation "prosthetic" invokes a replacement, a substitute, a removable attachment, and an addendum. Thus, prosthetic memories are new memories, different memories that may or may not appear to perform the same functions of healing or revision as memories held by those with direct experience of the events remembered. Sometimes these new memories replace older memories and most often they are addendums to earlier memories. New memories reimagine, reinvent, revise, and remember; the possibilities are limitless. Significantly, new memories ensure that the war is not forgotten.

Prosthetic also invokes amputation and its often-attendant phantom limb syndrome—the perception of feeling, often pain or discomfort, in the absent amputated limb. This haunting sensation of present absence gives the impression that the limb still exists. One of the most common cures for phantom limb syndrome is a mirror box wherein the patient places his or her parallel remaining limb and regards the reflection as the missing limb. Doing so provides the patient with a sense of being able to move the missing limb. Returning to a preamputation past provides a reenactment of movement, and a memory of the lost limb that often provides the "cure" of closure for patients suffering from phantom limb pain. Likewise, imaginative representations of the war at the turn of the twenty-first century reflect the past in the present. Public and private memorialization and memorial performances often seek to reenact or revisit the past in order to assuage the pain. Memories of the American War in Viet Nam at the turn of the century supplement the memories of the 1970s and 1980s. Yet, these earlier memories linger like a phantom limb.

Moreover, prosthetic memory acquired through memorialization by those with no direct experience of the war demonstrates that the memories of the war do not solely belong to those of a singular generation within particular countries that participated in or witnessed the war directly or from the home front. Prosthetic memory broadens the possibilities of remembrance. It circumvents identity politics and thereby suggests that memories of the past and memories of the American War in Viet Nam are transgenerational and transnational. Thus, I begin with a formulation of a collected cultural memory to demonstrate that transgenerational, transnational, and prosthetic memories of the war continue to be shaped and reshaped in imaginative representations of the war.

Situated within the tradition of memory theory, the discussion of memory and memorial in the following chapters aims also to delineate a definition of a collected cultural memory of the American War in Viet Nam. The formulation of collected cultural memory joins and transcends Marita Sturken's cultural memory, Alison Landsberg's prosthetic memory, and James Young's regard of memorial sites as places of collected, rather than collective, memories. In accordance with Young in his *Texture of Memory* (1993), "collective memory" signifies cohesion, whereas "collected memory" suggests the contentious nature of cultural memory (xi–xii). Collected memory is a compilation of multifaceted, sometimes competing, individual and group memories.

The term emerges from the insufficiencies of the phrase cultural memory in that memories of the war do not always coincide with the predominant thoughts of society. Thus the combination of "collective" and "cultural" results in a collected cultural memory. The terminology also imports the cultural emphasis of collected memory found in Sturken's theory of cultural memory as shared outside formal historical discourse and situated among culturally mediated negotiations. The concept of collected cultural memories, then, refers to a culturally mediated collection of multifaceted memories. Although there may be a cultural shift in the 1990s towards recuperation and healing, memories also exist that reject the forgetfulness necessary for recuperation. Memorial, cinematic, and literary representations of the war often represent a collection of contending memories and proffer the possibility of prosthetic memory.

RECUPERATION AND RECONCILIATION

The following chapters focus on poetry, prose narratives, and cinematic narratives created between the Persian Gulf War (1990–1991) and 2013, well into the "War on Terror" that began in 2001. Situating this exploration between these wars not only contemporizes the study, but also requires consideration of twenty-first-century cultural, rhetorical, and political perspectives about why memories of the American War in Viet Nam continue to haunt, to varying degrees, the United States' military, government, soldiers, and civilians.

Although there are countless memoirs, many of them superb, written at the turn of the millennium, such as Tobias Wolff's In Pharaoh's Army: Memories of the Lost War (1994), Albert French's Patches of Fire (1998), Nathaniel Tripp's Father Soldier Son: Memoir of a Platoon Leader in Vietnam (1998), Kien Nguyen's The Unwanted: A Memoir of Childhood (2002), Andrew Pham's Catfish and Mandala (2000) and The Eaves of Heaven (2008), David Donovan's Once A Warrior King: Memories of an Officer in Vietnam (2005), Lac Su's I Love Yous Are for White People (2009), and Karl Marlantes's Matterhorn (2011) and What It Is Like to Go to War (2011), among many others, memoirs receive minimal attention in this book, except when they are clearly related to the films discussed herein. Instead, imaginative representations take center stage. They are among the most highly mediated representations of the war, and mediated representation rests at the center of prosthetic memory.

My analysis of memorial sites, poetry, and narratives of recuperation and reconciliation in the following chapters relies on a general consensus in the field of Vietnam War studies that considers the shift in national American memory of the war from a sense of guilt in the 1970s, through the revisionist refighting of the war in the 1980s, to "kicking" the "Vietnam Syndrome" in the 1990s. Often, the key to recuperation and reconciliation is healing through recognition. In addition, reconciliation emphasizes the notion that everyone suffers in war. In reconciliationist texts American men and women suffer alike; however, as reconciliationist texts show, the suffering extends beyond Americans to include the Vietnamese from the northern DRVN and southern RVN. Reconciliation also often requires forgetfulness. Therefore, lack of healing and an understanding of the far-reaching consequences of the American War in Viet Nam undermine reconciliation. For example, consequences of the war exceed both American and Vietnamese suffering in Jessica Hagedorn's Dream Jungle (2003) discussed in chapter 7. Consequences of the war also include transgenerational American and Vietnamese memories and disillusionment, as well as the New Vietnam Syndrome that emerges, affecting the policies of and attitudes toward the War on Terror.

Chapter 1, "Reflections of Memory: Past Presence and Present Absence at the Vietnam Veterans Memorial," focuses on remembrance at the National Vietnam Veteran's Memorial (VVM) in Washington D.C. Although the VVM was dedicated in 1982, this study commences with the memorial because it became a catalyst for the turn-of-the-century narrative, cinematic, and poetic memories of the war. The chapter does not examine the controversy over Chinese American undergraduate architectural student Maya Lin's proposal, which won the design contest, because several studies, including the memorial project founders Jan Scruggs and Joel Swerdlow's book *To Heal a Nation* (1985), provide accounts and analysis of the debate over Lin's abstract design.[10] The chapter focuses instead on the memorial's aesthetic design, visitor interaction with the memorial (including the leaving of objects at the base of the memorial's walls), and the possibility of visitors creating prosthetic memories at the memorial. Memory theorist Pierre Nora's contention that an adversarial relationship exists between history (events) and memory (sites) informs the examination of memorials throughout the following chapters. Nora's concern is that memorial displaces the responsibility of memory onto the site or object; yet he also understands history as an incomplete and problematic reconstruction of that to which we no longer have access. Refusing to relegate the war to the forgotten past, the memorial's dynamic design, visitors' memorial performances, and poetry about the VVM culminate in a multifaceted collected cultural memory of the war that encourages prosthetic memory.

Chapter 2, "Poetic Remembrances at the Vietnam Veterans Memorial," examines what I term a "cycle of poetry" about visiting the VVM. These poems include W. D. Ehrhart's well- known "The Invasion of Grenada" (1984) and his lesser-known "Midnight at the Vietnam Veterans Memorial" (1993), Yusef Komunyakaa's "Facing It" (1988), and Doug Anderson's "The Wall" (1991). The chapter also discusses selections from Eugene Grollmes's obscure collection *At the Vietnam Veterans Memorial, Washington, D.C.: Between the Lines* (1988) and Lamonte B. Steptoe's "A Second Wall" (1990). By situating these poems at the VVM, a democratic space of memory, poets contribute to making memories of the war more accessible to those who did not directly experience it. The poetry serves as both mediated representations of remembering the war and as reflections on the VVM as a mediated remembrance of the war. The poems engage with the memorial's design—material, form, structure—and visitor interaction with the memorial. While the poems treat the same historical event, and each responds to remembrance at the VVM, some poems rebuff sentimental closure and others encourage the possibility of prosthetic memory. Set in the shared, democratic space of the memorial, those poems often present a fusion of past and present that joins individual memories in a collected cultural memory. Although many hoped the Vietnam Veterans

Memorial would be history's final chapter on the war, it instead generated further memories of the war that this study underscores.

Chapter 3, "Remembering Servicewomen: The Battle for the Vietnam Women's Memorial," emphasizes recuperation via representations that recognize women's war and postwar experiences. The chapter focuses on servicewomen's contribution to recuperation as portrayed in the Vietnam Women's Memorial (VWM), dedicated in 1993. The VWM has received little critical attention from scholars in the fields of memorial architecture, military history, cultural studies, and Vietnam War studies.[11] Hopefully, this oversight will be remedied because the VWM holds the potential to become a principal site for exploring American aesthetic representations of women and war. Educating the public about women's role in the war, the VWM provides a narrative to replace omission with recognition. The VWM's feminist origins, careful promotion, and the design itself engage the recuperative work of feminism. Although the VWM engages the political and historical failures to recognize women's military service in the war, its sculptural narrative—which calls attention to nurses' sometimes futile efforts to assist wounded and dying soldiers—evokes the central trauma that many American servicewomen experienced during and after the war. However, feminism also rests at the center of debate about the memorial. The memorial both succumbs to and resists patriarchal ideals of authenticity in order to legitimize military women's service in and responses to war.

Although the founders of the Vietnam Women's Memorial Fund hoped to provide a memorial for all women with any connection to the war, its sculpted figures characterize only military servicewomen who served in Viet Nam. Yet memories of the war also hold a profound psychological affect on American and Vietnamese civilian women, especially women who were married to servicemen and women who later married Vietnam veterans. Therefore, chapter 4, "Civilian Women: American and Vietnamese Married to Viet Nam," considers representations of the war's psychological affects on both American and Vietnamese civilian women. The chapter examines two representative fictional texts, Sandie Frazier's novel I Married Vietnam (1992) and Oliver Stone's film Heaven and Earth (1993). Frazier's postwar I Married Vietnam represents a small genre of sentimental novels by female authors who write of American women's lives after the war and center on their characters' relationships with American male veterans of the war. However, I Married Vietnam is unique in its treatment of memory, especially the power of traumatic memory transference and prosthetic memory. It is the very best of this genre; it is not a romance novel, but it is a love story. Like Frazier's novel, Oliver Stone's *Heaven and Earth* explores the commingling of memory between husband and wife. However, Stone portrays the psychological impact of the war on a civilian Vietnamese woman. Like Frazier's character Sam, Oliver Stone's Le Ly acquires prosthetic memories from her veteran husband's memories of the war; yet she also possesses her own direct memories of the war. Moreover, she serves—like the VWM's sculpted servicewomen—as a reconciliatory mediator between civilians and veterans, between Vietnamese and Americans, and between Vietnamese immigrant-refugees and those who remained in Viet Nam.

These narratives seek reconciliation between soldiers and civilians via recognition of women's wartime and postwar experiences. Moreover, they contribute to a collected cultural memory of the war resultant from both direct and prosthetic memories. These narratives reject forgetfulness by recognizing the psychological consequences of the war, beyond the battlefield, on American and Vietnamese service and civilian women.

Chapter 5, "Private Sites of American and Vietnamese Memory and Reconciliation in Viet Nam," examines individual memorial performances situated in Viet Nam. The Vietnam Veterans Memorial may provide a democratic space for shared memories; however, it remains a national space and a place where, unavoidably, national memory is one of many contending narratives. Private sites of memorial performances offer sanctuary from master narratives of national remembrance. The chapter pairs two Vietnamese novels, Bao Ninh's *The Sorrow of War* (1993) and Huong Thu Duong's *Novel Without a Name* (1995), with selections from Tim O'Brien's *The Things They Carried* (1990) and Sidney Furie's film *Going Back* (2001). The two Vietnamese novels are representative of Vietnamese war literature produced during and after the cultural relaxation period in Viet Nam known as *Doi Moi*. They also emphasize the relationship between place and memory in addition to private memorial sites in Viet Nam. Furie's *Going Back* was not a very popular film; however, it is a fictional representation of the many memoirs and documentaries about American veterans returning to Viet Nam, seeking out private memorial sites, and their attempts at healing via reconciliation with the past and with their former foes. All veterans of the war, the protagonists in these narratives visit specific sites of personal memory, usually the locale of particular deaths in the war. At these particular memory sites, memorial enactments, remembrances of the dead, and sometimes communion with the spirits of the dead provide invocations through which past and present merge. In the American narratives, witnesses with no direct access to memories of the war observe prosthetically mediated representations of the war through the memorial performances war veterans enact. Their newly attained memories reject relegating the war to the forgotten past. Moreover, these narratives, especially the Vietnamese novels, portray sites of memory as potential locations of reconciliation between the Vietnamese DRVN and RVN and between the Vietnamese and Americans. Thus, memories of the war in these turn-of-the-century narratives emphasize shared experience across enemy and soldier-civilian divisions.

REVISION AND REMEMBRANCE

In *Race and Reunion* (2001), historian David Blight argues that historical memory consists of deflections, evasions, and embittered and irreconcilable versions of experience. The phenomenon of regeneration and reconciliation that Blight identifies in literature and culture during the fifty years after the Civil War relies on various modes of remembrance and forgetfulness that the following chapters address. In *Mystic Chords of Memory* (1991), Michael Kammen contends that forgetfulness induces reconciliation and that contestation activates memory. Blight's and Kammen's work on memory and reconciliation provide models and theories for approaching the various modes of revision, forgetfulness, and remembrance of the American War in Viet Nam addressed in the following chapters. For example, Blight's understanding of the "Plantation School" of literature as presenting a more pleasing past informs my examination of the proliferation of World War II films in the 1990s. In addition, Blight's study of forgetfulness uncovers American traditions of making remembering safe. Remembering the war dead is easier than confronting the causes of war, particularly for the American Civil War and the American War in Viet Nam.

A collected cultural memory of the American War in Viet Nam unavoidably includes countless attempts to reframe the war as a noble cause. Therefore, chapter 6, "Forgetting the American War in Viet Nam: *We Were Soldiers*," argues that Randall Wallace's 2002 cinematic adaptation of Harold Moore and Joseph Galloway's memoir *We Were Soldiers Once . . . and Young* (1992) relies on the traditional generic conventions of the World War II combat film—battle tactics, leaders, and heroics—to recast the American War in Viet Nam as a "good war." The chapter begins by discussing the proliferation of American cultural remembrance of World War II at the turn of the millennium. As the New Vietnam Syndrome emerged and the battle over collective attitudes toward the "War on Terror" escalated, remembrance of the "good war," World War II, supplanted the desire to remember or forget the American War in Viet Nam.

Although Wallace's film is unique in its inclusive portrayal of civilian women on the American home front and proffers a more developed depiction of the PAVN than nearly any other American narrative of the war, it overlooks the cultural and political causes and consequences of the war in favor of representing the war as a fight for survival among "brothers in arms." By emphasizing the early battles and success stories of particular units, the film holds the potential to influence audiences to regard favorably the prospect of war. Moreover, Wallace's *We Were Soldiers* veils its revision and forgetfulness by attesting to its historical accuracy and the authenticity of experience. However, Moore and Galloway's subsequent memoir, *We Are Soldiers Still: A Journey Back to the Battlefields of Vietnam* (2008), rejects forgetfulness in favor of encouraging a postwar reconciliation based on mutual recognition between former American and Vietnamese foes. In addition, *We Are Soldiers Still* further clarifies the authors' negative assessment of the war as politically misguided, a parallel to their regard of the Iraq War. The book thereby reclaims a twenty-first-century remembrance of the war's aftermath in the shadow of the film's forgetfulness. Thus, even among narratives originating from the same authors, a collected cultural memory of the war is a contentious memory.

Chapter 7, "Unfinished Remembrance: Beyond the United States and Viet Nam—Jessica Hagedorn's *Dream Jungle* and Francis Ford Coppola's *Apocalypse Now Redux*," argues that the memory of the American War in Viet Nam exceeds the time, place, and space of the war. Situating memories of the war beyond America and Viet Nam contributes to the collected cultural memories of the war. The chapter pairs Jessica Hagedorn's novel *Dream Jungle* (2003) with Francis Ford Coppola's film *Apocalypse Now Redux* (2001). *Dream Jungle* interweaves fictional accounts of two 1970s controversies—the filming of *Apocalypse Now* and Manuel Elizalde Jr.'s 1971 "discovery" of a primitive tribe, the Tasaday, in the Philippines. Hagedorn's narrative primarily addresses the Philippines' colonial legacy wherein the memory of the American War in Viet Nam, via the filming of *Napalm Sunset*, her fictional double for *Apocalypse Now*, encroaches on the Philippines as an act of neocolonialism. In addition, *Dream Jungle* interrogates the meaning of *Apocalypse Now* and thereby questions the American War in Viet Nam.

Chapter 7 also examines Coppola's *Apocalypse Now: Redux* (2001) not merely for its twenty-first-century release date but, more important, because it, like Hagedorn's *Dream Jungle*, visits intertextual imperialist repetition on the

twenty-first century. Hagedorn reminds audiences of the Spanish colonization of the Philippines that preceded American colonization in order to
reveal American neocolonialism in the Philippines. Similarly, Coppola's *Redux*
reminds audiences of the French colonization of Viet Nam before American
militarism in Viet Nam. These two twenty-first-century narratives engage
with the enduring memory of the American War in Viet Nam by exploring
the cycle of telling and retelling colonial and neocolonial corruption. Their
repetitive need to retell the narratives of colonialism emphasizes the multifaceted memories of the American War in Viet Nam that exist well beyond
the literal and cultural battlefields of Viet Nam and the United States.

Chapter 8, "Vietnamese American Diaspora: Identity, Memory, and Repetition," demonstrates that memories of the American War in Viet Nam at
the turn of the twenty-first century are transnational and global memories.
Thus, this study addresses American, Vietnamese, Philippine, and Vietnamese
American texts as a means of exploring the major players in the war. Each
contribute to a collected cultural memory—a mediated gathering of polysemic
memories—of the war and its aftermath.

Moreover, chapter 8 focuses on Vietnamese American perspectives in
diasporic literature produced during the turn of the millennium emanating
from Vietnamese American authors of the 1.5 and second generations. The
"1.5 generation" refers to people who immigrate to another country in their
childhood or early teens. The literature chosen emphasizes diasporic identity,
interactions with American veterans of the war, repetition, and prosthetic
memory—thus, the significance of studying the 1.5- and second-generation
representations of memory in the war's aftermath. Three of the most widely-
read 1.5-generation and second-generation Vietnamese American authors
who illustrate issues of identity, interactions with American veterans of the
war, prosthetic memory, and repetition include Lan Cao in her *Monkey Bridge*
(1997), Andrew Lam in his three books, *Perfume Dreams: Reflections of the Vietnamese Diaspora* (2005), *East Eats West* (2010), and *Birds of Paradise Lost* (2013), and
GB Tran in his *Vietnamerica: A Family's Journey* (2010). This chapter traces the
influence that history, family, memory, and interactions with Americans and
the Vietnamese have on Vietnamese American diasporic identities. It also
explores how representations of prosthetic memory and repetition in these
texts reveal a transnational global memory, one that is rife with the possibilities of prosthetic memories that refuse to relegate the war, its aftermath, and
Vietnamese American diasporic experiences to the forgotten past.

The conclusion of this book—chapter 9, "Exit Strategy: The New Vietnam Syndrome"—imagines the possibilities and limitations of a future collected cultural memory of the American War in Viet Nam in the broader context of the "Global War on Terror," particularly the wars in Iraq and Afghanistan. The chapter addresses cultural memory's influence on the interrelationship between these wars and what I term the "New Vietnam Syndrome"—American reluctance to, and the seeming impossibility of, withdrawing from twenty-first-century wars for fear of reenacting the outcome of the American War in Viet Nam. Thus, the conclusion aims to demonstrate that the United States has not "kicked the Vietnam Syndrome" but that the war continues to resonate politically and militarily in the twenty-first-century War on Terror.

Although several earlier studies explore legacies of the American War in Viet Nam, no work published to date examines narratives, poetry, and memorials of the war published or dedicated between the Persian Gulf War (1990) and the War on Terror that began in 2001 as a means of examining the influence of contemporary war on remembrance of the war in Viet Nam. Most works examine representations of and political responses that appeared and occurred in the 1970s and 1980s. For example, John Hellmann's *American Myth and the Legacy of the Vietnam War* (1986) addresses the war in Viet Nam as an experience that called into question American myths of exceptionalism. Still other texts examine the literary or cinematic tradition of representing the war from the 1970s through the 1980s, emphasizing veteran characters, trauma, gender, or the revenge-plot revisionism of the 1980s.[12]

Few scholarly texts address post-1990 representations of the American War in Viet Nam. Although Guy Westwell's *War Cinema: Hollywood on the Front Line* (2006) discusses the emergence and dominance of World War II films in the 1990s, he dedicates only one chapter to contemporary films. Westwell's treatment of Vietnam War films, however, is limited to his discussion of *We Were Soldiers*. He does not include *Heaven and Earth* and *Going Back*, texts essential to the understanding of cultural memory treated in the following chapters. This study examines representations of both American and Vietnamese memory, as well as the possibilities of prosthetic memory. Moreover, the following chapters provide a contemporary perspective on recent narratives, poetry, and memorials that have received minimal attention in the field of Vietnam War studies.

Despite efforts at healing from the American War in Viet Nam, disillusionment with the myth of American exceptionalism continues to accompany a collected cultural memory of the war. Reconciliation, recognition, and recuperation fail to relegate the war to the forgotten past. Contemporary memorials, poetry, prose narratives, and cinematic narratives participate in a collected cultural remembrance of the war and continue to generate prosthetic memories of the American War in Viet Nam.

CHAPTER 1
✦ REFLECTIONS
OF MEMORY

PAST PRESENCE AND PRESENT ABSENCE AT THE
VIETNAM VETERANS MEMORIAL

The Vietnam Veterans Memorial (VVM) in Washington, D.C., serves as the nation's central symbolic memory location of the American War in Viet Nam. Situated on the National Mall between the Lincoln Memorial and the Washington Memorial, the VVM, also known as *The Wall*, provides a democratic space of remembrance. Dedicated in 1982 and designed by architect Maya Lin, the VVM lists the names of the 58,307 American servicemen and servicewomen killed in the American War in Viet Nam. Since its dedication, over four million annual visitors have deposited over fifty thousand objects of remembrance at the VVM. In leaving and viewing these objects, visitors contribute to and actively engage in an ongoing collected cultural memory of the war that broadens memories of the war to include personal memories in public space. Here, "collected" memory is distinct from "collective" memory, which indicates cohesion, while "collected memory" illustrates a compilation of multifaceted, sometime competing, individual and group memories. These interactions with the VVM result in the possibility of attaining prosthetic memory—newly acquired, individually felt memories of the war for those with no direct memories of or hereditary connection to the war.[1]

The statement of purpose for the VVM, created by the Vietnam Veterans Memorial Fund (VVMF), includes the following: "The purpose of the Vietnam veterans memorial is to recognize and honor those who served and died.... The Memorial will make no political statement regarding the war or its conduct. It will transcend those issues. The hope is that the creation of the Memorial will begin a healing process" (Scruggs and Swerdlow 53).

The statement's emphasis on healing indicates the perceived need on behalf of the VVMF for recuperation and reconciliation. Together, recuperation and reconciliation help reestablish national cohesion. The VVMF hoped that the memorial would "transcend" divisions over the war and "its conduct" and would not only recognize service and sacrifice but also reconcile veterans with civilians, especially those who participated in the antiwar movement. The desire for recuperation and reconciliation occurs within a specific historical context, during the Reagan administration and the age of the "Vietnam Syndrome"—Reagan's misnomer for antiwar sentiments and the national postwar unwillingness to intervene militarily in the Third World.[2] While, for some, the VVM's emphasis on healing, recuperation, and recognition may indeed succeed in transcending divisions over the war, the memorial's abstract design ultimately resists closure of the past. The VVM is a catalyst that encourages visitor participation in a collected cultural memory—a culturally mediated collection of multifaceted memories. More important, the memorial encourages the formation of prosthetic memories—newly acquired memories by those with no experiential or hereditary connection to the war. Prosthetic memories encourage ongoing memories that refuse to relegate the war to the forgotten past.

Maya Lin's abstract design of the Vietnam Veterans Memorial participates in and encourages a collected cultural memory via its reflective surface, its visceral imperative of the engraved names, and its nonlinear chronological approaches to representing time and memory. At the VVM visitors respond to and interact with the memorial's design through individual and communal acts of remembrance, thus participating in collected cultural and prosthetic memory. Enacting memorial performances, visitors make speeches, mount protests, take photos of or make charcoal rubbings on paper of the engraved names, and leave letters or other material items. The objects that visitors deposit at the VVM serve as material memory—objects that come to signify the continued presence of absent individuals. Visitors leave a varied collection of material memory objects that range from representing the American War in Viet Nam as futile to those representing the war as honorable sacrifice. These material memories and the names engraved on the VVM invoke the dead and possess, for some visitors, the possibility of communication with the dead. They hold the potential of dissolving the distance between past and present. Although these memorial performances take place at a national place of remembrance, a collected cultural memory emerges wherein multifaceted material and performative memories deny the possibility of a unified memory of the war. Moreover, visitors with no direct connection to the war who observe material and performative memories sometimes acquire prosthetic memories—in this case, an emotional connection to the war and the war dead.

The memorial's dynamic design and visitors' memorial performances at the VVM enter into a discourse of memory-making that results in a multifaceted collected cultural memory of the war that encourages prosthetic memory. The design and performances interconnectedly reflect one another and culminate in the creation of a new narrative approach to remembering the American War in Viet Nam. This narrative approach engages with recuperation and reconciliation, ultimately emphasizing memory of the war and refusing to relegate it to the forgotten past.

MATERIAL MEMORIES

Like the American War in Viet Nam, the memorial's abstract concept provoked controversy. The dispute over Maya Lin's design concerned how Americans should remember the war. The debate is well documented in Scruggs and Swerdlow's To Heal a Nation and often figures prominently in scholarly studies of the VVM.[3] The primary concern with Maya Lin's design was that it was too abstract. Some criticized the memorial for being too sober and therefore not properly honoring the dead. For example, during the process of final approval by the Fine Arts Commission, Vietnam veteran and member of the VVMF Tom Carhart made a statement to the commission calling Lin's design "a black gash of shame" (qtd. in Scruggs and Swerdlow 81–82). Joined by Ross Perot, who helped fund the design contest, Vietnam veteran and author James Webb, who also later served as a United States Senator (2007–2013), insisted on changes to the design. He called for the walls to be either made of white granite or to place them above ground. He also wanted to abandon the chronological listing of names and to add an American flag.

The movement against the memorial gained traction as negative publicity about it mounted. Media coverage of the debate revealed anxiety about Maya Lin's Asian American identity. The attacks on Lin took a great toll on her, resulting in her absence at the groundbreaking ceremony and the dedication of the memorial. They also influenced President Reagan, who, as historian Walter Hixon noted, did not attend the dedication ceremony in 1982 but did attend the dedication of the statue two years later instead. Finally, Secretary of the Interior James Watt determined that he would not clear the building permit for the memorial until the VVMF agreed to additions of a flag and a statue. The memorial would not be built without the addition of Fredrick Hart's *Three Fighting Men* sculpture.

Fredrick Hart's *Three Fighting Men* sculpture, dedicated in 1984, was included in the memorial design before groundbreaking as a compromise with those who felt the Vietnam Veterans Memorial was too bleak and, for some, too abstract. For example, Hart criticized the VVM's encouragement of visitor participation. He claimed that "people say you can bring whatever you want to Lin's memorial. But I call that brown bag aesthetics. I mean you better bring something, because there ain't nothing being served" (Hess 274). Yet what Hart called "brown bag aesthetics" is precisely the reason to privilege the VVM as a memorial that encourages ongoing memory. By urging visitors to engage actively with memory-making via the material objects they bring to the memorial, the VVM effectively engages collected cultural and prosthetic memory. The Vietnam Veteran's Memorial compels visitor interaction and participation, thereby prompting memory-making through the creation of new memories—prosthetic memories. Like the names on the memorial, the material memory objects addressed hereafter come to signify individuals from among the collective and encourage observers to create new meaning and memories of the war and the war dead.

Both the polished surface and the engraved names of the VVM possess a tactile quality that encourages visitors to touch the memorial. Touching an engraved name allows visitors to feel a sense of contact with the person whom the name represents. According to Lin's written description of the memorial, "these names, seemingly infinite in number, convey the sense of overwhelming numbers while unifying those individuals into a whole" (*Boundaries* 27). She has also said that the VVM "focuses on individual loss" to emphasize a private experience (*Grounds* 11, 9). Thus the VVM proffers a tension between an individual name and the collected names. Furthermore, visitors who make rubbings of the names take mementos of the memorial and the named dead soldier with them when they leave. Through the rubbings, the VVM and the memories of the war and war dead transcend the physical space of the memorial. For example, visitors often make rubbings of names to share with others who have not or cannot visit the VVM. Philosophical theory critic Karen S. Feldman understands the rubbings and their tactile properties as "evidence that the names are not just designations. The name is the presence . . . of the person" (300). Sometimes, the dead are more literally brought to the memorial, instead of symbolically brought home from the memorial. For example, there are at least three documented cases of human ashes left at the memorial. The Vietnam Veterans Memorial Collection (VVMC), discussed in more detail later, collects and archives objects left at the VVM. Human remains found in the accession boxes are cataloged and removed immediately whenever a staff member or researcher discovers them. According to the VVMC's 2008 draft of the "Scope of Collection Statement," these ashes are spread at the VVM after contacting next of kin.

Unlike the usual protocol of leaving flowers and flags, the range of memory objects deposited at the VVM constitutes competing personal memories intended to be shared and thereby to create a collected, rather than collective, cultural memory—a mediated gathering of polysemic memories.[4] While some objects suggest that the American War in Vietnam wasted lives, others signify sacrifice and purpose. Representing a collected cultural memory, objects comprise individual possessions once belonging to the dead: popular culture icons such as teddy bears or sports memorabilia, photographic images of the dead or their personal possessions (for example, automobiles, clothing, watches, or jewelry). Some objects represent past written reflections of those who are dead, such as copies of their letters sent home during the war. Visitors also leave objects as means of communication with the dead; these range from schoolchildren's assignments to write "dear dead soldier" letters, to tourists' or friends' notes scrawled on hotel stationary, to family members' highly personal letters filled with sorrow, anger, regret, apologies, and final farewells. Some objects are familiar military memorabilia that signify military service. These items include service badges, dog tags, prisoner of war (POW) and missing in action (MIA) remembrance bracelets, and combat boots.[5] While other objects such as commemorative pins, bumper stickers, or coins celebrate the memorial itself, still other objects left at the VVM, such as rocks and handcrafted mementoes, are obscure items left by anonymous visitors.[6] Furthermore, some visitors leave the VVM with commodified memories, souvenirs purchased from nearby vendors; these include replicas of POW bracelets or commemorative items.

Material memory objects constitute something like an objective correlative for the emotions called up in visitors by the VVM.[7] Individual possessions, cultural icons, and efforts of communication deposited at the VVM engage with the prewar past by signifying the hopes, likes, loves, and habits of the dead soldier to whom they once belonged. However, the material memories inexorably invoke the absence of that person. As cultural anthropologists Elizabeth Hallam and Jenny Hockey explain, memory objects summon characteristics of their owners and thus serve as substitutes for the absent body (14, 78). For example, objects left at a child's grave, such as toys, "maintain the material culture of childhood" (Hallam and Hockey 88). These objects evoke emotions associated with the play or innocence of childhood and the loss of a particular child. At the VVM memory objects correlate with the absent body and signify an individual from among the collective.

Moreover, material memory objects placed at the VVM call attention to an individual from among the collected names. For example, in *Carried to The Wall* (1998), Kristin Hass identifies the objects as "markers against the threat of the erasure of the memories of the war and its soldiers" (93). The material markers draw attention to one name among many on the memorial and, as Hass argues, "insistently work to recast the soldiers' identities" (93). Recasting identity allows the absent dead to become present. Consider Hallam and Hockey's explanation of the dual nature of memories as "past presence [and] present absence" (85): memories have the potential to dissolve the distance and duality between then and now, creating a fused perspective—simultaneity.

Material memories also create a convergence of private and public memorials. Memory objects simultaneously communicate individual and collective memory, or a collected cultural memory. Leaving material memory objects at the VVM enables visitors to share and transcend personal memory. Spilling over into the space of the public, material memories support the creation of new memories both for those who leave them, participants, and for those who see them, observers. Material memories compel observers to piece together a narrative memory, implicating them in remembering. Private memories of the war and the war dead thereby enter the domain of the public psyche.

Moreover, material remembrances deposited at the VVM generate prosthetic memories and encourage "post-memories," the term Marianne Hirsch uses when writing of Holocaust memories acquired by postwar generations (3). As Hass explains, visitors encountering material memories at the VVM attach narrative meaning to the object. The meanings of the objects to those who leave the items are accessible to observers insofar as the meaning is constituted by the discourse it enters, the context of remembering the American War in Viet Nam and the American war dead. Encountering material memories at the VVM as mediated representations of the war allows observers who have no "natural" or hereditary claim to the war's memory to incorporate that memory into their own archive of experience. Moreover, objects deposited at the VVM, such as letters to the dead from postwar generations with no direct organic or hereditary connection to the war, attest to the formation of prosthetic memory. In leaving memory objects, these visitors have formed a personal connection with the war dead, thus visitors form post-memories of the war. In leaving memory objects, those who were once observers now become participants in memory-making. Participants and observers sometimes engage equally with memory at the VVM, and many visitors acquire the dual perspective of participant and observer.

Through material memory the VVM becomes what memory theorist Pierre Nora identifies as a *lieux de mémoire*, a site of memory, on two levels—the memorial itself and the objects left at the memorial. The objects deposited at the VVM constitute a meta-memorial, a memorial within, or one that arises from a memorial. Nora describes a site of memory as a principal place or site in which collective memory is rooted where one can study "national feeling" (7). This sense of national feeling takes on an amalgamated form of multifaceted collective and individual memories. Material remembrances contend with one another, each representing diverse narratives to participants and to observers.

A PEOPLE'S MEMORIAL

Memorials do not provide remembrance by their mere existence. They should not simply remain in their material space but should somehow transcend that "space" so that observers are invited to participate in memory-making. Because the Vietnam Veterans Memorial encourages the participation of visitors, it is highly effective in invoking and creating memories. Just as memories of the American war in Viet Nam are not static, the VVM encourages continual participation in memory-making. The VVM truly is a people's memorial from conception and funding, to visitors' interaction with and reaction to the memorial, through poetry written in response to the memorial. The memorial encourages material and performative memories from a variety of visitors, ranging from those with direct memories of the war, to those with direct memories of the Viet Nam–generation experience, those with hereditary, familial memories, as well as those with no direct or hereditary memory of the war. The memorial design, visitors' responses to the VVM, and poetry about the memorial fulfill Jan Scruggs's hope for a "people's memorial."

In 1979, when Scruggs determined to build a memorial in memory of his fallen comrades, his concern was with forgetfulness. *To Heal a Nation* (1985) recounts Scruggs's inspiration for the memorial as stemming from a flashback to the war that he experienced after he saw the film *The Deer Hunter* (1979). The narrative explains that "[t]he flashbacks ended, but the faces continued to pile up in front of him. The names, he thought. The names. No one remembers their names" (Scruggs and Swerdlow 7). The inspiration for the VVM was an attempt to combat the collective amnesia that set in upon the signing of the Paris Peace Accords in 1973, two years before the fall of Saigon.[8] For America the war "officially" ended in 1973, and by 1975, the end of the Vietnamese Civil War, most Americans avoided memories of the war that divided the United States. Preventing complete government control over the creation of the memorial was also of importance for Scruggs and those involved with the Vietnam Veterans Memorial Fund (VVMF).

The VVMF's efforts to acquire the necessary funds for the memorial reflect its emphasis on individual citizen participation. An early letter from the mass mailings asking for donations includes the following passage: "All of us, regardless of how we felt about the war, can participate in building this memorial that says we care about the men and women who fought in Vietnam. If you give $20, it will sponsor the name of one Vietnam War veteran who gave his life in service to our country" (Scruggs and Swerdlow 23). The very nature of mass mailings used for the solicitation of funds indicates the desire for the VVM to be a "people's memorial." Providing the opportunity to sponsor a name on the VVM created a sense of participation for donors and particular individual remembrance.

Further still, the Vietnam Veterans Memorial Collection (VVMC) at the Museum Resource Center (MRCE) in Landover, Maryland, part of the National Parks Service, holds all of the objects deposited at the memorial. This archival museum collection demonstrates the overwhelming scope and lack of coherent memorial narrative in the extensive range of objects left at the VVM. Such a diverse collection demonstrates the multifaceted nature of a collected cultural memory. Organizations and visitors from across the globe leave objects at the VVM, and many of these objects do not clearly relate to the American War in Viet Nam.

Seeking to determine the extent to which visitors comment on other wars in the objects they leave at the VVM, I conducted hands-on research at the VVMC. I sought visual, textual, and material objects associated with the Global

War on Terror left at the VVM, hoping to provide empirical evidence that the public does indeed regard the memorial space as a democratic space of memory-making wherein they may comment on broader national and international issues—in this case, the Global War on Terror, particularly the Iraq War. I searched through approximately twenty-five boxes ranging from September 2002 through May 2003. Of the thousands of items observed, only fifteen clearly commented on the Persian Gulf War or the War on Terror. While such a low number indicates that the public did not overwhelmingly respond to the Global War on Terror at the Vietnam Veterans Memorial, it does demonstrate that there is some commentary on these events. For example, letters written by K–12 students often reference that we are now in a war. Other materials demonstrate the distinction between the antiwar movement of the 1960s and the balancing act of supporting troops while maintaining an antiwar stance that we observe in the twenty-first century.

Repetition and reproduction were the most common experiences in searching through these items. There are often multiple copies of the same poem or handmade service-badge reproductions. Likely these, placed along the length of the memorial, are left by a group of visitors on a single day. While many objects are duplicates, there are also unique objects left, such as hand-carved wooden plaques that reference the Persian Gulf War (1990–1991) or a business card stating "wish you were here to enjoy Baghdad with us." Still other objects, often letters or notes, mention that we are now at war or that the person who left the object "understands" and even that the "Illuminati" is to blame. Still, there were a few twenty-first-century "Support our Troops" signs, a "No War in Iraq" sign, and a pair of desert combat boots. One theme reigned supreme over all—patriotism. This was particularly clear in the "Proud to be an American" signs, notes, and T-shirts; the same sentiment peppers schoolchildren's letters. So, in many ways, the memorial does reflect the most prevalent sentiments of the time. These objects were left in late 2002 and early 2003, and they do demonstrate that the Vietnam Veterans Memorial is a "People's Memorial."

AESTHETIC MEMORY • A LIVING MEMORIAL

The memorial's design, however, tells a different narrative. Evoking emotions of loss and suffering rather than representing heroism, the Vietnam Veterans Memorial differs greatly from hallmark Classical Greek and Roman architectural styles associated with the Commission of Fine Arts and the American

Battle Monuments Commission (Piehler 174). For example, historian Kurt Piehler asserts that the VVM's focus on individual names breaks with Classical memorial imagery that most often includes a "heroic-style statuary" (174). The VVM consists of two horizontal walls sloped into the earth, meeting at an angle of 125 degrees. Each wall, or arm, of the memorial contains seventy polished black granite panels engraved with the names of the dead. The panels range in height from a few inches at each end, to just above ten feet where the two sides meet in the shape of an inverted V. The panels bear the names of the 58,307 war dead. Names engraved on the reflective panels are arranged not alphabetically but in chronological order according to date of death.

The inverted V shape of the memorial, the numbered panels, and the inscription of names culminate to create a book of the dead. As Maya Lin understands the design, "the panels open like a book . . . [they] are numbered like the pages in a book" (Grounds 13). Like a book, the memorial's two inscriptions on the far eastern and western panels serve as a prologue and epilogue to the memorial.[9] Along with these inscriptions, the text of the VVM culminates with the names, material, and form of the memorial in a "convergence between the notions of text and art and content" (13). Literary scholar Stephen Greenblatt further understands that "to cut words into matter, to transform matter into a book to be read, is the central memorializing act" (27). Creating a narrative of the war in stone from the names of the dead and missing holds a permanency that is there for all to read. The act of reading produces the possibility of forming new memories. Moreover, the chronological listing of names creates a relationship between past and present time, place, and memory inscribed in the names. The memorial lists the names of those who died together next to one another. Thus veterans visiting the memorial will likely encounter the names of several individuals they once knew on a singular panel that, in turn, signifies a particular place and time in memory.

Despite the familiar, Freytag-pyramid, narrative structural appearance of the inverted V-shaped memorial, the chronological listing of names does not follow that seemingly predictable order; alternately, it disrupts a Western narrative order (fig. 1). Rather than beginning with the date of the first American military death in 1959, the outermost ends of the memorial walls begin with the war's climax of 1968. The west wall of the memorial rises from the year 1968 to the year the war ended in 1975, while the east wall descends from 1959 to 1968. Each outermost end of the memorial's walls begins in medias res, and the memorial reaches its greatest height and narrative climax with the beginning

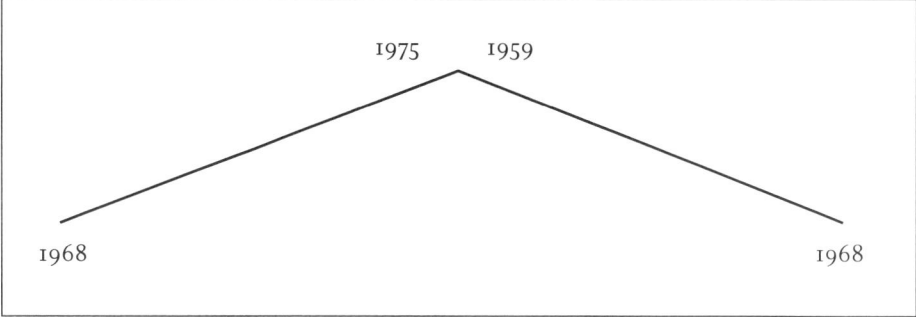

FIG. 1. CHRONOLOGICAL LISTING AT THE VIETNAM VETERANS MEMORIAL.
COURTESY OF THE AUTHOR.

FIG. 2. APEXES OF THE VIETNAM VETERANS MEMORIAL LOOKING
EAST AND WEST. LIBRARY OF CONGRESS.

and the end of the American War in Viet Nam. The memorial's chronology is in counterdistinction to Western expectations of chronological ordering by starting at 1968 and moving upward toward the culmination of 1975/1959 at the height of the memorial and then descending back down toward 1968.

Because the memorial's chronological display does not follow an expected Western linear plot of development, visitors experience a fusion of time, a simultaneity of past and present that exists both in the VVM's reflective material, enveloping structure, and ordering of dates. While visitors may choose to enter the memorial at either end designated with the date 1968, they unavoidably encounter a circular narrative arc. This circularity seems to reject closure and finality and to encourage continued remembrance of the war by influencing visitor interaction with the memorial. The apex of the memorial signals both the first and last American military deaths of the war, invoking the fusion of historical moments nearly a decade apart. The dates and names of the first and last deaths reflect onto and into one another via the memorial's reflective panels (fig. 2). The VVM's apex also reflects the east and west walls onto and into one another, symbolically reflecting the joining of the East, Viet Nam, and the West, the United States, by the war.

Circular chronology induces visitors to participate in an ancient, non-Western form of memorialization. In her *Toni Morrison and the Idea of Africa* (2008), literary scholar La Vinia Delois Jennings analyzes a "four moments of the sun" cosmogram to explore a non-Western spatialization of time "as governed by nature, from east to west or right to left" (3,18). She explains, "The counterclockwise spiral of the solar moments suggests a backward movement that spatializes time as it recedes into the past" (19). African in origin, the cosmogram connects with Eastern philosophy. Engaging with this spatialized time, and thereby the past made present, visitors at the VVM must "read" the memorial, not by simply reading the engraved names but by interpreting the material, form, and space of the memorial. As literary critic Donald Ringnalda suggests, visitors wishing to read the memorial from the first death in 1959 to the last death in 1975 must start at the mirrored apex of the monument at 1959; move east toward 1968; cross the green to the west side of the monument, again encountering 1968; and proceed toward 1975, returning to the center of the memorial (236–37). To read, or experience, the memorial in Western chronological order, visitors must actively interpret the chronology to make sense of it against the form, the incline, and decline of the inverted V-shaped monument and encounter a non-Western cosmology.

As the chronological ordering of the VVM denotes the circularity of past and present, so too does visitors' relation to the memorial. For example, Jan Scruggs and Joel Swerdlow, founders of the Vietnam Veterans Memorial Fund, describe the two sides of the memorial as part of a circle, which the "living person who visits . . . through his presence fills in the part of the circle that has been omitted" (77). Maya Lin agrees; she does not think of the memorial as V-shaped but rather as a circle "to be completed by the thoughts and feelings people bring" (Palmer xviii). The visitor's physical reflections in and mental reflections on the memorial become part of the chronology or narrative memory of the war. They are the living half of the memorial.

Maya Lin's Chinese ancestry influenced her design of the memorial to incorporate elements of Eastern philosophy's conceptions of time, death, and memory.[10] Her inclusion of these elements illustrates that the memorial comprises subliminal cultural markers of what many of its critics, including Donald Ringnalda, say it lacks—representations of the Vietnamese (240). The VVM's inscription makes no reference to the Vietnamese; the memorial is dedicated to the living, the dead, and the missing Americans who served in the war. The memorial's design, however, does include a subtle reference to the Vietnamese. According to Scruggs and Swerdlow, East Asian philosophy regards time as cyclical, informing the memorial's depiction of life and death as part of a continuous circle (77). For example, Lin describes [the memorial] as a boundary between the living and the dead" (Palmer xviii). Lin's understanding of the memorial as a liminal space supports the possibility of communication with the dead and continued remembrance of the war.

According to Lin's Eastern aesthetic, time is inseparable from this circle at the VVM where we enter a "dialogue [not just with the contemporary, but also] with those before and beyond our time" (*Maya Lin: A Strong Clear Vision*). Lin's description of visitor connection to those "before and beyond" their time indicates her desire to encourage prosthetic memories. The VVM encourages visitors to participate in a collective cultural memory by piecing the narrative together and filling in the void of the circle of the life and memory cycle. With time and history unbound, memory radiates like sound waves, not in a linear direction but refracting in multiple directions as it encounters other memories. Lin further explains that "although we can be defined by our brief physical time, we have the ability to make that time extend far beyond our physical existence. . . . We are part of a collective consciousness connected through time by works, images, thoughts, and writings" (*Maya Lin: A Strong Clear*

Vision). The reflective surface of the memorial effectively realizes Lin's exten-
sion of time, unbounded reflection, and refraction. For example, as Ringnalda
argues, the scope of the memorial reflects its surroundings, particularly the
Washington and Lincoln Monuments, in a compression of history (236–39).
The two sides of the memorial reflect each other and their surroundings—
other memorials, the flag, and visitors—into one another and infinitely into
the apex of the memorial, creating an illusion that one can walk into the apex,
penetrate the wall, and be enfolded into a book of the dead. The engulfing
reflection of the VVM invites visitors to realize their participation in living
remembrance. The image is especially poignant at night, when the walkway's
subtle light reflects into and up the center walls, creating a reflection of the
walkway into and beyond the surface of the memorial.

The reflective surface of the polished granite invokes the qualities of a
living memorial apropos of Maya Lin's description a previous passage. The
reflection envelops visitors as they encounter the VVM. They become part of
the memorial via their own living image reflected on its surface. The memorial's reflective panels create a composition that includes both the names of
the dead and reflections of the living, creating a vibrant reciprocity and unity
between the living and the dead that again reinforces the expansion of time
Lin discusses earlier. Literary scholar Grant F. Scott remarks that "whereas the
other monuments [Washington and Lincoln] are eerily self-sufficient, boasting forms that are clearly closed, the VVM necessitates our existence and our
gaze for the completion of its aesthetic" (39). A visitor's gaze completes the
memorial's reflective aesthetic when a visitor sees his or her body reflected
onto the memorial. At the VVM visitors see their bodies reflected on the walls
seemingly behind the names of the dead. Thus visitors are inscribed, if only
momentarily, with the names of the dead; therefore, the dead transcend the
static permanence of engraving. They become enveloped in the memorial and
thereby merge with a collected cultural memory of the war. Visitors' memories,
as Scott interprets the memorial, are not self-sufficient, closed, or final.

In his essay "Window or Mirror," artist Levi Smith contends that regarding
the memorial's reflective surface as a mirror brings the past via the names to
the present (106). Alternatively, as a window to the past, the surface allows
viewers to see the names beyond their reflections (106). Smith refers to those
who visit a specific individual name listed on the memorial as belonging to
the category of those who consider the surface as a window, arguing that they
"often ignore or resist broader interpretations" of the VVM's reflective quali-

ties (111). Some of this group who come to view a specific name or names are the Vietnam veterans who tend to visit the memorial at night, where "they find comfort in the presence of their dead comrades" (111). Smith identifies a second group of visitors—those who experience a "release from the past" when they see their present surroundings reflected in the memorial (111). Smith's distinctions are not as clear as he might hope, however. As Lin argues, because of its reflective surface, the memorial is not static but a "moving composition" (*Maya Lin: A Strong Clear Vision*). As a moving composition, the memorial, the dead it memorializes, and the war it remembers refuse to be relegated to the forgotten past. The memorial therefore may, in a singular moment, reflect both past and present. In the following chapter, I identify a "cycle of poetry" about the VVM that also simultaneously functions as both window and mirror—"depending on the light."[11]

CHAPTER 2
♦ POETIC REMEMBRANCES AT THE VIETNAM VETERANS MEMORIAL

My clouded reflection eyes me . . .
I turn this way—the stone lets me go.
I turn that way—I'm inside
the Vietnam Veterans Memorial
again, depending on the light to make a difference.

—Yusef Komunyakaa, "Facing It"

Poems written by Vietnam veterans about the Vietnam Veterans Memorial meditate on the memorial as an impetus of memory and thereby engage in and evaluate the modes of memory-making at the VVM discussed in the previous chapter. The poets and their poems instruct visitors about the possibilities and limitations of the memorial's design, the memorial as mediated representation of the war, and the potential for prosthetic memory. Poetry about the VVM self-consciously contemplates the memorial's materials, form, and structure, as well as individual and group interaction with the memorial and memory objects that visitors leave there. Vietnam veterans often write these poems, and they frequently employ a veteran as speaker. Vietnam veteran Yusef Komunyakaa's widely anthologized poem "Facing It" (1988) rests at the center of a "cycle of poetry" about visiting the VVM. The cycle of VVM poems includes major contributors to Vietnam War poetry: W. D. Ehrhart's "The Invasion of Grenada" (1984) and "Midnight at the Vietnam Veterans Memorial" (1993) and Doug Anderson's 1991 "The Wall." It also consists of Eugene Grollmes's obscure collection *At the Vietnam Veterans Memorial, Washington, D.C.: Between the Lines* (1988) and Lamonte B. Steptoe's "A Second Wall" (1990). All published in the decade following the 1982 dedication of Vietnam Veterans Memorial, these poems remember the war at a time when President Ronald

Reagan referred to the "Vietnam Syndrome" and called on Americans to re-evaluate their attitudes toward the American War in Viet Nam. In the midst of Reaganesque Cold War certitudes, American memories of the war took on amalgamated forms ranging from emphasis on the misunderstood renegade Vietnam veteran portrayed by John Rambo (Sylvester Stallone) in *First Blood* (Ted Kotcheff, 1982) to Reagan's "noble cause." While the poems treat the same historical event and each responds to remembrance at the VVM, they also demonstrate varying attitudes about the war and its contemporary legacies. Some poems reject sentimental closure, while others indict prosthetic memory as insincere. Thus the cycle of poems participates in a multifaceted collected cultural memory.

While the poets self-consciously explore the possibilities and limitations of achieving a collected cultural memory, the poems they write serve as mediated representations of the war that provide opportunities for prosthetic memory. The poems are often didactic; they demonstrate for their audiences means of interacting with the Vietnam Veterans Memorial. Speakers in their poems visit the memorial in pilgrimage fashion to confront their memories and commune with the dead. Often the poems describe sensory memories, those arousing sight, taste, smell, sound, and touch. The most powerful poems include a sixth sense that resides in the mind's eye. Set in the shared space of the memorial, poetry about the VVM engages with a collected cultural memory by emphasizing the commingling of individual and collected memories. Again, "collected" memory is distinct from "collective" memory which indicates cohesion, while "collected memory" signifies multifaceted memories.

Vietnam veteran Yusef Komunyakaa's "Facing It," written more than decade after the end of the war, appears in his *Dien Cai Dau* (1988), which literally means "crazy," a Vietnamese phrase used to describe American soldiers during the war. In fact, the bravado of some American soldiers led them to consider the description a compliment. "Facing It" is the final poem of the *Dien Cai Dau* collection, but it was the first Komunyakaa wrote. This image-laden retrospective prompted him to write other memory poems about his experiences as a soldier in Viet Nam (Houghtaling). The final poem in the collection, prompted by an encounter with the Vietnam Veterans Memorial, serves as the beginning of memory.

"Facing It" enacts a collected cultural memory that the VVM's design encourages. Brimming with sensory images, the poem contains thirty-one lines of free verse in a single stanza describing a Vietnam veteran's visit to the

Vietnam Veterans Memorial. The Vietnam veteran speaker, often associated with Komunyakaa, describes visitors interacting with the memorial, the nature of the memorial's reflection in relation to identity and memory, and the possibilities and failures of remembrance that the memorial possesses. He has a heightened awareness of his reflection; he observes other visitors and surroundings in the reflection; he sees a name and then experiences a flashback; he reflects on the memorial as a "moving composition"; and he fluctuates between past and present via the reflection.

Through a series of juxtapositions—past and present, stone and flesh, the dead and the living, night and day, and self and other—the speaker in "Facing It" engages with the past presence and present absence that visitors encounter at the VVM.[1] Komunyakaa's chosen binaries call attention to the paradoxical nature of the VVM; it reflects the past war and the war dead while simultaneously, and literally, reflecting present visitors. In the poem, the VVM signifies loss and the trauma of the past at the same moment that it encourages visitors to become a present part of that void when confronted with their living reflection in the memorial. Komunyakaa's choice to write the poem in the present tense enhances the reader's sense of immediacy. In the poem, as at the VVM, public and private histories collide while time collapses and expands. Inviting the reader to associate with his position as a Vietnam veteran standing before the VVM, the speaker shares his memorial experience with generations who have no direct access to memories of the war. The poem functions as a mediated representation of remembering the war, thereby encouraging prosthetic memory. In the context of President Reagan's so-called Vietnam Syndrome and "noble cause" revisionism and the popular culture of the 1980s, Komunyakaa writes against forgetful revision.

Like the VVM, "Facing It" invokes the past while reflecting the present. The poem begins with the speaker being absorbed into the past, into the memorial: "My black face fades, / hiding inside the black granite" (1–2). Present identity succumbs to memorial memory. Writing in a series of juxtapositions, the speaker enters into a dialogue with self: "I said I wouldn't. . . no tears. / I'm stone. / I'm flesh" (3–5). In these lines, the literal denial and acceptance of emotions commingles with the metaphorical memorial past. The speaker reflects the experiences of visitors to the VVM. Seeing themselves reflected in the memorial, they complete Maya Lin's circle of remembrance.

The speaker becomes engulfed in the memorial when the reflection creates a distance between observer and the observed. Komunyakaa writes, "My clouded reflection eyes me" (6). Observed by his reflection in the memorial, the speaker becomes aware of his participation in the memorial. He is both inside and outside the memorial, in the past and in the present. Komunyakaa writes, "I turn / this way—the stone lets me go, / I turn that way—I'm inside / the Vietnam Veterans Memorial / again, *depending on the light to make a difference*" (8–13, emphasis added). He constructs a fused perspective for his speaker. Depending on the light, he is in the memorial—or in the past. Alternatively, depending on the light, he is reflected by the memorial—in the present. Emphasizing immediacy, Komunyakaa positions readers with him at the VVM when he writes "this way" and "that way," rather than "one way" and "another way."

Like many Vietnam veteran visitors, Komunyakaa's speaker "half-expect[s] to find [his] own letters like smoke" on the memorial (15–16). The expectation represents a common theme in postwar representations, survivor's guilt and a symbolic death of the self—*I died over there*. Still, the speaker does not achieve a definitive sense of unity with the dead or the living. Seemingly held in limbo between past and present, death and life, the speaker's experience at the memorial duplicates the effect of the VVM's reflection.

Enacting the memorial's visceral imperative, the speaker touches a name and past becomes present. However, the speaker does not experience a prewar memory of the living but rather a memory of the wartime past, the moment of death in a "booby trap's white flash" (18). Sensory memory takes hold; visual and tactile senses at the memorial prompt the senses of the mind's eye, creating a memory that is faceless, consumed by the violent image of the booby trap. The image of a flash invokes a traumatic flashback, a fusion of time. Contributing to new memories of the war's aftermath, the speaker's momentary traumatic flashback breaks with the 1980s stereotype of the crazed veteran becoming violently enraged when experiencing a flashback, as Rambo does in *First Blood*. In the following line of "Facing It," boundaries between past and present fluctuate as speaker returns to the present, where "names shimmer on a woman's blouse" (19). Depending on the light, the names shimmer dynamically, as if they are not permanently fixed on the memorial's panels; however, when the woman walks away, the names return to their static position. Between the flashback and return to the present, the speaker encounters Maya Lin's "moving composition" (*Maya Lin: A Strong Clear Vision*). The poem's meta-composition in response to the moving composition of the VVM calls attention to the moving and static position of the names and memory, thereby emphasizing the textual and artistic composition of the memorial.

Komunyakaa further explores fusion at the memorial—its simultaneous reflection of past and present, the dead and the living—and the duality of meaning in his textual composition by raising questions of identity when he introduces a white veteran. Readers might wonder what the two veterans share, or if the speaker and white veteran reconcile racial tensions that were exported from the United States via the war to Viet Nam. One answer is that the two share a common position as Vietnam veteran visitors at the VVM. Yet the white vet functions as "other" on several levels. Komunyakaa writes that "a white vet's image floats / closer to me, then his pale eyes / look through mine. I'm a window" (25–27). Critics reference these lines most frequently when trying to determine the sense of or lack of unity in "Facing It." Thomas Marvin, for example, acknowledges that it may appear, at least for a moment, that the two veterans—white and black—look through the same eyes and share the same perspective (7). However, Marvin contends that in light of the racial tensions throughout the poems in Dien Cai Dau that Komunyakaa is invisible to the white veteran (7).

Komunyakaa instructs his audience that veterans who visit the memorial may confront the traumas and tensions they experienced during the war, whether it be the "booby trap's white flash," racial tensions, or amputation. Thus the memorial, for Komunyakaa's speaker, is a window to the past. According to Levi Smith's account of the window and mirror discussed in chapter 1, regarding the black veteran as a window might place the white veteran among the group of visitors who regard the reflective surface of the memorial as a window to the past. The white veteran could simply represent a veteran of the war who is lost in his own memories and active engagement with the memorial. It is also possible to read the white veteran as a dead other. His "image floats" like that of a ghost. At a minimum, the white veteran haunts the poem with the image of amputation. Komunyakaa writes that "he's lost his right arm / inside the stone" (28–29). The memorial dismembers the image or, at least, depicts the dismembered veteran through reflection. Like the speaker of the poem, the white veteran holds a binary position—he is both inside the memorial, in the past, and a reflection of the memorial, in the present.

During a November 2006 reading at the University of Tennessee–Knoxville, Komunyakaa spoke of his forthcoming work, noting that he was writing poetry from the perspective of a white veteran, a speaker he considers his alter ego. The alter ego may be a double that informs the reading of the white vet in "Facing It." Depending on the light, both speaker and white veteran are inside or outside the memorial; depending on the light, they are self or other; or, depending on the light, they are both part of the same moving composition.

Although critics often do not see much hope for healing from the war in "Facing It," citing either a lack of recovery or a pattern of promise and disappointment, some regard the conclusion of the poem as an "act of love" (Stein 10). In the final lines of the poem, the speaker encounters a woman and a boy visiting the memorial. The woman, "trying to erase names," elicits fears of forgetfulness (30). Immediately, however, in the next and final line of the poem, Komunyakaa writes, "no she's brushing a boy's hair" (31). According to some critics, Komunyakaa brings his reader back to the everyday, and back to the active present moment of observation, in the mother's gesture, "affirm[ing] sanity and life in the face of the insanity of war" (Gotera 299). He certainly invokes the future of remembrance, however uncertain, through the figure of the boy. However, the hope some critics read in the poem is not assured because "Facing It" lacks final punctuation.[2] The poem's open ending reflects the VVM's lack of closure, its refusal to relegate the war to the forgotten past. In addition, Komunyakaa states that the last line is meant to be an "open ended release" (Blue Notes 37).

The narrative movement of "Facing It" shifts from individual to communal experience at the VVM, again suggesting that memories of the war are not isolated and will not necessarily fade with the passing of a generation. The poem represents the self-reflection that a visitor experiences when standing at the VVM's apex. The walls infinitely reflect onto and thereby into each other. "Facing It" begins with the individual facing himself in the memorial's reflection, shifts to observing others in the memorial's reflection, and ends with the speaker and white veteran commingling in the memorial's reflection. The poem enacts cultural memory, engages in sensory memory, prompts artistic response, and contemplates the positions of self and other in remembrance. Komunyakaa faces the Vietnam Veterans Memorial, a mediated representation of the war and the war dead, and creates his own poetically mediated representation of remembrance. The poem functions for its readers as the memorial does for the poet; it creates a memory of the war by encouraging visitors to interact with the memorial and confront their direct or prosthetic memories of the war and the war dead.

One of the reasons "Facing It" is one of the most memorable poems about visiting the VVM is because it articulates the boundless qualities of time in the memorial. The poem includes reflection, flashback, dismembering, remembering, a veteran visitor, and civilian visitors—features present in nearly every poem that emerges in response to the VVM and Komunyakaa's poem. The cycle of poems often sentimentalize, reenact, or extend Komunyakaa's exploration of memory at the VVM. Indeed, one might say that the reinvention of Komunyakaa's "Facing It" illustrates the multifaceted nature of a collected cultural memory.

The array of responses to the memorial is difficult to capture in a single poem. Friends of the Vietnam Veterans Memorial published Eugene Grollmes's ambitious yet relatively obscure collection *At the Vietnam Veterans Memorial, Washington, D.C.: Between the Lines* in 1988, the same year as Komunyakaa's *Dien Cai Dau*. Grollmes's poems attempt to represent the wide range of visitors and responses to the VVM. The assemblage of poems attests to representational challenges that most poems about the VVM encounter: how to represent the successes and failures of collected cultural and prosthetic memory that the memorial encourages. Grollmes found it necessary to compile cultural memories in thirty poems. The collection includes descriptions of visitors participating in remembrance, experiencing loss and sorrow, communing with the dead, and gaining a sense of healing. Grollmes catalogues the numbers and types of visitors to the memorial, thus depicting the VVM as a memory destination. Poetry about the VVM predicates the active process of memory on the journey to the memorial. The VVM serves as a place of memory. Maya Lin said of the memorial, "I don't make objects; I make places" (*Grounds* 13). Grollmes's collection reflects themes of Komunyakaa's "Facing It" and those that the following poetry about the VVM address—flashbacks, the need for continued memorialization and remembering, and the possibilities and limitations of prosthetic memory, hope, and healing.

Poetry about visiting the VVM engages with the memorial's invocation of a fused past and present via the names of the dead. In Doug Anderson's "The Wall" (1991), a visit to the VVM transports Anderson's Vietnam veteran speaker to the past. After enacting the ritual of finding a name in the memorial's directory index, the speaker experiences a flashback. The memory is highly personal; the name is that of "the first man / [He] could not help," yet the flashback occurs upon seeing the name in the index, not on the memorial's panels (11–12). The name invokes a memory associated with the loss of that individual. As in Komunyakaa's "Facing It," the name conjures a visual memory. Anderson's flashback, however, transcends the visual, including memories of smell and sound. He writes, "for a moment, the tree splintering / in front of me, smell of blood and cordite, his lips turning blue, / the gasp of a lung filling with blood" (12–14). Thus the name, placed chronologically according to the personal moment of death, conjures a precise memory of place and circumstance of violent imagery. For the Vietnam veteran speaker, the memory conjures the visceral, sensuous nature of past becoming momentarily present. Yet Anderson also suggests that memories of the war transcend the war's historically delineated ending. He depicts veterans' homecoming as a realization that "for us the war / had just begun, that for years we would be picking through the shards, / the war pursuing us everywhere, our dreams, our lives. . . chasing us" (20–23). In the poem, as at the VVM, past and present are continuous and fluctuating.

Poetry about visiting the VVM not only illustrates the fusion of past and present that occurs at the VVM and offers audiences immediate moments of veterans bearing witness to trauma, the poems also communicate a narrative of ongoing remembrance that the VVM encourages. For example, in "The Wall," Anderson invokes the "three million Vietnamese, [and] four million [names of] Cambodians," civilians and allies, absent from the memorial, asking, "how long a wall?" if more death and suffering of the war were memorialized (25–26). Again, he summons the war's violent and psychological consequences beyond its historical ending by alluding to postwar consequences of the Khmer Rouge in Cambodia.[3]

Lamont Steptoe's "A Second Wall" (1990) also calls for further memorialization, not of the Vietnamese, however, but of surviving American veterans. Textually similar, although much shorter and less image laden than Komunyakaa's "Facing It," Steptoe's poem of twenty short, abrupt lines resembles Komunyakaa's open verse, truncated lines, and lack of final end punctuation. Writing in military metaphor, Steptoe invokes veterans' psychological suffering. His opening line calls for "A / second wall for those who cracked . . . by the knife of memory and nightmare" (1–8). Among the poems, Steptoe's "knife of memory" is the most explicit depiction of memory as painful. Like Doug Anderson, Steptoe suggests the surprise at returning home to realize that there was still a "most concealed ambush . . . wait[ing] / secretly for years . . . the one that hid / in the tunnels of the spirit" (14–20). Steptoe points to the unending psychological effects of the war. Haunting memories of the war—for these Vietnam veteran poets, their speakers, and some visitors to the memorial in their poems—corresponds to the VVM design's rejection of closure and forgetfulness.

Nonetheless, the poets address concerns of forgetfulness and interrogate the possibilities and limitations of prosthetic memory—acquired via mediated representation by those with no direct experience in the event(s) remembered—at the VVM. Grollmes, for example, criticizes some who visit the VVM in "Tourists." He describes visitors in summer outfitted with "colorful / Maps of other monuments in town" (21–22), who see "History. Mere history soon fading into . . . / Nice weather to be out" (20–21). Grollmes rejects prosthetic memory among observer-visitors; he hastily assumes they have forgotten the war and the dead as "mere history." However, Grollmes rightly notes that some observer-visitors are tourists simply pausing at the VVM only to "Tell their friends they . . . saw 'The Wall' Yet all they see is names / And marble . . ." (3–5). This touristic goal is not unusual at any of the memorials on the Washington Mall and is certainly explicitly visible at the Three Fighting Men sculpture, where it is not uncommon for groups of families or children to file in front of the sculpture for a scrapbook photograph. Interestingly, Grollmes's tourists see marble rather than granite, attesting to Grollmes's accusations that these visitors are not very observant or reflective. Grollmes's example exposes the limitations of prosthetic memory. There remains a cultural "you had to be there" argument about remembering the war. As Grollmes represents them, these visitors see only the empirical names and dates; they do not experience the memories that he likely considers appropriate and authentic. The authenticity of experience continues to hold sway over the authority of memory. Grollmes's poem attests to the fear of misremembering: simply encountering a mediated memory, or experiential site, does not guarantee that individuals acquire prosthetic memories. Nor does the attainment of these new memories satisfy requirements held by some for authentic memory.

Engaging with the positive possibilities of prosthetic memory, however, Doug Anderson's "The Wall" describes tourists with a more sympathetic understanding than those in Grollmes's poem. Anderson regards visitors' actions as products of the memorial. He characterizes the VVM as a place of uncertainty, memory, and potential rebirth. Describing visitors' reactions to the memorial, Anderson writes:

> A place of whispers, and tourists wander confused,
> are hesitant to photograph, seeing themselves reflected so.
> How are we to be, they seem to ask, and what is this?
> The young ask especially, threatened by this invitation to grieve. (3–5)

Unlike Grollmes, Anderson recognizes confusion and hesitancy not as ignorance or forgetfulness, but as encountering an "invitation to grieve." He continues, revealing the memorial's powerful implication of visitors in its reflection, describing a "stone [that] draws the surrounding monuments / into contention, [and] shames them with the suggestion that we are not stone, / but reflections of the earth, before and behind these names" (8–10). Engaging with Komunyakaa's "I'm stone / I'm flesh" (3), Anderson stresses the human element of memorialization at the VVM: "we are not stone." He also carefully instructs visitors to understand their liminal position in relation to the memorial. They, "we," are "before and behind these names." Reflected into the memorial, visitors in the poem and at the VVM see their likenesses on and behind the engraved names.

Anderson acknowledges the intermingling of personal and historical memory at the VVM that allows those who have no personal, direct connection to the war to form their own prosthetic memories. The most poignant example follows when Anderson describes "A girl too young to know this war, / [who] sobs nonetheless, so precise are these fifty-eight thousand facts" (17–18). Unlike Grollmes and Ehrhart, Anderson denies that the empirical alienates visitors with no direct connection to the war. Rather, Anderson calls attention to the power of the number of names to represent loss. He champions prosthetic memories enabled by the mediated representation of the war and the war dead at the VVM.

In addition to exploring mediated memories, poetry about the VVM also meditates on the tensions between hope and healing and a false sense of closure. Anderson's "The Wall," despite its emphasis on psychological suffering, sorrow, and prosthetic memory, contains hope and ends with potential redemption. The memorial that "from a distance seems a scar, / [is rather] the crook of an arm to cradle a head" (1–2). Here, Anderson engages with the debate over the monument's efficacy, directly responding to Vietnam veteran and former Vietnam Veteran Memorial Fund volunteer Tom Carhart, who in his Fine Arts Commission hearing statement critiqued the VVM as a "black gash of shame" (Scruggs and Swerdlow 82). In the final lines of the poem, the memorial becomes a "gazing stone of possibility, / womb of Kali, and not least, the night we wander in becoming whole" (29–30). Although an ambiguous figure for Anderson, Kali signifies creation, healing, and wholeness.[4] Anderson further emphasizes the healing possibilities of the memorial while avoiding simplistic sentimentality by pairing wholeness with the night, rather than with morning—the expected pairing. Like Komunyakaa, Anderson complicates the ending of his poem.

Unlike these other poems, W. D. Ehrhart's poem "Midnight at the Vietnam Veterans Memorial" (1993) avoids Ehrhart's own psychological suffering as a consequence of the war, sentimentality, and a hopeful ending. Known as the renegade Vietnam veteran poet, Ehrhart upholds his reputation in his blunt critique of the war and his implied critique of the VVM. He writes a sparse narrative of eighteen lines.

> Fifty-eight thousand American dead,
> average age: nineteen years, six months.
> get a driver's license,
> graduate from high school,
> die.
> All that's left of them
> we've turned to stone.
> what they never got to be
> grows dimmer by the year.
>
> But in the moon's dim light
> when no one's here,
> the names rise up, step down
> and start the long procession home
> to what they left undone,
> to what they loved, to anywhere
> that's not this silent
> wall of kids, this
> smell of rotting dreams.

Like Grollmes and Anderson, Ehrhart employs the empirical to transmit his message. He describes lives as short lived. Moreover, when he writes of loss—"What they never got to be / grows dimmer by the year"—he describes not just the loss of possibilities, hopes, and dreams, but an inevitable failure of remembrance (8–9). He portrays the memorial as a place of fleeting memory; he writes, "All that's left of them / we've turned to stone" (6–7). Yet Ehrhart does not champion forgetfulness. Like Steptoe, Ehrhart reminds his audience of the consequences of the war that he believes are not explicitly memorialized at the VVM.

Setting his poem at midnight, Ehrhart engages with the memorial's gravesite qualities. He invokes the ghosts of the dead at midnight when "the names rise up, step down / and start the long procession home" (12–13). For Ehrhart, as for some visitors to the VVM, the names signify the individual and take on a ghostly quality. However, unlike an expected sentimental journey toward peace, the names flee "to anywhere / that's not this silent / wall of kids, this / smell of rotting dreams" (15–18). Invoking senseless loss, Ehrhart utilizes a sparse and simple language, "silent" and "kids." Calling attention to the possibility that war memorials offer false healing, Ehrhart unabashedly condemns maintaining a sacred attitude toward the VVM, describing it as a place that "smell[s] of rotting dreams."

For Ehrhart, the VVM is not a site for sorrowful remembrance of the dead; it is a place of cold, hard numbers, silence, and "rotting dreams." Ehrhart refuses to allow cultural expectations of war memorials to influence his antiwar stance. Like Grollmes's excessive critique of tourists, Ehrhart rejects what he considers the memorial's false healing, arguing as he does in his 1984 "Invasion of Grenada" that he did not wish for a memorial "not even one as sober as that / vast black wall of broken lives" (1–3) but rather an "end to monuments," an end to war (15).

Although many hoped that the Vietnam Veterans Memorial would be the final chapter on the war, poetry set at the Vietnam Veterans Memorial reflects the many tensions implicit in a collected cultural memory associated with the memorial. The cycle of poems that emerge in response to the memorial and modes of memorialization and memory at the VVM represents the memorial as a nexus of multifaceted emotions and memories. Komunyakaa's "Facing It" envelops those with and without direct memories in a singular memorial moment. Anderson's "The Wall" praises the memorial, arguing that "we are not stone / but reflections of earth, before and behind these names" (9–10), whereas Ehrhart maintains that the memories of the dead are "turned to stone" (7). Grollmes exhibits disdain for ignorant tourists, while Anderson recognizes the emotional impact of prosthetic memory. Anderson and Steptoe each encourage further memorialization of the psychological impact of the war on civilians and postwar life. Each of these poems represents the memorial's power to engage visitors—both participants and observers—in memory-making. That the poems take place, and memories converge, at the VVM demonstrates that both the memorial and these poems serve as markers against forgetfulness. The poets self-consciously depict memory as an active process of performance and heightened awareness that engages with past presence and present absence. The poems, like the memorial, function as mediated representations of the war and the war dead. They encourage readers and visitors to engage with memories of the war and to form new memories; understood together, they reveal the multifaceted, rather than unitary, nature of a collected cultural memory. Moreover, as differing memories of the war engaged with contentions over the war itself, as well as fears of misremembering and even forgetting the American War in Viet Nam, a need for further recognition arose among American civilian and servicewomen who participated in the war. They sought their own recognition and recuperation via a women's memorial.

CHAPTER 3
⋆ REMEMBERING SERVICEWOMEN

THE BATTLE FOR THE VIETNAM WOMEN'S MEMORIAL

The Vietnam Veterans Memorials on the Mall in Washington, D.C., form a political memorial triage.[1] The sequence of official approval for and dedication of these memorials suggests the practice in disaster medical emergencies of sorting patients by the seriousness and type of injury in order to prioritize treatment. With respect to the Vietnam Veterans Memorials, women were the last to receive treatment. Dedicated in 1982, Maya Lin's inverted V-shaped design, the Vietnam Veterans Memorial (VVM), engraved with the names of the dead, continues to receive the most critical attention from scholars in the fields of memorial architecture, military history, cultural studies, and Vietnam War studies. The Vietnam Veterans Memorial serves as the cultural and national site for postwar recuperation for veterans of the war and for reconciliation between veterans and civilians. Fredrick Hart's sculpture, *Three Fighting Men*, dedicated in 1984, was a controversial addition to Lin's design (fig. 3). By providing a realistic figuring of servicemen, the addition placated those who deemed the VVM too abstract and depressing. As I have noted, the debate is well documented in Scruggs and Swerdlow's *To Heal a Nation* and in many other studies of the Vietnam Veterans Memorial.[2] The primary concern with Maya Lin's design was that it was abstract instead of a realistic representation. After extensive and discouraging controversy, the memorial would not be built without the addition of an American flag and Hart's statue.[3]

In response to the fissures in the American mythic exceptionalism brought about by the American War in Viet Nam and the "Vietnam Syndrome"—a postwar national unwillingness to pursue military intervention in the third world—Americans sought recuperation via reconciliation and healing.[4] The Vietnam Veterans Memorial and the addition of the *Three Fighting Men* sculpture exemplify those attempts at recuperation, reconciliation, and healing. However, the American reconciliationist narrative movement coalesced with the inclusion of women's experiences and perspectives established at the 1993 dedication of the Vietnam Women's Memorial (VWM).

Glenna Goodacre's sculpture-in-the-round encourages recuperation and reconciliation via recognition of the untold history of American servicewomen in the war (fig. 4). Recognition of American servicewomen's participation in the war was the primary mission for the female Vietnam veteran founders of the Vietnam Women's Memorial Project (VWMP), currently known as the Vietnam Women's Memorial Foundation, Inc.[5] Their vision of a memorial recognizing women's military service during the American War in Viet Nam arose in response to the Vietnam Veterans Memorial and the concessional addition of *Three Fighting Men*.

FIG. 3. FREDERICK HART'S *THREE FIGHTING MEN*, WASHINGTON, D.C. LIBRARY OF CONGRESS.

FIG. 4. GLENNA GOODACRE'S VIETNAM WOMEN'S MEMORIAL,
WASHINGTON, D.C. LIBRARY OF CONGRESS.

The VWM has received little critical attention from scholars in the fields
of memorial architecture, military history, cultural studies, and Vietnam War
studies.[6] This is likely due to the contradictions many feminists faced in
regard to the memorial when they questioned how one could memorialize
women's service in a war that most feminists opposed. However, the VWM
does serve as a principal site for exploring American aesthetic representations of women and war and should be examined as such. The VWM engages
the political and historical failures to recognize women's military service
in the war, while its sculptural narrative—which calls attention to nurses'
endeavors to provide relief for dying soldiers—evokes the central trauma
that most American servicewomen experienced during and after the war. At
times resisting and conceding to patriarchal ideals of authenticity and work
in order to legitimize military women's service in and responses to war, the

VWM's feminist origins and careful promotion, as well as the design itself, engage the recuperative work of feminism. However, this feminist aesthetic is challenged by the tension about feminist and military service that surfaced in the debate over the clearance for the memorial, as seen in promotional materials and a hearing before the Senate Subcommittee on Public Lands, National Parks and Forests, which considered authorizing construction of a statue at the Vietnam Veterans Memorial.

RECOGNITION

During the American War in Viet Nam, between ten thousand and eleven thousand American women served "in country"—in Viet Nam—in military and civilian roles. All volunteers, military servicewomen cared for the wounded during medical evacuations, in the Army Nurse Corps, and as medical specialists and support staff in mobile army surgical hospitals (MASH units). Civilian women served in the Red Cross to provide welfare services—counseling, recreational activities, and drug-abuse treatment— for the injured and able-bodied alike. Civilian women worked as journalists covering the war and, as appointees of the Department of Defense Special Services, attended to troop morale and recreation. From the first category, eight military servicewomen died in the war and their names are engraved on the Vietnam Veterans Memorial Wall (Evans 16). Of the second category, nearly sixty civilian women, including journalists and missionaries, died in Viet Nam between 1964 and 1975 (Evans 16). Although American servicewomen experienced fewer casualties than servicemen, they shared many of the same wide-ranging war experiences.

Women's military service in Viet Nam exposed them to both the dangers and carnage of war. Like male soldiers, servicewomen completed their tours of duty by abruptly returning to civilian life, to which they found it difficult to readjust. Before the 1990s few studies existed on the connection between exposure to death, dangers of the combat zone, and psychological distress among military servicewomen (Fontana, Schwartz, and Rosenheck 169). It was not until after a 1990 report of a National Vietnam Veterans' Readjustment Study resulting from a 1983 congressionally mandated investigation into post-traumatic stress disorder (PTSD) among Vietnam veterans, including women, that findings surfaced concluding that exposure to death and combat among servicewomen frequently resulted in PTSD.[7] Moreover, women veterans received little to no support from the Veterans Administration, "whose hospitals often lacked the facilities to give women the most basic health care" such as routine gynecological exams (Mithers 78, Bonior, Champlin, and Kolly 159–60).

After returning from Viet Nam to the United States, servicewomen experienced isolation akin to that commonly associated with alienated male combat veterans.[8] Women's war and postwar memoirs and oral histories, for example, often represent their postwar stateside experiences as rife with hostility from the antiwar movement or indifference to their service and war experiences from family and friends.[9] In the mid-1980s, the silence about women veterans seemed to break with the publication of several memoirs, oral histories, and the 1988 premiere of the stereotypically suspect television series China Beach, whose main characters included a combat nurse, a Red Cross volunteer, a USO entertainer, and a "prostitute/black marketer" (Mithers 87). However, according to Vietnam Veteran and VWMP founder Diane Carlson Evans, until the dedication of the Vietnam Women's Memorial in 1993, American servicewomen felt alienated and ignored, and were ultimately unrecognized for their participation in the war and the psychological effects they had suffered (2). Since the dedication of the VWM, the Women in Military Service for America Memorial building, dedicated in 1997 and located at the ceremonial entrance to Arlington National Cemetery, serves as a memorial to all United States servicewomen, past, present, and future. Despite efforts to broaden their recorded experiences, servicewomen remain significantly underrepresented in sculptural memorial locations, celluloid memorials, and textual narratives. Moreover, the availability of women's accounts of the American War in Viet Nam declined further when their recorded recollections turn to their postwar experiences and their responses to the Vietnam Veterans Memorials.

MEMORIAL MEMORY

The Vietnam Women's Memorial (VWM), Glenna Goodacre's sculpture-in-the-round, figures three female nurses and a wounded male soldier. In the sculpture, a nurse kneeling over medical supplies and a fallen helmet looks as though she may be praying or is despairing over the uselessness of her supplies to save the wounded serviceman. A second nurse, looking to the sky, seemingly searches for a helicopter or spiritual help. She grasps the elbow of a third nurse, who cradles the head of the male soldier lying prostrate with a bandage over his eyes on a pile of sandbags. In its sculpted figures, the VWM presents a narrative that tenuously represents hope and despair. The figures call attention to the challenges of saving dying soldiers—the central psychological trauma that many American servicewomen experienced during the war and one that continues to haunt their postwar memories. The women do not appear to fear the possibility of attack but rather sacrifice their own safety in efforts to help the wounded male soldier.

The sculptural narrative of the Vietnam Women's Memorial provides a feminine aesthetic within the larger framework of traditional masculine, heroic war memorials. In conjunction with postmodern aesthetics, feminism provides narrative tools to begin changing gendered representations of war in a manner that permits multiple positions for the individual and the community. Yet the VWM both resists and concedes to patriarchal ideologies of universal truths in war. Just as the history of the memorial's creation reveals the legitimizing work necessary for its acceptance, so does the sculpture itself, insofar as it mimetically figures women's bodies and the work those bodies perform—caring for wounded or dying *male* soldiers in an attempt to authenticate women's wartime service.

The VWM negotiates recognition, recuperative feminism, political agency, memory, and postmodernism's crisis of representation. Scholars such as Linda Hutcheon and Barbara Creed raise important questions concerning the possibilities and limitations of feminist recuperation in the age of postmodernism. In *The Politics of Postmodernism* (1993), Hutcheon understands postmodernism as disruptive yet complicit in its critique, whereas feminism calls for change and political agency (151–52). As she applies her assessment against the VWM, the risks of accommodation in feminism's recuperative work emerge. Is it possible that recuperative work at the VWM, because it relies on legitimation, undermines recuperative feminism? Although postmodernism and feminism deal directly with the crisis of representation (Creed 398), feminism's project of telling history through women's experiences can, as it does at the VWM, find itself overwhelmed by a grand narrative impulse, or *consistent history*, laden with patriarchal ideologies of authenticity (truth) and progress (work).

In keeping with traditional heroic memorial aesthetics, the VWM consists of realistic figures cast in bronze. Yet Donald Ringnalda, in *Fighting and Writing the Vietnam War* (1994), maintains that despite the realism of the bronze figures, the memorial "lends itself in no way to the conventional validation of war" (235). He directs attention to the sculpted faces, explaining that their expressions indicate helplessness:

A nurse holding a dying soldier looks on him tenderly, but she is saddened beyond language. The soldier himself has a Goya-like expression of terror and pain. . . . Instead of protecting him from "incoming," the sandbags he lies on will likely be his deathbed. Another woman looks off to the horizon, mouth agape, as if screaming for help that won't help the soldier even if it comes. Behind these three figures—invisible, from a unidimensional perspective—a third woman kneels prayerfully; but in view of the memorial's totality, these would seem to be unanswerable prayers. (235)

Ringnalda offers a compelling reading of the powerlessness and futility evident in the VWM's narrative that has come to signify the American War in Viet Nam. However, he overlooks the authenticity trap of the memorial's legitimizing figuring of the work that servicewomen perform in war. A striking disparity exists between representing servicemen's and servicewomen's active participation in war. For example, the sculpted soldiers in Hart's *Three Fighting Men*, cast realistically in bronze, are not figured at work but seem to stand in waiting. Most critics agree that the men are returning from the battlefield exhausted. The realistic, albeit larger-than-life, figuring of the male soldiers fulfills demands of authenticity; however, the servicewomen must be at *work*. Here emerges a feminist recuperative project trampled by legitimation. Servicewomen must justify their service and memory, even in the memorial.

Although the VWM "avoid[s] overt allusions to motherhood" by breaking with the tradition of figuring gown-donned women of wartime memorials (Piehler 178), the memorial does exhibit Josephine Donovan's "conditions that appear to have shaped traditional women's experience and practice in the past" (100). These conditions include a colonized mentality that tends to silence women; a domestic sphere accounting for the repetitive, cyclical, interruptible nature of women's work; a creation for use rather than exchange; an emphasis on physiological experiences, especially childrearing, a practice of holding and waiting; and a psychological maturation of relationships (100–104). The VWM's sculpted women engage in the work of holding, waiting, and praying. One nurse holds the injured soldier, while the others seem to wait and pray. The memorial represents the physiological and psychological experiences of injury and healing of the past in the present. It signifies a moment suspended in time. In accordance with psychological maturation, the memorial emphasizes community. The woman searching the sky engages in mutual support by placing her hand on the shoulder of the woman holding the prostrate soldier.

The positioning of the prostrate soldier and the attending nurse's embrace at the VWM invokes Michelangelo's Pietà and its associated sentiments of glorious sacrifice (fig. 5). Goodacre's male soldier lies prostrate, with one arm dangling, in the nurse's arms while she despairingly gazes down upon him. The pose is reminiscent of Mary's gaze of resignation as she holds the body of Jesus after his crucifixion in Michelangelo's sculpture. Goodacre's nurse duplicates Mary's silent, maternal suffering. As caretaker, the nurse alleviates suffering and soothes the passage between life and death. The VWM thereby feminizes the liminal space between life and death. Regardless of the similarities between the two sculptures, Michelangelo's youthful Madonna has a serene facial expression as opposed to the weary furrowed brow of the at-

FIG. 5. MICHELANGELO'S *PIETÀ* AT ST. PETER'S BASILICA, ROME. PHOTO BY STANISLOV TRAYKOV.

tending nurse and the distress of her companions. Although the VWM figures sacrifice as central to its representation of the war, it does not necessarily validate that sacrifice. The women are not simply maternally feminized; they move beyond Michelangelo's Jesus and Mary by offering a sense of interconnectedness, in the circular form of the VWM. In fact, the memorial has come to be called the "Circle of Healing."[10] The memorial's circular narrative joins feminist and postmodern aesthetic rejection of linear master narratives. The sculpture forms a circular narrative with no clear starting point and, most important, no end (Ringnalda 235). Because the memorial narrative has no end, it encourages a continuous open narrative akin to Maya Lin's circular chronology at the Vietnam Veterans Memorial.[11]

The open narrative of the VWM further surpasses patriarchal memorial traditions by encouraging visitors to enter the space of the memorial in order to view all three women. This is especially true of the kneeling nurse, often unseen in photographs of the memorial (see fig 4). It is impossible to view the entire memorial without viewing it from all vantage points. Thus visitors walk around the memorial, stepping beyond their comfortable place on the boundary as observers into the space of the memorial. The relationship between the VWM and visitors transcends object/observer positioning because the memorial involves the viewer in a kinetic relationship to the sculpted bodies of its female subjects. The postures and facial expressions of sculpted female figures of the VWM denote their confrontations with traumatic physical injury and their ensuing psychological trauma. As literary critic Carol Acton explains, nurses are both observers and participants in warfare's trauma of injury (65). So, too, Goodacre's sculpted servicewomen metaphorically mediate between participant and observer. They participate in attempts at healing and observe the wounded male soldier, while experiencing their own psychological wounds. The figures serve as a mediated representation of the physical and psychological traumas of the American War in Viet Nam. Acton further understands the three women of the VWM as looking at unseen trauma—that is, "deliberately placed outside the [visitor's] gaze" (62). Although invited to follow her skyward gaze, visitors do not know if the standing nurse awaits assistance from humans—a medevac helicopter—or the divine. The kneeling nurse, whose distraught face is obscured unless the visitor also kneels, stares helplessly at her medical equipment. According to Goodacre in her "Statement on the Women's Memorial," the kneeling nurse's posture "reflect[s] her despair, frustrations, and all the horrors of war" (39).

The central nurse looking down upon the prostrate male soldier sees a condition to which visitors have no clear narrative access. Although Goodacre explains that she "want[s] this to be a monument to the living," insisting that the wounded male soldier "will live," his fate is not necessarily clear to visitors who have not read her statement (39). The bandage that covers much of wounded soldier's face creates an "everyman" identity and conceals narrative access to his condition, leaving visitors uncertain about whether he is wounded, dying, or dead. Despite her narrative intent, Goodacre also wrote of the memorial that "the figures and their roles are intentionally vague, creating opportunities for interpretation for each viewer" (39). A multiple and tenuous aesthetic emerges in Goodacre's positioning of these service-women as paradoxically exposing and shrouding the trauma beyond their gaze. The VWM servicewomen thus simultaneously reveal and conceal the extent of trauma injuries that servicewomen witnessed during the war and psychological traumas they experienced during and after the war. Although the memorial represents servicewomen in their wartime roles, the postures and expressions of the sculpted figures invoke the memory of war, thus providing one possibility for the memorial to transcend its historical specificity.

LEGITIMATION

The history of the Vietnam Women's Memorial's creation delineates the legitimizing work necessary for congressional legislation, the secretary of the interior's authorization, and approval from federal regulatory commissions: the Fine Arts Commission, the National Capital Planning Commission, and the National Capital Memorial Commission (Evans 7). Promotional materials and public support for the Vietnam Women's Memorial, established in human-interest articles and produced by the Vietnam Women's Memorial Project, asserted that history had repeatedly disregarded the roles of women in war and specified that the women's memorial would fill the void of silenced stories.[12] In response to postwar lack of recognition and the subsequent isolation that grew out of that deficiency, Vietnam veteran nurse Diane Carlson Evans founded the VWMP. The necessity of validating women's military service in Viet Nam surfaced in the recuperative, feminist project at work in the controversy over the memorial proposal.

When Evans established the VWMP in 1984, it was discovered that the Department of Defense had not kept a definitive, official record of the number of women who served in the American War in Viet Nam and that postwar psychological support structures and veterans' groups for women were virtually nonexistent. Women veterans were physically isolated from one another and psychologically detached from the general public, which was not aware of the women's participation in the war. Indeed, as some oral history collections such as Keith Walker's *A Piece of My Heart* (1985) and Ron Steinman's *Women in Vietnam* (2000) demonstrate, a sense of shame and alienation discouraged many servicewomen from sharing their veteran status with friends and sometimes their husbands. Evans believed that a memorial would not only recognize women's military service during the American War in Viet Nam but would also provide an impetus for women to gather, create support systems, and share stories.

In addition to educating the public about women's roles during the war, the VWMP emphasized women's postwar experiences of psychological detachment from family and friends and physical isolation from each other. The stated objectives of the VWMP were to locate the women who had served, to facilitate research on women's service in the war, to educate the American public about women's military service in Viet Nam, and to erect a monument for female Vietnam veterans on the grounds of the Vietnam Veterans Memorial (Evans 3–4). For the VWMP, activism, information gathering, and education became the means of countering political and historical neglect and achieving recognition for servicewomen.

Ultimately rejected by the Fine Arts Commission, the initial memorial design figured a sculpted female nurse, known as "The Lady" or "The Nurse," carrying her helmet and medical supplies. Evans and sculptor Roger Brodin intended to sculpt a face on the statue that projected a look of "tiredness, strength, and compassion" that would represent a nurse returned from Viet Nam, rather than the heightened alertness of a nurse in combat (Marling and Wetenhall 353). Sharing similarities with Hart's mimetic *Three Fighting Men* sculpture at the Vietnam Veterans Memorial, the figure proposed for "The Nurse" was weary, in uniform, and carrying authentic military paraphernalia.

The proposal for "The Nurse" was unique for a war memorial in its aim to represent postwar experience in a sculpted body. Washington, D.C., is riddled with memorials figuring a heroic posture of a once great man deemed worthy of a postmortem memorial. Examples include, but are not limited to, equestrian sculptures of former presidents and figurative sculptures of Christopher Columbus, George Thomas, and Winfield Scott Hancock. American war memorials commonly emphasize the dead by listing names, as the VVM does, or by employing symbols to represent the number of American war dead—that is, gold stars at the World War II memorial and combat boots in *Eyes Wide Open*, the American Friends Service Committee's Iraq and Afghanistan exhibit. Such memorials do not embody the postwar experience of the living and, therefore, do not figure the living body as a vehicle of memorial communication. To some extent, symbolic memorials may provide alternatives to the falsely authentic, historically specific, mimetic sculptures of the body figured in *Three Fighting Men*. However, encouraging representations of postwar experiences at war memorials permits memorials to speak not only for the past but for the present and future as well.

The proposal for "The Nurse," however, was not rejected for its aesthetic implications but for the very idea of a Vietnam Women's Memorial. Objections to the VWM, led by Robert Doubek, the Vietnam Veterans Memorial Fund project director, and J. Carter Brown, the former chairman of the Fine Arts Commission during the vetting process of the Vietnam Veterans Memorial, argued against the women's memorial on the basis that it would only encourage other ethnic and specialized veterans' groups to seek a memorial of their own. Their line of thinking took popular hold, appearing in numerous testimonies, interviews, and newspaper commentaries.[13] Opponents shared Brown's concern that the Mall in Washington would be overrun with statues and monuments, becoming, as Brown suggested, "Disneyfied" or "ghettoized" (Marling and Wetenhall 358). To use these words perpetuates patriarchal hierarchies. Brown unequivocally asserted that a women's memorial would be child's play, postmodern kitsch, unworthy of the Mall's hallowed, white, upper-class, patriarchal ground. Brown further argued that special-interest groups, such as those representing military scout dogs, were mounting support for a memorial of their own.[14] While scout dogs served a variety of roles in Viet Nam, ranging from mine detection to tracking the enemy to locating cadavers, the VWMP members were understandably outraged at the comparison of women's military service to that of service dogs.[15] The equation undermines women's roles in war and speaks to the VWMP's primary concerns with recuperation of women's military history and recognition of women's military service in Viet Nam.

Those who opposed the women's memorial understood that a recuperative, feminist undertaking was at stake. As designer of *Three Fighting Men* and a member of the Fine Arts Commission, Fredrick Hart appropriately disqualified himself from voting on the VWM proposal (Evans 8). He did not, however, refrain from arguing against a women's memorial on the grounds that his *Three Fighting Men* represents all veterans, regardless of gender. Brown agreed, deeming Hart's sculpture "symbolic of humankind and everyone who served" (Evans 8). Yet Hart's sculpture unsuccessfully symbolizes *everyone*; it fails to include women. It depicts three male soldiers: a Latino American, an Anglo American, and an African American. Because Hart's realist sculpture figures only male soldiers, members of the VWMP maintained that a sculpture of a woman was a necessary addition to the Vietnam Veterans Memorials. In addition to Hart's comments, a letter from Maya Lin was read at the Fine Arts Commission hearing as final resistance to the proposed women's memorial. Because she considered her design, commonly known as *The Wall*, as complete and inclusive, Lin objected to "individual concessions" and any further additions to *The Wall*, noting that she had consistently opposed any supplements to her design, including Hart's sculpture (8).

Proponents of the women's memorial responded to opposition by engaging with Hart's description of his design as "consistent with history" (2). For example, Evans argued that American servicewomen "slip into history unrecognized and forgotten" and that Hart's male-centered *consistent history* erroneously leads the public to believe that only men serve in war (Evans 2). Furthermore, Karal Marling and John Wetenhall, in "The Sexual Politics of Memory," defend the women's memorial on the grounds that *Three Fighting Men* "already compromise[s] *The Wall*'s inclusive embrace by its omission of women" (362). In 1987, after much debate, the Fine Arts Commission rejected the women's memorial proposal. After this initial rejection, the VWMP opened a design contest and continued to promote the project.

Emphasizing a recuperative mission, rhetoric of recognition and honor pervade the VWMP's promotional material. For example, Evans's VWMP interviews debunk the myth that women do not serve, or *significantly* serve, in war. She recalls that "the most predictable question was 'were you ever rocketed or attacked?' We would negate the myth and defy the stereotype on both counts. Yes, women were there, and yes, they were wounded and killed" (6). To combat forgetfulness, denial, or ignorance, Evans argued that the VWM would fulfill a "tremendous responsibility to the people of America," to share servicewomen's war experiences with the public (9).

Although the VWMP aimed to discredit myths that women did not significantly serve during the war, the project's rhetoric is not consistently reconciliatory. In 1988, as part of a congressional lobbying effort, the VWMP released a promotional poster illustrated with a woman's name on a dog tag and the divisive statement, "Not all women wore love beads in the '60s" (fig. 6). Thousands of these posters were sent out across America. They became petitions that volunteers asked Americans at veterans' groups, shopping malls, and street corners to sign. For example, at least twenty-five thousand were sent to national veterans' conventions that summer (Evans 12). According to Evans, "Legislators became so tired of receiving the tubes they said 'no more!' They had gotten the message" (12).

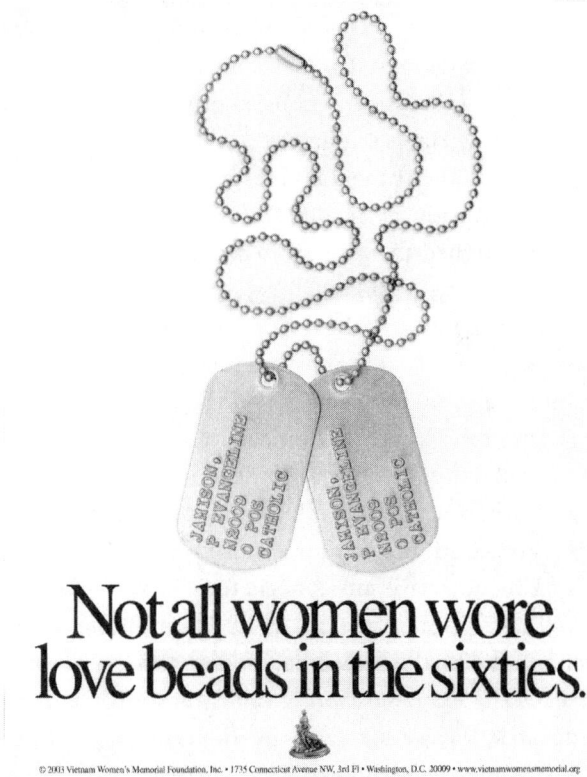

Not all women wore love beads in the sixties.

© 2003 Vietnam Women's Memorial Foundation, Inc. • 1735 Connecticut Avenue NW, 3rd Fl • Washington, D.C. 20009 • www.vietnamwomensmemorial.org

FIG. 6. VIETNAM WOMEN'S MEMORIAL PROJECT PROMOTIONAL POSTER. COPYRIGHT © 2003 VIETNAM WOMEN'S MEMORIAL FOUNDATION, INC., AND COURTESY OF THE UNIVERSITY OF VIRGINIA SCHOOL OF NURSING, ELEANOR CROWDER BJORING CENTER FOR NURSING HISTORICAL INQUIRY.

Unfortunately, the poster's rhetoric revives old battles over the war by segregating servicewomen from antiwar activists. The poster may be an attempt to discredit cultural myths that all women were opposed to, and therefore enemies of, male soldiers who served in the war.[16] However, the poster undermines the purported goal of the VWM as a memorial for all women with *any* connection to war (Ringnalda 235). The conciliatory endeavor inherent in the women's memorial project fails by relying on patriarchal ideals of authenticity in experience. The poster is aggressive in its claims of female sacrifice and "real work" by demeaning the antiwar movement. In effect, the poster encourages an inconsistent history by failing to recognize antiwar groups with close ties to the war, such as G.I.s Against the War, Gold Star Mothers Against the War, and Vietnam Veterans Against the War.[17] Furthermore, the VWMP continues to sell the image on T-shirts and coffee mugs, prolonging division among service and civilian women of the war era and perpetuating negative myths associated with the antiwar movement.[18] Regrettably, the poster undermines the recuperative and reconciliatory goals of the memorial. The poster's consistency with history—the patriarchal order—excludes women, especially women from the antiwar movement, from the community of veterans.

Legislators responded positively to the VWMP and the posters surely played a role in this as they did in February 1988, when proponents and opponents gave testimony in a hearing before the Senate Subcommittee on Public Lands, National Parks and Forests, which was considering authorization for the VVMP to construct a statue at the Vietnam Veterans Memorial.[19] Among over twenty speakers, the very first statement on the bill, S. 2042, referenced the poster as a call from the American people to build the memorial. This statement was made by Dave Durenberger, U.S. senator of Minnesota, a cosponsor along with Senator Alan Cranston of California. This bill and the hearing arose from the 1987 rejections by the Commission of Fine Arts against the proposal for a women's memorial. In his testimony, Senator Durenberger emphasized the public support for the memorial, noting the many letters he received from Vietnam veterans across the country. Most important, he referenced the "Love Beads" poster. He was given a copy of the poster, signed by many of his constituents, when he arrived at the hearing. Although he referred to the poster as a "new form of petition," he further highlighted the "telling side of the poster" (United States 8). As he quoted the text on the poster, he stressed "commitment" and willingness to serve in Vietnam. His statement echoes the rhetoric of the poster, demeaning the antiwar movement. In addition to making its way into the hearing, the poster must have influenced support for the bill, considering that there were thirty-one supporters of the legislation on January 19, according to Senator Barbara Mikulski's statement, and by February 23 there were fifty-two senators sponsoring the bill (153, 140). Such support is likely a result of the poster. After all, as Evans noted, legislators received the message.

The battle over the Vietnam Women's Memorial was also a public airing of the tension among feminists. Indeed, many feminists opposed the American War in Viet Nam, yet they confronted an ethical contradiction about how best to represent women's military service in relation to a war they opposed. In a double bind, Evans explains that she was "described as a radical feminist . . . using the Vietnam dead to further [her] cause" (4). She received "hate mail, threats, and angry phone calls" (4). Ultimately, she frames the mission of the VWM as a feminist mission when she writes, "Many people were comfortable with the popular stereotype of the all-male American military. For adversaries we were providing a new emblematic definition of women they were eager to impugn" (4).

However, not all feminists supported the memorial. Testimony from a feminist perspective at the hearing before the subcommittee included opponents to the VWMP. Noting that the memorial would be an addition or afterthought, several speakers, including male and female military veterans, argued that singling women out was actually a form of discrimination, not an effort toward equality. Still others perceived that the statue of a nurse as a separate entity at the Vietnam Veterans Memorial would "suggest that women played . . . a subsidiary role," as Shelley Mastran, a scholar of the American cultural landscape, claimed (134). She further contended that a memorial should be build, but elsewhere, and that it should "represent the women who fought their own battles at home . . . [because they] also serve who only stand and wait" (134–35). Maya Lin thoughtfully suggested that the desire for the women's memorial was a response to the addition of Fredrick Hart's Three Fighting Men as an attempt to "equalize or neutralize the power" of that sculpture, resulting in a "misdirected attempt at equality for women" (123). She further questioned whether "an addition to an addition [was] the best and most honorable way of paying homage" to female veterans (123). Lin's comment stands at the center of the feminist debate over the VWM is an ineffectual means of recognizing the equality of women and their military service, which is still easing its way into military policy since the Pentagon lifted the ban on women in combat in 2013.

Despite these contentious issues, the VWM was fully approved in 1991 by the Commission of Fine Arts, the National Capital Memorial Commission, and the National Capital Planning Commission. Yet testimony like that of those who supported the memorial at the hearing continue in the Annual Storytelling Project, which now occurs twice a year, on Memorial Day and Veteran's Day.

STORYTELLING

Besides the VWM's sculptural narrative of women's war experiences, the Annual Storytelling Project at the VWM encourages further narrative accounts, including postwar experiences. A typical ceremony at the VWM's Annual Veteran's Day service includes a daylong educational service entitled "Vietnam: In Their Own Words; Storytelling at the Vietnam Woman's Memorial." Speakers range from servicewomen of the American War in Viet Nam to women who served with the Red Cross in Viet Nam to civilian women, including schoolteachers, filmmakers, and writers. The importance of the title, "In Their Own Words," reveals the recuperative feminist aims of the sharing of women's stories. In spite of the many possible ambiguous readings of the memorial design, political agency emerges in the shared narratives of these women. The Storytelling Project generates alternate voices to the patriarchal traditions. By joining the VWM with larger issues of women and war, these narratives provide a means for women's war experiences to transcend historical and memorial specificity. The women's shared stories and the Vietnam Women's Memorial thus become mediated memories accessible to the larger cultural community.

The ten-year battle for the VWM's creation calls attention to the ambiguous nature of political agency for women. The VWMP and the VWM confront political and historical failures to recognize women's military service in the war. Aesthetically, the memorial both relies on and transcends patriarchal values of authenticity and work. Utilizing traditional bronze material and a realistic figuring of bodies at work, the VWM invokes patriarchal tradition. The memorial thus authenticates women's military service in the war via the tradition's dictates. However, the VWM's sculptural narrative maintains an aesthetic limbo between healing and closure and an ongoing remembrance. The circular narrative and emphasis on community allows for a joining of feminist and postmodernist aesthetics at the memorial that operate, in part, to overcome the perceived validation necessary for memorializing women's military service in the war. The Vietnam Women's Memorial's primary achievement and contribution to the memory of the war includes recognizing servicewomen's participation in the war. Although the VWM legitimizes and mimetically represents recognition for women's participation and military service in the war in patriarchal terms, the memorial's aesthetic also transcends those terms. Finally, the memorial ultimately contests patriarchal means of legitimation in its encouragement of an ongoing womens' narrative through storytelling. Thus the VWM participates in a collected cultural memory. Here, "collected" memories do not signify the cohesion of "collective" memory but rather a gathering of multiple and sometimes competing memories. A collected cultural memory holds some possibility of making memories of the war more accessible to those with no direct experience in the war.

Still, the Vietnam Women's Memorial primarily emphasizes the war experiences of American servicewomen with direct experience and memories of the war. However, as the following chapter will explore, other written and cinematic narratives focus on both the direct war memories and prosthetic war memories—memories acquired via mediated representation by those with no direct experience in or hereditary connection to the war—of civilian women in both America and Viet Nam.

CHAPTER 4
⋆ CIVILIAN WOMEN

AMERICAN AND VIETNAMESE
MARRIED TO VIET NAM

Although the founders of the Vietnam Women's Memorial hoped to provide a memorial for all women with any connection to the war, its sculpted figures characterize only military servicewomen who served in Viet Nam. It does not figure civilian women journalists and morale contingents. Nor does the memorial allude to American and Vietnamese civilian women on the home fronts. Yet memories of the war also hold a profound psychological effect on civilian women, especially women who were married to servicemen and women who later married Vietnam veterans. Moreover, the war obviously altered the lives of Vietnamese civilian women.

At the turn of the millennium, memorial, cinematic, and written narratives depicting women's experiences in the American War in Viet Nam have encouraged recuperation and reconciliation. Recuperation, however, is not simply achieved via recognition but also through reconciliation. In addition to recognition, reconciliationist narratives promote the perception that "everyone"—servicemen, servicewomen, and civilians—suffers in war. Moreover, in reconciliationist narratives of the war, wartime and postwar psychological suffering extends beyond Americans to include those from the northern Democratic Republic of Viet Nam (DRVN) and those from the southern Republic of Viet Nam (RVN). Reconciliationist representations of women affected by the war also materialize beyond the battlefield, thus encompassing the war and postwar experiences of American servicemen and American and Vietnamese civilian women.

Sandie Frazier's novel *I Married Vietnam* (1992) and Oliver Stone's *Heaven and Earth* (1993), a narrative film based on Le Ly Hayslip's autobiographies *When Heaven and Earth Changed Places: A Vietnamese Woman's Journey from War to Peace*

(1989) and *Child of War, Woman of Peace* (1993) serve as representative narratives of civilian women's relationship to and memories of the war. Frazier's *I Married Vietnam* explores the postwar experiences and prosthetic memory of a civilian American woman who marries a Vietnam veteran after the war. Stone's *Heaven and Earth* presents the direct memories of a civilian Vietnamese woman who marries an American serviceman. Each considers the memories of women who do not directly participate in warfare. Just as earlier war narratives, films, and memorials engage in the search for meaning in the face of overwhelming death, these narratives serve as examples of reconciliation that elude the causes of the war in favor of examining the wide range of psychological and cultural effects of war. However, unlike their predecessors, these narratives examine women's memories of the war. The main female characters in these narratives also operate as audience to veterans' confessions and thus as reconciliatory mediators between veterans and civilians via the women's own prosthetic and direct memories of the war. Ultimately, *I Married Vietnam* and *Heaven and Earth* remember women's experiences and explore women's memories in order to encourage reconciliation between servicemen and servicewomen, between servicemen and civilian women, and between Americans and the Vietnamese. Together, recuperation and reconciliation as represented in *I Married Vietnam* and *Heaven and Earth* culminate in a collected cultural memory of the war derived from both direct and prosthetic memories. Again, "collected" memories are distinct from the unity that "collective" memory invokes; instead, "collected" memories account for multiple and often competing memories.

I Married Vietnam represents the very best among a small genre of sentimental novels and memoirs written by women about women's lives during and after the war that center on their relationships with male soldiers. Like others of its kind, Frazier's novel offers a narrative through which to understand the suffering and sacrifices of the postwar wives of Vietnam veterans. However, *I Married Vietnam* is unique because it is not a romance novel, like so many others written by women about being married to Vietnam veterans. It is also unique in its treatment of memory, especially the power of traumatic memory transference and prosthetic memory—individually felt cultural memory. Unlike nurses' memoirs and most narratives about wives' experiences, however, Frazier's novel does not follow her main character or her relationship with her husband through the changes of war. Instead, Frazier writes of the war's effects beyond the battlefield. Her female character, Sam, meets African American veteran Jeremy Freeman after his tour of duty in Viet Nam. The war and his veteran status serve as Freeman's postwar identity and thus Sam "marries Vietnam."

The novel chronicles Freeman's life beginning with his birth, sketches a childhood of familial, economic, and racial challenges in Mississippi, includes accounts of his enlistment and military training, incorporates a stream-of-consciousness montage of his combat experiences in Vietnam, details his return home, and depicts his addiction to heroin as a result of his physical and psychological injuries during the war. This first third of the novel employs a third-person narrator. These chapters begin with Jeremy's name, noted as "Freeman" during his military service. In many respects, the narrative is conventional in its recounting of Freeman's challenges finding employment because of his veteran status, its presentation of the Veterans Administration as incompetent, and its depiction of Freeman as a prisoner of his memories and self-preserving isolation. The novel details Freeman's difficulties with addiction, violence, and severely physical flashbacks.

Freeman is a stereotypically isolated veteran. Concerning stereotypes of Vietnam veterans, literary critic Toby Herzog asserts, "Americans attempting to reconcile with traumatized Vietnam Veterans construct images of these individuals to fit myths, stereotypes, reality, or social, political, ideological, and literary agendas" (113–14). Thus, representations of Vietnam veterans often fall into one stereotype or a combination of three that Herzog outlines: the Blank Page, the Tripwire, and the Interstate Nomad (113–14). The Blank Page is all things to all people: a survivor who is completely void of any self-identity. The Tripwire veteran keeps a distance from the community, the tripwire signifying a noisemaker as distant warning. This stereotype can also be considered a "bunkered in" veteran. The Interstate Nomad is the type of veteran who lacks community and continuously wanders in search of this impossibility. Freeman's detached character constitutes a combination of the distancing Tripwire and wandering Interstate Nomad veteran.

Despite its characteristic rendering of Freeman, *I Married Vietnam* is unique in its emphasis on Sam's experiences and its depiction of Sam's prosthetic memories of the war. As opposed to the third-person narration that provides Freeman's background, the last third of the novel shifts to a first-person narration that gives voice to Sam's life with Freeman. Her narrative begins with, "I was nothing when I met Freeman" (159). The following chapters begin with "we" and "our." The shift in opening lines of each chapter points to the central theme of the novel, that Sam "married Vietnam." Sam and Freeman develop a conjoined identity deeply associated with their fused memories of the war.

Although Freeman is reluctant to divulge his memories of the war, twenty years after the conflict he begins to share his memories with Sam, and she thereby experiences mediated memories. Trauma and literary scholar Kalí Tal's influential *Worlds of Hurt* (1996) addresses this desire to communicate to others traumatic memories in what she terms a "Literature of Trauma," a literature "written from the need to tell and retell the story of the traumatic experience, to make it 'real' both to the victim and to the community" that does not directly experience the trauma (21). Although Freeman performs a confessional speech act, he and Sam do not fall into what Foucault would identify as a power relationship between confessant—the person confessing their wrongs—and confessor—the authority who hears the confession—because the act does not inscribe Sam as authoritative power. Yes, Sam's first-person narration positions her as "author," but she serves as mediator between Freeman and the reader, as she does not hold any authority over Freeman. In fact, she suffers violence and physical abuse resulting from Freeman's power over her. Further, she functions as a confessor who takes on the wrongs of the confessant. Not only does Sam "take the burden off [Freeman's] back as he begins to talk to [her] and [she] listen[s]. [She] take[s] his sins on as [her] own" (210). As audience to Freeman's confessions and memories, Sam encounters her own prosthetic memories of the war. She narrates, "I know Freeman's pain so intensely that it has become my own. When he suffers, I suffer" (201). Taking on Freeman's memories and sins as her own, Sam serves as a reconciliatory mediator between Freeman and Frazier's audience.

When Freeman repeatedly shares his memories of the war, Sam experiences memory sensations, acquiring a proximity-induced posttraumatic stress disorder (PTSD). PTSD is generally defined as a "response, sometimes delayed, to an overwhelming event or events, which takes the form of repeated, intrusive hallucinations, dreams, thoughts or behaviors stemming from the event" (Caruth 4). According to the American Psychiatric Association's *Diagnostic and Statistical Manual of Mental Disorders* (1994), the wide-ranging and some-times paradoxical indications of PTSD include reliving a traumatic event through flashbacks, nightmares, and invasive memories; avoiding situations reminiscent of the event; lack of emotions; anxiety and difficulty sleeping; impulse control; alienation and intimacy problems; and substance abuse. Sam's proximity-induced PTSD occurs when, for example, Freeman shares his memories with Sam and she begins to "smell, taste, and see what he [repeatedly] was telling" (201). Sam also experiences the war via Freeman's memories and dreams. She "can feel his dreams, in [her] subconscious" (208). "PTS, battle fatigue, shell shocked, whatever you call it, affects not only Freeman but me as well," she says. "We are both products of Vietnam" (201). When Sam explains that she and Freeman are "products of Vietnam," she speaks of their status as part of the so-called Vietnam Generation; however, she also attests to the power of prosthetic memory. Sam and Freeman are irrevocably haunted by the war; the war is part of them. Although the novel figures Freeman as Viet Nam, as the war and memories that Sam married, she too is Viet Nam.

When she attends a belated "Coming Home" parade, Sam attempts, like the sculpted women of the Vietnam Women's Memorial discussed in the preceding chapter, to fulfill the role of reconciliatory mediator between veterans and civilians.[1] Although she cannot convince Freeman to participate or observe, Sam attends the parade, applauds the veterans, and fantasizes about Freeman marching with the others. The parade signifies recognition and a collective, momentary, living memorial. Freeman later confesses that he was uneasy about participating in the parade because "He was afraid of the names you would call him again, 'baby killer, monster, murderer'" (218 emphasis added). At times, Sam directly addresses Frazier's audience, as above, with accusations and lessons. Here the novel confronts the old divisions between soldiers and the antiwar movement that the Vietnam Women's Memorial Project took advantage of with their "love beads" poster.[2] Sam reveals her anger with the civilian population; she lays blame on them for Freeman's ongoing lack of recuperation, recognition, and reconciliation. However, to Freeman, Sam describes the parade as a time of reconciliation and recognition. She explains that there was no derision but rather "a lot of love in the air" (218). Thus the novel itself participates in a collected cultural memory of reconciliation. It gives voice to past anger toward the antiwar movement and represents the present parade as holding the potential to heal divisions between veterans and civilians.

Although the parade was intended to offer healing and Sam's presence might have helped both Freeman and herself to feel a sense of recuperation, it holds only a momentary sense of reconciliation. I Married Vietnam does not impart clear answers or a closed narrative. The novel ends with Freeman's deserting Sam, as he often did. He leaves her with the memories of the war and the uncertainty of her future with Freeman. Upon hearing of the death of another

Vietnam veteran, the novel closes with Sam wondering when she will "bury Vietnam" (222). Sam, however, will never "bury Vietnam" as it has become part of her life experience. She has acquired individually felt memories of the war, a proximity-induced PTSD that constitutes her prosthetic memory. Despite Sam's mediating role between veteran and civilians, the novel rejects recuperation for Freeman located in the recognition of the parade. Freeman and Sam are still irrevocably psychologically affected by the memories of the war. Frazier thus explores the effects of prosthetic memories and the cultural impossibility of relegating the war to the forgotten past.

VIETNAMESE WOMEN, RECONCILIATORY MEDIATOR

Like Frazier, Oliver Stone cinematically explores the commingling of memory between husband and wife in *Heaven and Earth* (1993). Both narratives call attention to the postwar lives of those married to American veterans of the war. The veteran characters in each narrative experience PTSD, and through sharing their memories of the war, so too do their wives acquire indirect but individually felt prosthetic memories of their husbands' war experiences. The wives also undergo a proximity-induced PTSD. As in Frazier's I *Married Vietnam*, husband and wife in *Heaven and Earth* share in the traumas and memories of war. Stone, however, addresses the impact of the war on a civilian Vietnamese woman, Le Ly. Like Frazier's character Sam, Ly acquires prosthetic memories from her veteran husband's memories of the war. However, Ly also possesses direct memories of the war. Moreover, she operates—like the sculpted servicewomen of the VWM discussed in the previous chapter—as a reconciliatory mediator between civilians and veterans, between Vietnamese and Americans, and between Vietnamese immigrant-refugees and those who remained in Viet Nam.

Following Stone's *Platoon* (1986) and *Born on the Fourth of July* (1989), *Heaven and Earth* (1993) is the third of an informal Vietnam War trilogy. *Heaven and Earth* presents a mediated representation of a Vietnamese woman's experiences in its adaptation of Le Ly Hayslip's *When Heaven and Earth Changed Places: A Vietnamese Woman's Journey from War to Peace* (1989) and *Child of War, Woman of Peace* (1993). Like many of Stone's films, *Heaven and Earth* remembers the war with Stone's trademark emphasis on historical breadth and authenticity. The film participates in the culture wars concerning how best to remember the war. Stone said he hoped the film would respond to "the blind militarism and mindless revisionism of the Vietnam War . . . that has snaked its way into our culture over the past decade or so, in which the conflict is refought in comic book style with a brand-new ending . . . we win!" (qtd. in Kagan 208). Rejecting a narrow, revisionist memory of the war, Stone broadens a collected cultural memory of the war to include representations of Vietnamese memory. However, in broadening collected cultural memory, Stone employs the story of only one woman, Le Ly, who symbolically bears the collective pain of the Vietnamese.

True to Stone's typical epic structure, the narrative spans several decades, from the prewar years to postwar life, while creating a circuitous journey from Viet Nam to America and ending with a return to Viet Nam. The film contains both the micro, Le Ly's life, and the macro, the history of Viet Nam from the 1950s French colonial rule to the late 1980s. Stone frames the film with text noting that the film is based on the true events of Le Ly Hayslip's life, mentioning both her creation of the East Meets West Foundation and her war and postwar memoirs.[3]

Heaven and Earth is also an evacuee-immigration narrative. The film explores the successes and failures of the American dream from a Vietnamese woman's perspective. Ly is initially overwhelmed and later disillusioned with America. She does not immediately find a happy land of opportunity and acceptance upon her arrival in the United States. Instead, she encounters alienation, rejection, strife, and abuse. Often the film is about Ly's loss of identity. However, by the end of the film, Ly has come into her own independence and now has the strength to confront her prewar past and the familial obligation she feels toward her ancestors when she makes a return visit to Viet Nam.

Although the story originates from a woman and is dedicated to Stone's mother, the film, like *Platoon*, "reshape[s] a Vietnamese women's story as one of an American veteran's struggle with guilt" (Sturken 121). In keeping with the 1970s and 1980s mainstream cinematic narrative representations of the war, Stone's film offers yet another negative representation of a disturbed Vietnam veteran. The American War in Viet Nam comes home to America through the character of Le Ly's husband, Steve Butler, and his domestic violence.

Nonetheless, the film depicts a Vietnamese woman in a more positive and complex manner than previous negatively stereotypical fictional representations. For example, Kalí Tal in "The Mind at War: Images of Women in Vietnam Novels by Combat Veterans" demonstrates that in many novels about the war "the Asian woman character has no real life before she meets her soldier and none that is pursued after; these women seem to fade painlessly (through death, desertion, or transfer of affection) out of existence. Asian women are mirrored as whore, or whore-with-a-heart-of-gold, or inscrutable lover, or will-less mistress" (77). Alternatively, *Heaven and Earth* portrays Le Ly's life before and after the war and before and after her relationship with Steve. The film is very much about her problematical experiences as a civilian woman during the war, her postwar life in America, her memories of the war, and her position as reconciliatory mediator.

The film's theme of liminal identity, as the title indicates, places Ly in the position of reconciliatory mediator between veterans and civilians, and between Americans and the Vietnamese. Like the sculpted women of the Vietnam Women's Memorial and Frazier's female character, Ly mediates between spheres of war and peace.[4] Throughout the narrative Ly finds herself caught between Viet Nam—family, ancestors, loyalties, land, home, violence, war, and ultimately peace—and America—Steve, peace, a new life, opportunity, and more violence. Ly's character represents potential psychological and spiritual healing for the Vietnamese, thereby providing possible recuperation for Americans and reconciliation between Vietnamese and Americans. She serves as the means of reconciliation between these worlds and between the United States and Viet Nam. Early in the film, and in her life, Ly comes to understand her liminal position. For example, in the opening sequence of the film, Ly explains that in Vietnamese Buddhist tradition heaven is the father, earth the mother, and the people live in between. As war encroaches, Ly, her family, and her village in the Central Highlands find themselves caught in a civil war. After the arrival of Americans and the challenges of being under the control of South Viet Nam's Army of the Republic of Viet Nam (ARVN) and the Americans during the day, then Viet Cong control at night, Ly and her mother leave the village for what was then the South Vietnamese capital, Saigon.[5]

War disrupts and ultimately destroys the pastoral ideal and thus the ancestral memorial binds of Ly's childhood, creating a disjuncture in her life. The destruction of the pastoral is twofold: familial and ancestral. As Ly's father explains, the family plants rice near the cemetery so that the following generations will eat the rice that contains the wisdom of the ancestors. Thus, destruction of the land dishonors the memory of the ancestors and fractures the connection between past and present. When Ly leaves the village, she is severed from her past, her ancestors, and much of her family. Here, Stone draws attention to the displacement and fragmented community and family ties that many Vietnamese experienced throughout the war years and beyond.

It is that devastation to those connections, to her village, to its people, and to her brothers who joined the Viet Cong that haunts Ly's dreams and memory visions.

Ly's memory visions, threaded throughout the film, represent both direct and prosthetic memories. Figured in black and white and suspending narrative movement, Ly's dreams and memory visions occur both while she is sleeping and awake. Often recurring and repetitive, her dreams and memory visions indicate traumatic memory or PTSD. Ly's memory visions parallel trauma scholar Cathy Caruth's understanding of PTSD in that they are recurring and acquire "the form repeated, intrusive hallucinations, dreams, thoughts or behaviors" (4). Ly's memory visions further correlate with Caruth's Freudian understanding of traumatic memory in that they are belated and refuse "to be simply located in [their] insistent appearance outside the boundaries of any single place or time" (9). For example, Ly experiences a repeated memory vision wherein she witnesses her brother's death, a death she does not witness in waking life. Her family was not officially informed of his death; however, a local "wizard" confirms the family's fears after examining her two brothers' umbilical cords. The wizard informs the family of one brother's restless spirit but not the nature of his death. Ly's memory visions, however, represent the death of that brother. In these visions, Ly and her brother are in a flying helicopter being tortured by American soldiers. Her brother will not acquiesce and is thrown from the helicopter.

The helicopter signifies American encroachment early in the film. When American troops first arrive in Ly's village, she and her father are in the rice paddies. The camera, positioned from the perspective of the helicopter, frames Ly from above. As the wind from the chopper's blades whips the grass and water, Ly is uncertain whether to crouch or stand as she gazes up at the helicopter. It is a frightening moment. Ly's father protectively runs to her and pulls her away. As Vietnam veteran and war literature scholar Philip Biedler in "The Last Huey" argues, in American memory, second only to the Vietnam Veterans Memorial, the helicopter operates as "the 'image' of American 'performance' [in the war] . . . a way of constructing a history out of the twinned resources of memory and imagination" (5). As Michael Herr describes it in his book Dispatches (1977), it is a "saver-destroyer, provider-waster" (8). In Heaven and Earth the helicopter signals the arrival of Americans and the ensuing destruction of Ly's village; yet later it rescues her from a battle zone, beginning her escape journey to Saigon at the end of the war.

Across genres the helicopter functions as a material memory and is a significant symbol of collected cultural memories.[6] Consider its use in popular American films of the war: it serves as John Wayne's taxi in The Green Berets (1968); it is accompanied by Richard Wagner's "Ride of the Valkyries" (1870) in an attack on a village in Francis Ford Coppola's Apocalypse Now (1978); it rescues Chris Taylor from being overrun by enemy forces in Oliver Stone's Platoon (1986); it is the historical focus of the new cavalry in Randall Wallace's We Were Soldiers (2002). In memoirs and novels of the war, echoes of the helicopter's whump-whump operates as an archetype of the war, and encroaches upon veterans' nightmares and waking memories in Bamboo Bed (William Eastlake, 1969), Dog Soldiers (Robert Stone, 1974), Meditations in Green (Stephen Wright, 1983), and Machine Dreams (Jayne Phillips, 1999), among many others. Moreover, the photograph of the last helicopter evacuating Americans

FIG. 7. DURING THE FALL OF SAIGON, A CIA EMPLOYEE (PROBABLY O. B. HARNAGE) HELPS VIETNAMESE EVACUEES ONTO AN AIR AMERICA HELICOPTER FROM THE TOP OF 22 GIA LONG STREET, A HALF-MILE FROM THE U.S. EMBASSY. COPYRIGHT BETTMANN/CORBIS/AP IMAGES.

and Vietnamese during the fall of Saigon in 1975 resonates as an official and unforgettable memory of the war in the American consciousness (fig. 7).[7]

This phantom chopper, known as the last Huey, is compulsively reproduced in narratives and photographs, as well as in documentary, narrative, and art films. In *Heaven and Earth* Oliver Stone contributes to a collected cultural memory of the war, broadening the savior-destroyer memory of the helicopter to include a civilian Vietnamese response to the memory machine.

Besides her helicopter memory visions, Ly repetitively returns to her former village in her memory visions. Also presented in black and white, Ly's village is a wasteland of the pastoral destroyed. In *The Great War and Modern Memory* (1975), Paul Fussell observes that wars take place within nature and therefore representations of war are necessarily antipastoral (231). Riddled with images of amputation, Ly's memory visions invoke T. S. Eliot's "The Waste Land" (1922). The scene, although rural, recalls Eliot's "Unreal City" as though Ly is thinking, "I had not thought death had undone so many. / Sighs, short and infrequent, were exhaled, / And each man fixed his eyes before his feet" (63–65). The people Ly observes move slowly, if at all, and, without expression, rarely meet her gaze.

East meets West in *Heaven and Earth* when Ly encounters Steve, her future American husband, and their nightmare memories intermingle. Soon after they meet, Steve stays the night in Ly's room in Da Nang and experiences a nightmare about the atrocities he has committed in the war. His dream, also black and white, comprises his experiences as a Black Ops assassin, Ly's memory visions of amputees in her village, and an image of Ly's bleeding face. Here, Steve confronts his dual position as what Vietnam veteran authors Jan Barry, Basil Paquet, and Larry Rottmann have termed "agent-victim" of the war (iii). Although Steve participated in violence and atrocity, he also suffers the consequences of his brutal actions and the difficulty of identifying the enemy during the war. As viewers learn later, he had, in his own words, "assassinated" women as well as men.[8] Like Sam and Freeman in Frazier's novel, Ly's and Steve's memories meld, coming together as one memory. Ly and Steve are opposing sides of the same coin of violence and trauma, a theme that becomes apparent later in the film.

Like Frazier's Freeman, Steve is a stereotypically disturbed veteran. According to Toby Herzog's delineation of the Interstate Nomad, the Trip Wire, and the Blank Page veteran outlined earlier, Steve falls into the latter category. The Blank Page, as "all things to all people," results in a limitless "collage of conflicting images and labels," ranging from the "heroic" to "crybabies" to "agents of violence" (Herzog 115). Steve's troubled character contributes to a collected cultural memory of the war's violent consequences. A heavy drinker, he is violent and obsessed with guns. Throughout their turbulent marriage, Ly and Steve often fight. During one particular argument about his purchase and ownership of guns and a disagreement about exposing their sons to firearms, the fight escalates. Steve puts a gun to Ly's head. A black and white flashback of previous war-related violence in her life ensues. When these visions occur, time is suspended as Ly's past traumas and memories collide with the present violence. Her memory visions have the power to make the past present. Immediately, in a tearful apology, Steve confesses his wartime atrocities to Ly. His assassination memories, figured in black and white, punctuate his confessions. Like Freeman telling Sam of his war experiences, Steve's confessions serve to accentuate the widening circle of the war's effects beyond the battlefield.

After recounting his crimes, Steve puts the gun in his mouth; Ly stops him. She tries to explain that they are the same, that they have "different skin, same suffering." She explains that she was a soldier in past lives and, just like Steve, has bad karma. Moments such as these figure Ly as a victim who carries the burden of forgiving American veterans. Ly and Steve suffer psychologically as a consequence of the war; each suffers from PTSD. Both Ly and Steve experience the repetition of memory visions and flashbacks. Ultimately, in the midst of divorce and a custody battle, Steve commits suicide, yet another indicator of PTSD.

The melding of Ly's and Steve's memories in the film represent the collected nature of memory. They are always figured in black and white and include the repetitive images indicative of PTSD. Ly's memory visions, threaded throughout the film, include actual memories, dreams, and hallucinations. The aesthetic quality of these memory visions indicates the nonlinear quality of memory. As they are presented in a film that is a retrospective of the war, both the memory visions and the film participate in an ongoing collected cultural memory of the war that emphasizes a commingling of past and present.

During these troubled times, Ly consults a Buddhist monk who stresses the necessity of forgiveness. He reinforces Ly's self-perception as mediator and potential healer. If she as victim carries the burden of forgiveness, then it is through the Vietnamese experience that America might achieve reconciliation with Viet Nam. The monk further reinforces the film's rendering of time and memory when he teaches Ly about the cyclical nature of life. He advises her that the future and past are the same and thus provides the philosophical frame for the film's ending, where Ly returns to Viet Nam.

While many memory representations of the war addressed here extend beyond the end of the war, as does *Heaven and Earth*, the film also reaches into the ancestral past, bringing it forward as part of present life and memory. When Ly returns to her village, she continues to feel a sense of alienation. Her surviving brother punctuates this disjuncture when he recounts how the end of the war did not bring peace but instead more fighting and suffering. In 1978 the People's Army of Viet Nam (PAVN) invaded and occupied Cambodia in response to Khmer Rouge attacks, and in 1979 China invaded northern Viet Nam in reaction to a perceived threat to the security of Southeast Asia resulting from a Vietnamese and USSR Treaty of Friendship and Cooperation.[9] Although this dialogue holds true to Stone's emphasis on historical breadth in his films, it also serves to remind viewers that the war and its attendant suffering did not end with the fall of Saigon. Ly's search for closure as late as the mid-1980s attests to this. However, despite her brother's recriminations, she visits the graves of her ancestors and finds peace with her father's spirit. She is no longer haunted by memory visions. Ly's mother grants her forgiveness, understanding Ly's return as a completion of an ancestral circle. Her mother says that the circle, the past, is now complete. Thus, the end of the film achieves a sense of reconciliatory closure.

Stone frames the end of the film with Ly narrating that the "Buddhist masters were right. Nothing happens without cause. . . . The gift of suffering is to bring us closer to God, to teach us to be strong when we are weak; to be brave when we are afraid; to be wise in the midst of confusion and to let go of that which we can no longer hold." *Heaven and Earth* instructs that reconciliation is possible because contending parties endure mutual psychological suffering. In part, the ending of the film shares similarities with post–American Civil War sentimental literature. As historian David Blight in *Race and Reunion* argues, sentimental reconciliationist Civil War literature attempts to return to a romanticized past (217). Blight contends that the "Plantation School," for example, replaces the realities of the war with intersectional marriages of reconciliation, thus transforming the war into a romance (217). Ly and Steve's marriage signifies reconciliation between America and Viet Nam. However, their reconciliationist marriage does not end the narrative and does not permit forgetfulness, but rather heightens memories of the war for both. Furthermore, their marriage ends in disaster. Finally, Ly also understands that although she "had come home . . . home had changed and [she] would always be in between . . . heaven and earth . . . it is [her] fate." While Ly's narration attempts to desimplify the film's easy ending, the narrative movement leaves a powerful impression of peace fulfilled.

Ultimately, the film leaves audiences with the idea that reconciliation and recuperation depend on recognizing the suffering in war beyond the American experience. The film adds to a collected cultural memory of the war in its response to the revision of the war that Stone identified—overlooking the Vietnamese experience. Although it tends to reinforce the stereotypical suffering Vietnam veteran, the film also offers a representation of a Vietnamese woman's memories of the war. Ly serves as a mediator; she provides a potential cure for the so-called Vietnam Syndrome: reconciliation between Americans and the Vietnamese, between the Vietnamese from the northern Democratic Republic of Viet Nam and those from the southern Republic of Viet Nam, and between Vietnamese refugees and their country.

AGAINST AND WITHIN THE TRADITION

Because they explore representations of civilian women's war and postwar experiences, Sandie Frazier's I Married Vietnam and Oliver Stone's Heaven and Earth participate in an ongoing collected cultural memory of the war derived from both direct and prosthetic memories—individually felt cultural memories. They contribute new perspectives, voices, and experiences of civilian women from both America and Vietnam. These narratives reject forgetfulness by recognizing the psychological consequences of the war, beyond the battlefield, on American and Vietnamese civilian women. Each seeks recuperation via recognition.

While sometimes sentimental, I Married Vietnam depicts ongoing remembrance in its recuperative recognition of the postwar memories of a Vietnam veteran and the fusion of his memories with his wife's prosthetic memories of the war. Heaven and Earth recognizes the psychological affects of war on a Vietnamese woman via her direct and mediated memories of the war and their fusion with her Vietnam veteran husband's memories.

It is possible to view Heaven and Earth as limited, despite the narrative's potential broadening of viewers' memories of the war. As Pat Dowell in Cineaste noted, Stone also risked simplifying Hayslip's account, Eastern philosophy, and Buddhism, "serv[ing] to Americanize the story by taming its more uncertain ideological moments" (56). Le Ly Hayslip identifies two deficiencies in the film. The first relates to limited portrayal of Vietnamese daily life (184). Her second disappointment concerns deleted scenes depicting incidents of American brutality she witnessed that "soiled the American military's record" in Viet Nam (185). Nonetheless, Hayslip defends the film, claiming that "better than any other feature film from Hollywood, Oliver Stone's *Heaven and Earth* shows a Vietnamese perspective of the Vietnam War" (178).

While the film has its sometimes "Americanized" limitations, just as *I Married Vietnam* may have some sentimental shortcomings, each contributes to a collected cultural memory of the war that suggest community, circularity, and ongoing remembrance. Moreover, these works, each originating from women's experiences and narratives, participate in an ongoing collected cultural memory by figuring the memories of American and Vietnamese civilian women as vital to a more inclusive and transnational, contemporary memory of the American War in Viet Nam.

As perspectives and memories of the war broaden at the turn of the twenty-first century to include civilian women, cultural memory of the war takes a significant look back to the country of Viet Nam before considering Vietnamese veterans perspectives on the war. Returning to Viet Nam in search of private locations of memory in Viet Nam, narrative representations discussed in the following chapter posit American and Vietnamese veterans finding themselves confronted with a commingling of past and present.

CHAPTER 5
◆ PRIVATE SITES OF AMERICAN AND VIETNAMESE MEMORY AND RECONCILIATION IN VIET NAM

> There was a map of Vietnam on the wall of my apartment
> in Saigon. . . . That map was a marvel, especially now that
> it wasn't real anymore. . . . It had been left there years before by
> another tenant, probably a Frenchman. . . . Vietnam was divided
> into its older territories. . . . If dead ground could come back and
> haunt you the way dead people do, they'd have been able to mark
> my map CURRENT and burn the ones they'd been using since '64,
> but count on it, nothing like that was ever going to happen.
> It was late '67 now, even the most detailed maps didn't reveal
> much anymore; reading them was like trying to read the faces
> of the Vietnamese, and that was like trying to read the wind. We
> knew that the uses of information were flexible, different pieces
> of ground told different stories to different people. We also knew
> that for years now there had been no country here but the war.
>
> —Michael Herr, *Dispatches* 3

While America's national sites of memory, specifically the Vietnam Veterans Memorials, serve as mediated representations of the war that encourage collected cultural and prosthetic memories acquired by those with no direct experience of the American War in Viet Nam, so too do specific locations in Viet Nam. Although Michael Herr speculates that "if dead ground could . . . haunt," Le Ly Hayslip's immigrant-refugee narrative as represented in Oliver Stone's *Heaven and Earth* examined in the previous chapter demonstrates that, in Viet Nam, "dead ground" can haunt the living. Yet American cultural constructs of the war delineate Michael Herr's "there had been no country here but the war" with the singular word "Vietnam." The word "Vietnam" has come to signify a war that affected America rather than identifying a country that has a long history of wars fought for and over the independence and unification of the country. Norman Mailer's *Why Are We in Vietnam?* (1967), for example, understands the so-called "Vietnam experience" as a national consciousness of impending calamity. While memory always negotiates a relationship with the past, meaning diverse things to people in different times, places, and cultures, "Vietnam" consistently evokes the American War in Viet Nam from the American perspective, instead of Viet Nam the country.

However, at the turn of the century, narratives that promote reconciliation complicate America's collected cultural memory of the war. "Collected" memories do not indicate the cohesion associated with "collective" memory but rather a gathering of disparate memories. Reconciliationist narratives perpetuate the perception that "everyone" suffers in war, even those who "won" the war, the northern Democratic Republic of Viet Nam (DRVN). Seeking recuperation via recognition and participating in an ongoing collected cultural memory, American and Vietnamese reconciliationist narratives figure depictions and memories of Viet Nam and the Vietnamese as vital to a collected cultural memory of the war. As reconciliationist cinematic and written narratives of the American War in Viet Nam begin to portray experiences of the Vietnamese in the DRVN and southern Republic of Viet Nam (RVN), "Vietnam" transforms from a war into a country, Viet Nam, a place where the United States was once at war, a place that was and is home to Vietnamese veterans, and a place that has since changed. Moreover, representations of Vietnamese memories of the war are not limited to immigrant-refugee narratives. English translations of works produced by Vietnamese veterans of the war—members of the People's Army of the Republic of Viet Nam (PAVN), America's former enemies—like their American counterparts, also explore direct and prosthetic memories of the war. In mediated representations of war memories, American and PAVN veterans alike illustrate Herr's observation that "different pieces of ground told different stories to different people." These narratives demonstrate that memory and the possibility of communication with the dead surface at specific sites of private memory in Viet Nam. Thus these veterans return to locations in Viet Nam not officially designated as sites of memory to enact memorial performances—tactile, bodily, or material engagement with the symbolic past.

Tim O'Brien's metafictional novel *The Things They Carried* (1998), Sidney Furie's narrative film *Going Back* (2001), Bao Ninh's metafictional memoir *The Sorrow of War* (1993), and Huong Thu Duong's fictional *Novel Without a Name* (1995) explore private memorial performances in Viet Nam enacted by American and PAVN veterans of the war. Located beyond America's physical borders, private memorial sites and performances in these works transcend American national sites of remembrance. Narratives addressed here, by American and Vietnamese directors and authors, emphasize return—going back to specific places in Viet Nam. These sites of memory transform into private memorials through the return visits, the memorial performances veterans enact, and material memory—objects that come to signify individuals—with which visitors engage.[1] It seems that Michael Herr's "dead ground" can haunt the living. At private sites of memory, memories of and communication with the dead provide invocations through which past and present merge.

Private memorial performances may appear, at first, to be highly individualized; however, these carefully situated moments encourage mediated memory via civilian witnesses. Although reliant on a specific site of private memory closely associated with the dead, private memorial performances encourage prosthetic memory—individually felt cultural memories acquired via mediated representation, such as these memorial performances by those with no direct memory of the war. Their presence during private memorial performances allows witnesses to acquire new memories of the war. Memorial performances also advance reconciliation between former enemies or reconciliation between those who directly participated in the fighting with civilians. In American reconciliationist works, witnesses with no direct memory of the war accompany the veterans to locales of private memory and witness veterans' enactments of private memorial performances. Witnesses to the postwar memorial performances include American women and children and Vietnamese veterans and civilians. The American narratives thus explicitly explore the possibilities and limitations of prosthetic memory. While the Vietnamese novels do not include witnesses to private memorial performances, they alternately explore direct memory, which emphasizes reconciliation between the living and the dead in addition to encouraging reconciliation between former enemies, PAVN soldiers, and soldiers of South Viet Nam's Army of the Republic of Viet Nam (ARVN), as well as between PAVN soldiers and Americans.

Narratives from both the American and the PAVN perspectives include both private memorial enactments and encounters between enemies and former enemies that promote reconciliation. For example, in Tim O'Brien's *The Things They Carried*, a pair of Native American moccasins, returned to the soil where a soldier died, signify his body in a symbolic burial. The American veteran conducts his memorial performance while his daughter and Vietnamese farmers observe. O'Brien thus engages with the possibilities of prosthetic memory and reconciliation. In Sidney Furie's fictional *Going Back*, American veterans return to the site of a friendly fire incident to reenact their memories, just as many American veterans of the war have done since the mid-1990s and continue to do well into the twenty-first century. In addition, American and Vietnamese civilian witnesses accompany Furie's characters participating in this reenactment. In Bao Ninh's *The Sorrow of War*, the "Jungle of Screaming Souls" makes communication with the dead unavoidable while wartime encounters with the enemy promote reconciliation. Duong's *Novel Without a Name* also depicts place— specifically the "Gorge of Lost Souls" and the "Valley of Seven Innocents"—as a fluid boundary between the living and the dead. While Bao Ninh implicitly encourages reconciliation between former enemies via his protagonist's empathy for the enemy, Duong is the most explicit advocate of reconciliation because her novel unequivocally critiques the reasons for fighting in the war on behalf of all parties, the DRVN, the RVN, and the United States.

These representative narratives also either implicitly or explicitly petition for reconciliation among the living and the dead and among former wartime enemies. In each of these reconciliatory works, communication with the dead generates a fusion of past and present, past presence and present absence. Private memorial performances that occur at private memorial sites in Viet Nam, as represented in American and Vietnamese cinematic and written narratives, encourage reconciliation between the past and present, between American servicemen and civilians, between Americans and the Vietnamese, between the living and the dead, and between the DRVN and RVN. Moreover, private memorial performances augment master narratives of American and Vietnamese national remembrance, thus creating not a collective, nor a cultural memory, but a collected cultural memory of the war that, at times, encourages newly formed prosthetic memories among witnesses.

(RE)VISITING VIET NAM

Tim O'Brien's *The Things They Carried* (1990) resists generic categorization. The collected stories in *The Things They Carried* present the war experiences of Tim

O'Brien, the author's fictional double referred to simply as "Tim," and his fellow soldiers. O'Brien emphasizes the importance of the text as a "work of fiction" in an informal subtitle. This fictional distinction is of great import for O'Brien as is evident in his widely anthologized "How to Tell a True War Story" from The Things They Carried, wherein he writes, "In any war story, but especially a true one, it's difficult to separate what happened from what seemed to happen" (71).

Immediately, and continuously throughout the novel, O'Brien forefronts the relationship between truth, memory, and the limits of writing about war. The various stories in The Things They Carried are linked but not necessarily interdependent; it is possible to read the stories in any order. An example of their interconnectivity, however, centers on narrations of deaths. Often a depiction of a character's death is rewritten in several different stories in the work. Sometimes the occurrence is retold from a different point of view, or the story changes: details may be added, or the narrator may revise the account, explaining that the event did not occur as previously narrated. Literary critic Catherine Calloway argues for the importance of this "technique that actively engages the readers in the process of textual creation" (253). Similar to the circular chronology of the Vietnam Veterans Memorial, O'Brien's narrative structure does not reward passive observation but encourages readers to participate actively in reconstructing memories of the war.[2] As such, The Things They Carried is one of O'Brien's most self-conscious explorations of writing about war and rendering memory. Although his entire work meditates on the rendering of memory, private memorial performance insistent on place, out of which an encouragement of prosthetic memory arises, will provide the focus of what follows.

The most vital private site of memory in The Things They Carried is the location of the death of Kiowa—an American soldier in Viet Nam. O'Brien's audience, according to chapter chronology, first learns of Kiowa's death in "Speaking of Courage" through Vietnam veteran Norman Bowker's internal recollection of the incident. Norman's postwar longing to communicate his memory of Kiowa's death motivates him to envision an intimate conversation with his father, wherein Norman describes his own sense of failure for not saving Kiowa. The soldiers had set up camp on what appeared to be a muddy field on the bank of the Song Tra Bong River. The mud was actually the village toilet—a sewage field. That night, as mortar shells pounded the field, the sludge shifted and swelled, enveloping the men:

> The field was boiling... all those years of waste.... [Norman] heard somebody
> screaming. It was Kiowa... in the glow he saw Kiowa's wide-open eyes settling
> down into the scum.... He could not describe what happened next, not ever,
> but he would've tried anyway. He would've spoken carefully so as to make it real
> for anyone who would listen. There were bubbles where Kiowa's head should've
> been.... He pulled hard but Kiowa was gone, and then suddenly he felt himself
> going, too... the stink was everywhere—it was inside him, in his lungs—and
> he could no longer tolerate it.... He released Kiowa's boot and watched it slide
> away.... He was alone. (149)

In order to bear witness, to remember Kiowa's death, Norman imagines the
challenges and obligation of communicating that which eludes articulation:
"He could not describe what happened next, not ever, but he would've tried
anyway." Norman's memory requires an audience, if imaginary. He reflects,
"He would've spoken carefully so as to make it real for anyone who would
listen." Literary and trauma scholar Kalí Tal's seminal *Worlds of Hurt* (1996)
examines the necessity of communicating traumatic memories in what she
terms a "Literature of Trauma" (21). According to Tal, this literature of trauma is
"written from the need to tell and retell the story of the traumatic experience,
to make it 'real' both to the victim and to the community" (21). The need to
make memories "real" for an audience recurs in turn-of-the-century American memorial, cinematic, and written narratives of the war. Concerned with
truth and accuracy, the war veteran characters also worry about forgetfulness.
Hoping to make the memory "real" for the audience is not simply a matter
of making it believable; it is about creating a felt experience. Some Vietnam
veteran characters, such as Norman, are consumed with creating a mediated
memory that will encourage prosthetic memory.

Perhaps because of the difficulty of communicating the emotional and
symbolic significance of Kiowa's death, O'Brien revisits the memory two
chapters later in one entitled "In the Field," wherein he recounts the search
for Kiowa's body. While the men search for Kiowa, an unnamed soldier in-
ternally recalls witnessing Kiowa's death. Because the retelling is so similar
to Bowker's recollection of the event, this anonymous narrator may very well
be Bowker. This narrator saw the arm, wristwatch, boot, and "bubbles where
Kiowa's head should have been" (O'Brien 171). Just as Bowker did, he "remembered grabbing the boot... pulling hard... and how finally he had to whisper
his friend's name and let go and watch the boot slide away" (171). He feels
responsible for Kiowa's death. He remembers pulling on Kiowa against the

impossible suction of the sludge. He sees the bubbles of Kiowa's last breath. Bowker and this anonymous narrator share the same mutable memory. This very same memory affects O'Brien's fictional double, Tim, as well. The site of Kiowa's death signifies the senselessness of the war. Kiowa dies by drowning in a field of human waste, not by engaging the enemy. As American soldiers during the war would term it, Kiowa is "wasted." The lack of sacrifice creates a meaningless death except that is it precisely very meaningful for O'Brien's purpose to reveal the futility, negligence, and absurdity of the war. The field becomes symbolic of the war, and thus the site of Kiowa's death beckons Tim back to Viet Nam to conduct a private memorial performance.

Near the end of *The Things They Carried*, in the chapter entitled "Field Trip," Tim returns to Viet Nam with his ten-year-old daughter Kathleen, hoping to share with her "a small piece of her father's history" (182). They visit the requisite organized tourist sites of the war: the mausoleum of Ho Chi Minh—president of the Democratic Republic of Viet Nam from 1945 until his death in 1969. They also visit the underground tunnel complex at Củ Chi in Ho Chi Minh City—formerly Saigon, the capital of the southern RVN—that represent the ingenuity, perseverance, and insurgency of the "Viet Cong" in South Viet Nam. Kathleen is the second-generation audience through which her Vietnam-veteran father hopes to convey his memories. Kathleen's presence makes prosthetic memory possible, yet she also serves as a foil to Tim's remembrance of the place because "the war was as remote to her as cavemen and dinosaurs" (183). Here, then, resides the same difficulty Norman imagines, making distressing memories of the war "real" for those with no direct memory of the war. After they visit public memorial sites and near the end of their trip, Tim takes his daughter to his private site of memory, the field where Kiowa died. He brings her there to "show her the Vietnam that kept [him] awake at night" (184).

However, this site with "no ghosts" fails to conjure spontaneous remembrance as it does in other narratives addressed in this chapter (181). The field is not how Tim remembers it. Surprised at the "too ordinary," nonthreatening atmosphere of the field, Tim encounters a disturbing distinction between the "Vietnam" of the past and the Viet Nam of the present. Tim encounters what literary scholar Julia Bleakney distinguishes as the disruption between "Nam," the physical place where the war occurred and the place of their memories, and Viet Nam, the country that has existed before and after the American War (147–48). The disruption of place, time, and memory creates in Tim a self-conscious "awkwardness of remembering" (O'Brien 184). He encounters the difficulty of conjuring emotion: "it simply wasn't there" (184). The emotion is absent, as is the war. However, the war is a present absence and absent presence. It is impossible to escape "Nam" because it is within Tim's memories and therefore ubiquitous. Thus true to O'Brien's contradictory form, the site, despite its initial failures, provides a place for private memorial performance. The field embodies memory; it serves as a kind of archeological site. Tim reflects, "Below the earth, the relics of our presence were no doubt still there, the canteens and bandoliers and mess kits" (184). The U.S. military relics buried in the land signify the hidden presence of material memories. These relics of the war not only serve as subterranean material memories but also signify the land's power to devour both the tangible and intangible "things" the soldiers carried. Of course, beneath the surface lay hidden dangers such as unexploded land ordinance that have killed and injured over forty thousand Vietnamese since 1975. Tim does not think of this, but the land still holds dangers.

Tim conducts a reenactment of Kiowa's death in a private memorial performance at this private site of memory. Immersing himself in the marshland stream in a baptismal scene, Tim pushes Kiowa's moccasins into the sludge, "letting them slide away [as] tiny bubbles broke along the surface" (186). Tim's memorial performance reenacts Kiowa's death by duplicating the bubbles on the surface that formed when Kiowa himself drowned beneath the mud. The moccasins serve as material memory—objects that invoke the present absence of occurrences, places, and people of the past. In this instance the moccasins signify the body of Kiowa returned to the place of his death.

In this private memorial performance, O'Brien invokes the limitations of memory and language. Tim "tried to think of something decent to say, something meaningful and right, but nothing came" (186). Finally, he utters, "there it is," the same phrase Tim and his fellow soldiers repeatedly used to explain death during the war (186). Despite Tim's inability to say anything more "meaningful," this simple phrase, in its repetition, is significant because it demonstrates the limits of language and rejects simplistic sentimentality. He "wanted to tell Kiowa that he'd been a great friend . . . but all [he] could do was slap hands with the water" (187). Although O'Brien suggests the failure of memorialization, perhaps these limitations of memory and language serve as the impetus for Tim's memorial performance.

The memorial performance joins the past, present, and future through Kathleen's presence. The moccasins, as material memory, invoke the past.

Tim's memories and his memorial enactment signify simultaneously the past and present. As witness to her father's private memorial performance, Kathleen acquires a prosthetic memory of the war. Thus she holds what Marianne Hirsch, when writing of the Holocaust, calls "post-memories," which represents both the present and future remembrance of the war (3). Yet her newly acquired memory of the war makes her "nervous"; she does not fully understand her father's actions or memories (O'Brien 186). Kathleen, however, is not the only witness.

The Vietnamese farmers who observe Tim's memorial enactment provide an opportunity for reconciliation between Americans and the Vietnamese. As one farmer solemnly watches from a distance, Tim "felt something go shut in [his] heart while something else swung open" (187). Tim feels a sense of kinship with the farmer, thinking that the farmer may wish to exchange war stories. They do not speak, but Tim feels that the farmer understands the memorial performance. The farmer stands watch with shovel raised "grimly, like a flag" in a moment of reverence before continuing with his work (187). There is, however, a sense of closure. When Kathleen asks her father if the farmer is angry, Tim responds, "'No . . . all that's finished'" (188). The memorial performance provides an end to an era for Tim. He reflects, "I'd gone under with Kiowa, and now after two decades I'd finally worked my way out . . . the war was over" (187). Yet, because of Kathleen's presence and her prosthetic memory, the memorial performance does not simply relegate the war to the forgotten past.

Tim's memorial performance is simultaneously temporal and permanent. The act itself is momentary and located in a place of flux—marshland water that transmutes into swelling sludge in the rainy season. The memorial performance is one of the many mutable memories of Kiowa's death. However, the memorial site is also permanent in that it is the origin of Kiowa's death. Moreover, the moccasins create a symbolic burial for Kiowa; they have been added to the archeological site of memory that contains both the tangible objects and intangible emotions of memory. As a private lieux de mémoire, or site of memory, the field does not provide a national site of remembrance but rather mingles with the memories of Tim, the Vietnamese farmers, and the second-generation, prosthetic memory held by Kathleen.[3]

In the American narratives of the war at the turn of the millennium, mediating memory is nearly as important as the return to the site of memory. In both The Things They Carried and in Sidney Furie's narrative film Going Back

(2001), veterans' memorial performances require witnesses that previously had no direct access to that particular memory and also often those with no direct memory of the war. Yet these two narratives are distinct in that Tim's memorial performance in *The Things They Carried* fails to transport him to the past, whereas in *Going Back* returning to sites of memory and enacting memorial performances more completely blur distinctions between past and present.

Going Back presents, as the title suggests, American veterans of the war on a return visit to Viet Nam. In a probable attempt to increase audience appeal, the title of this independent Canadian film became *Under Heavy Fire* for television and DVD distribution. Despite directorial experience—Sidney Furie wrote and directed one of the earliest films about the American War in Vietnam, *The Boys in Company C* (1978)—*Going Back* was not distributed in the United States. Likely because of its minimal distribution and because it is riddled with acting and cinematic weaknesses, the film received little attention from film reviewers. The minor attention *Going Back* did garner was primarily negative. For example, Jeet Heer of the *National Post* understood the film as a "well-meaning but ultimately unengaging melodrama" (PM7) and *Toronto Star* reviewer Peter Howell's straightforward critique saw the film "suffer[ing] from bad acting, slack directing and a melodramatic script, but. . . not a complete waste of time [because] Furie also attempts to show the Viet Cong's side of the story, which is fascinating but too ambitious for this film" (E05).

Although these critiques of the film are accurate, the film still holds several particular strengths. *Going Back* is representative of the thousands of American veterans who have returned to Viet Nam in hopes of finding healing and closure. Many American veterans have returned to Viet Nam to visit. The first chapter of anthropologist Christina Schwenkel's *The American War in Contemporary Vietnam: Transnational Remembrance and Representation* (2009) examines the mounting phenomenon of American veterans returning to Vietnam in hopes of achieving healing, reconciliation, and closure. Schwenkel also explores war tourism in Vietnam, analyzing many of the public sites of memory that the veteran characters in the previous discussion visit. Memoirs such as Andrew X. Pham's *Catfish and Mandala: A Two-Wheeled Voyage Through the Landscape and Memory of Vietnam* (1999), David Lamb's *Vietnam, Now: A Reporter Returns* (2003), Larry Heinemann's *Black Virgin Mountain: A Return to Vietnam* (2005), and Wayne Karlin's *Wandering Souls: Journeys with the Dead and Living in Viet Nam* (2009) chronicle the emotional journeys of Americans and Vietnamese Americans returning to Vietnam and their reflections on the evolving relationship between America and Vietnam.

Wandering Souls is especially poignant because, in presenting it as a dual bi-
ography, Karlin intertwines the stories of a psychologically wounded veteran,
Homer Steedly, and a North Vietnamese soldier, Hoang Ngoc Dam. Steedly
abruptly encountered Dam on a jungle trail in 1969 and shot him from a
distance. When searching for Dam's body, Steedly finds only Dam's journal,
which remained in Steedly's mother's attic for thirty-five years. Dam was the
only man Steedly killed in such proximity and this contributed to his posttraumatic stress. In reconciliatory fashion, Karlin highlights the similarities
between Homer and Dam: their family histories dating back to World War II,
political parallels, and the simple fact that both were farm boys when they
entered the military. Karlin also illustrates moments of courage and honor
in recounting Steedly's service in the war as he shares moments of his own
reconciliatory interactions with Vietnamese writers he has met.

Karlin presents both men as wandering souls. Dam is a wandering soul
because his family does not know what happened to him; his remains have
not been returned to the ancestral burial grounds. Steedly cannot afford—
monetarily or psychologically—to return Dam's journal, so Karlin does so
in his stead. This act of reconciliation and reparation results in a search for
Dam's remains and culminates in Steedly's return to Viet Nam to help Dam's
family conduct a burial ceremony for what they presume to be Dam's bones,
wherein Homer serves as a pallbearer, literally carrying the weight of the man
he killed. *Wandering Souls* provides a more intimate portrayal of the recuperated
remains of the Vietnamese dead than social anthropologist Heonik Kwon
offers in *Ghosts of War in Vietnam* (2008), as discussed in the following section
about Vietnamese literature.

However, Karlin ethically remembers not only the joining of past and present for those who participated in the American War in Viet Nam but also
America's twenty-first-century wars. He ends the book in his own hometown,
where the community has gathered, just as they did in Dam's village, to bury a
soldier who died in the Afghanistan War. Thus, Karlin leaves readers a remembrance of not just the American War in Viet Nam but also the War on Terror.

Going Back also serves as yet another attempt at reconciliation, it addresses
private sites of memory, it champions prosthetic memory, and it attempts to
import the emotional drama that American veterans experience when they
make return visits to Viet Nam. In the film, former marines of Echo Company revisit Viet Nam at the invitation of a television network that covered
Echo Company during the war. Their journey serves as a kind of fact-finding

mission to dissipate the fog of war and regenerate memories of a particular battle. This battle ended in friendly fire because of incorrect bombing coordinates that the main character, Captain Ramsey, was falsely accused of calling in erroneously. The purpose of the return visit is to reconcile divergent memories of the day in question. Despite unenthusiastic reviews, the film participates in a collected cultural memory of the war in its exploration of memory's entanglement with truth, place as imperative for reenacting accurate memory, and reconciliation between Americans and the Vietnamese.

Going Back contains several aesthetic layers as a means of suggesting the elusive nature of accurate memory. It includes a fictional documentary film set in the present, fictional wartime footage, characters' interior memories of the war, a black and white nightmare scene, and a black and white opening sequence depicting the battle in question. Furie renders all other memories in color. Using these various cinematic formats to signify multiple modes of memory and representation, *Going Back* distinguishes the battle in question from other memories while also placing great emphasis on place, memory, and truth.

The film delineates genre, purpose, audience, and memory as an active process in an early moment in the film wherein viewers are introduced to the main female character, journalist Kathleen Martin, who explains the truth-seeking impetus of the American veterans' return visit. Walking beside a camera recording the returning veterans' arrival in Viet Nam, Kathleen's introductory monologue explains that, during the war, her television network conducted a series of nightly visits with Echo Company and that they are now bringing back the "remnants" of what was the "hardest hit" company of the war. Her choice of pronouns invites her viewers, and Furie's audience, to participate in the return visit explaining, "we will walk beside them and so will you" on their first visit to Viet Nam since the war. The fictional documentary is a self-conscious, mediated memory that aims to make memories of the war more accessible to its audience. Thus, like *Going Back*, the documentary within the film invites audiences to reexperience Viet Nam with the veterans, thereby encouraging newly formed prosthetic memories via the documentary as mediated representation.

Kathleen's character signifies civilian audience, facilitator, and mediator for the Vietnam veterans' memories. Like Sam in Sandie Frazier's *I Married Vietnam* and female nurses during the war, Kathleen and the documentary medium perform reconciliatory purposes by mediating positions between veterans and a civilian audience.[4] She encourages the veterans to explore their past and their present reasons for being in Viet Nam, and she recommends that they reenact the friendly fire incident as a means of discovering the truth behind the veterans' memories. In response, everyone except Captain Ramsey repeatedly and enthusiastically chant for "the truth." Because of the inconclusive court-martial, differing accounts of the incident, and the fog of war that shrouds memories, the men determine to conduct their own "investigation" via reenactment. Their memory journey through Viet Nam will culminate in their return to the location of the friendly fire incident.

Besides calling attention to mediated memory and the search for truth via reenactment, *Going Back* accentuates reconciliation between Americans and the Vietnamese. Immediately following the veterans' arrival to Viet Nam, they attend a welcoming reception in Ho Chi Minh City, formerly Saigon. During the welcoming speech, a Vietnamese dignitary invites reconciliation between the United States and Viet Nam, explaining that "for life, for peace, for the future, we must try to *forget the past* and greet each other with open arms" (emphasis added). Here, the key to peace and reconciliation is forgetfulness. The Vietnamese dignitary's advancement of closure complements the Americans' search for truth. Although they will need to conjure the past, the Americans will do so with the primary objective of achieving closure. Captain Ramsey responds, speaking of his desire for peace, saying, "war destroys everything." His encompassing statement reflects the basis of reconciliation—everyone and "everything" suffers in war.

In their search for closure, the American veterans revisit officially designated tourist sites of remembrance that provide opportunities for reconciliation between American and Vietnamese veterans of the war. Their geo-memory tour of Viet Nam constitutes what tourism scholars John Lennon and Malcolm Foley term "dark tourism"—travel to sites of death and disaster. Yes, Tim O'Brien's fictional double also takes his daughter on a similar tour of Viet Nam; however, they also visit Ho Chi Minh's mausoleum unlike the veterans in *Going Back*. The veterans revisit the Củ Chi tunnels, their former base, and the city of Huế, just South of the wartime border between the northern DRVN and southern RVN, where they fought during the 1968 TET Offensive, the Communist attack on the RVN during the lunar New Year ceasefire.[5] The narrative unrealistically, yet purposefully locates their memories of the war at official sites of memory in Viet Nam in order to construct episodes of reconciliation. For example, at the Củ Chi tunnels the American veterans meet a Vietnamese woman who was one of only three survivors of her battalion. She recognizes two of the former marines because, according to the subsequent memory scene, the Americans provided her with medical treatment and spared her life, coincidentally, during a battle at these very tunnels. She expresses her gratitude and the men feel a sense of recognition in seeing the living embodiment of their wartime compassion. Their reconciliation with the Vietnamese woman recognizes wartime affliction on behalf of both the Vietnamese and American veterans and acknowledges one of the more compassionate moments and memories of the war.

Another such reconciliatory episode attempts to incorporate a Vietnamese perspective into the film's rendering of memory. One of the former marines returns a diary he found on an enemy corpse to the wife of that fallen Vietnamese soldier. In a seemingly twenty-first-century phenomenon, Randall Wallace's We Were Soldiers (2002) discussed in the following chapter, depicts a similar scene of reconciliation with former enemies' wives. In Going Back the wife voices the Vietnamese perspective on the war, explaining that they fought for "love of country," whereas she believed that the Americans fought out of "hatred," presumably for her people. The return of the diary, however, seemingly reconciles these differences with the American veteran's gesture of compassion. However, the scene is more ambiguous and open to interpretation. The film gives voice to a negative Vietnamese view of the United States military presence during the war and breaks with most American fictional representations of the Vietnamese as cruelly inhuman.[6] While Going Back primarily depicts the Vietnamese in a positive, reconciliatory manner, this scene complicates the film's simplistic rendering of reconciliation.

Official sites of remembrance also conjure private memories, encourage catharsis, and provide wartime context for the friendly fire incident. Memory scenes evoked by visiting particular locations in Viet Nam demonstrate that, during the war, the men encountered a multitude of challenging wartime situations, including the deaths of their "brothers in arms" and the torture and killing of civilians committed by their allies, the Army of the Republic of Viet Nam soldiers. To excavate the truth behind their memories, the characters stress the importance of chronologically revisiting sites and recalling events that led to the friendly fire incident. They self-consciously engage with memory as an active process of narration.

As the veterans approach their reenactment destination, anger and resentment build, erupting in an argument about whether they should leave the village via the road or by crossing nearby rice paddies. The argument parallels their dispute on the day in question during the war. The film cuts between the present reenactment and color memory as some men refuse Captain Ramsey's order to leave the village by way of the road. They no longer trust his judgment and begin the cross the rice paddies.

In the present postwar setting, the men in the rice paddy conduct private memorials for their fallen fellow soldiers. Ray, who is now a preacher, creates a makeshift memorial that replicates a Battlefield Cross Memorial erected for wartime ceremonies honoring the dead. The Battlefield Cross Memorial consists of the fallen soldier's helmet hung from a standing firearm with boots placed at the base. Icons of material memory, these temporal wartime memorials display material objects corresponding to parts of the body. The boots at its base signify feet; the helmet denotes the head; and the firearm suggests an upright body. Ray reproduces a similar battlefield memorial when he places a branch into the ground from which to hang the dog tags of the fallen. Here, as in O'Brien's The Things They Carried, material objects represent the lost. Ray then calls the names of his fallen comrades, apologizes for their deaths, and asks for their forgiveness. Ray's memorial enactment resembles the Vietnam Veterans Memorial, where the names, like material objects, come to signify individuals.[7] Ray's performative utterance commemorates the dead and allows Ray to bear witness to his survivor's guilt. Like Tim in O'Brien's The Things They Carried, Ray's memorial performance takes place at the origin of death. The place of death is a site of memory that holds the possibility of communicating with the dead because it is implicitly where the soul or spirit resides, as will be explicated further in the following discussion of Vietnamese novels below. Ray's invocation of the dead creates a present absence wherein past and present merge. Much like the mirror box employed to ease phantom limb syndrome (discussed in the introduction), the Memorial Cross mirrors the body of fallen soldiers. Each reenacts and reflects the past as present in an attempt to provide the "cure" of closure.

The present reenactment of the battle in question also serves as the mirror box and Memorial Cross do when past and present merge psychologically and cinematically. Furie intercuts scenes of the here and now with wartime scenes. Place soon transports the men to the past. When the film cuts to the memory scene of the day in question, Captain Ramsey learns that an enemy ambush is waiting for his men on the other side of the rice patty. As he tries to warn his men of the danger, Ramsey relays bombing coordinates to the radioman who, in the confusion of the battle, calls in the wrong coordinates. Before the men crossing the paddies in the present reenactment discover that the friendly fire incident was not Captain Ramsey's fault, things fall apart and emotions of guilt and anger transport the men into the past. Yet their reenactment occurs in a limbo between past and present. As with O'Brien's character, Tim, they experience what Julia Bleakney considers a disruption between "Nam," the place where the war occurred and the place of their memories, and Viet Nam, the country (147–48). One of the men anguishes over the reenactment not being "right" because there should be "a leg there. . . . an arm here." The veterans' present distress overwhelms them as they lament the loss of their fellow soldiers by crying out the names of the dead and angrily scream accusations at Ramsey. Violence ensues as two of the men in the rice paddy reveal their previously hidden firearms and begin to shoot toward Ramsey and the men who remained by his side on the road. Several men are wounded and the journalist, Kathleen, screams for a "chopper," participating as one of the group in her use of the military vernacular. Just as it was during the war, the helicopter is once again their savior.[8]

The reenactment of memory creates a prosthetic memory for civilian witnesses as the past overwhelms the present. The new memory now includes Kathleen and the son of one of the fallen American soldiers, who signifies a second-generation audience yet receives very little attention in the film despite living in Viet Nam and accompanying the veterans throughout their return visit. Because of the lack of attention this second-generation character receives, it is no wonder that the *National Post* film critic, Jeet Heer, found that the film's "tonal disharmony is increased by the introduction of unnecessary subplots about . . . a young man searching for information about his [dead] father" (PM7). For a film about memory, it is a shame that this second-generation character should really be cut from the narrative. Nonetheless, Kathleen and the son experience a mediated memory in the reenactment, as well as a direct memory of the present violence that erupts during the reenactment. However, the focus is on Kathleen, as love interest, and civilian witness. In the next scene when the veterans confess their remorse for blaming Ramsey for the deaths of their comrades and for their violent flashback, Kathleen cries with them. In post-catharsis moments, veterans and civilians suffer alike, creating a new understanding and reconciliation between them.

Now that Kathleen shares a direct memory with the men, they regard her as part of their experiential, authoritative, "you-had-to-be there" veterans' circle.

A pervasive problematic of privileging an exclusionary authenticity of experience that recurs in literary and cultural productions and attitudes toward war that precludes prosthetic memory is thus reinforced when Kathleen, now having her own personal experiences, is welcomed into the veterans' group.[9] She also participates in the erasure of truth. She reassures the veterans that the tape of the reenactment gone awry was "accidentally" placed on a magnet. Just as the initial incident in the rice paddies eluded documented truth, so do the present-day shootings. Since no one was killed and the occurrence reunites the veterans, there are no legal consequences and the memory remains accessible only for those who directly experienced the incident. Of course, the film's audience also witnesses the event via the twofold mediated representation—the reenactment and the film. Moreover, the present-day violence ironically reestablishes order for the veterans. Ramsey, now exonerated, regains among his fellow veterans his rank, his authority, his men's trust and belief in him, and his position as a figurative father. The men are no longer upset that the bombing coordinates were incorrect but rather that they suspected their once-respected leader of the error. As feminist critic and Vietnam War scholar Susan Jeffords suggests, images of the figurative father in "Vietnam-oriented" narratives portray "decisive and active father-figures who are able to protect and reunite a frayed domestic scenario" (138). The exoneration of Ramsey and disregard for others' mistakes unifies the men and reestablishes their socio-domestic order. Thus, *Going Back* exemplifies a limiting discourse of sentimental closure. The love interest between Captain Ramsey and Kathleen contributes to reestablishing socio-domestic order and the sentimental theme of the film's closing. Now that Kathleen, as civilian, understands the veterans, her romantic relationship with Ramsey helps reestablish order, a sense of normalcy, and a reconciliation between civilians and veterans.

The closing montage of the film further attempts to encapsulate the American War in Viet Nam both as it was and as it is remembered. The overriding theme, past and present, is that of "brothers in arms." The film's closing shots cut between images of the Vietnamese agrarian lifestyle and happy wartime memories of the marines providing medical care to Vietnamese children, baptizing one of the soldiers, drinking in bars, carousing with women, and playing basketball. Yet the montage also depicts memorial performances enacted during and after the war. Perhaps to clarify Ray's construction of the private memorial in the rice paddy, *Going Back* depicts a Battlefield Memorial

Cross ceremony with a helmet resting atop a rifle supported with combat boots. Further still, in the postwar present, Captain Ramsey, accompanied by Kathleen, visits a temple and reads the names of the American dead from Echo Company. Ramsey's performative memorial utterance in Viet Nam shares similarities with the reading of the names of the dead on the Vietnam Veterans Memorial as performed by individual visitors and groups at anniversary ceremonies. His private memorial reflects the fusion between Eastern and Western modes of memorialization that occurs at the Vietnam Veterans Memorial.[10] Finally, his memorial performance reinforces the film's emphasis on memory sites and the location of death as a place where souls reside.

The film promotes the concept that reconciliation, healing, and recuperation are possible if American veterans return to Viet Nam. While this has held true for some veterans more than others, this understanding of return is significant in a collected cultural memory of the war—both in the United States and in Vietnam. However, American veterans do not just return to visit Viet Nam; some have also relocated to Viet Nam, both part-time and year-round. Often, these veterans speak of the need to give back to Vietnam or to make up for the damage they did while serving in a military capacity. For example, in a November 2013 *Christian Science Monitor* cover story, a veteran named Greg Kleven shares a remarkable story about being the first American to live in Ho Chi Minh City after the war. He moved there in 1991, and he and his veteran brother have become the American voices of English-language education in Vietnam (Rhee, "Why US Veterans"). American veterans living in Vietnam serve not only as teachers but strive to help other American veterans heal from the war. For example, American veterans Suel Jones and Chuck Palazzo now live in Da Nang and help run the first overseas chapter of Veterans for Peace; Ed Stiteler is president of Vietnam Battlefield Tours; and Bill Ervin runs his own travel agency in Vietnam. Chuck Searcy, who lives in Hanoi, helped organize Project Renew, a Vietnamese-international group that removed unexploded ordinance. These veterans also assist in healing the Vietnamese and the country, particularly victims of unexploded ordinance and those suffering from the effects of herbicides such as Agent Orange.

Of course, Vietnamese Americans—or *Việt Kiều*, as they are called in Viet Nam—have also returned to live at least part-time in Viet Nam. For example, in his first collection of essays, *Perfume Dreams: Reflections of the Vietnamese Diaspora* (2005), Vietnamese-American journalist Andrew Lam writes about his return visits to Viet Nam. PBS also produced a documentary, *My Journey Home* (2004), following the stories of three Americans, Armando Peña, writer Faith Adiele, and journalist Andrew Lam as they return to their ancestral homelands—Mexico, Nigeria, and Vietnam, respectively. Lam also writes about his Vietnamese American friends and acquaintances who live in Viet Nam; frequently, they have successful businesses in the country. Still others, who immigrated to countries like France, have also returned to live in Viet Nam. However, as Lam notes, there are many, such as his father, who will never return to Viet Nam as long as it is a Communist country. Thus, reconciliation does not seem to be a possibility for some of the war's participants.

VIETNAMESE MEMORIAL PERFORMANCES AND RECONCILIATION

Like O'Brien's collection and Furie's film, two Vietnamese novels—Bao Ninh's *The Sorrow of War* (1991, English translation 1993) and Huong Thu Duong's *Novel Without a Name* (1990, English translation 1995)—figure the locality of death as both a site of memory and as a location where souls reside. In these novels, however, sites of memory are also where souls remain despite survivors' efforts to complete funerary rites. Bao Ninh and Duong share similar backgrounds: both are North Vietnamese, and each participated in the PAVN's war efforts during the American War in Viet Nam. Bao Ninh served with the "Glorious 27th Youth Brigade," which later came to be known as the "Lost Battalion," of whose original five hundred members only ten survived. Duong's service in the Communist Youth Brigade, entertaining front-line soldiers as a theatrical performer, exposed her to life among the PAVN troops and to U.S. bombing raids. Like Bao Ninh, Huong Thu Duong survived the war while her unit endured many casualties; she is one of three survivors of her original unit of forty members (Searle 227). Often paired and written at nearly the same time, *The Sorrow of War* and *Novel Without a Name* both express the point of view of their protagonist PAVN soldiers, both novels include memory sites and address reconciliation, and both novels appeared during the *Doi Moi,* or "Renovation," period in Viet Nam, a time of economic liberalization and internationalization as well as relaxation in cultural policy. In Duong's earlier *Paradise of the Blind* (1988, English translation 1993), a satire of the Communist Party in Viet Nam and the first Vietnamese novel translated into English and published in the United States, a "Note about the Author" explains, "In

1987 . . . the Vietnamese Communist Party called on writers and journalists to shake off the stiff, official Marxist style that had been imposed on them and encouraged them to reassert their traditional roles as social critics" (268). Writers, intellectuals, and artists, including Duong and Bao Ninh, responded; however, the work that surfaced, because it critiqued Vietnamese government and society, proved more than the Communist Party anticipated. These two novels exemplify postwar Vietnamese literature written from the perspective of the North Vietnamese that Doi Moi made possible.

Although Bao Ninh's and Duong's wartime service secured their postwar lives in Communist-ruled Viet Nam, they chose to question their government's policies through war literature. The bitter depictions of Vietnamese society in Duong's writing, in addition to her human rights activism in the 1980s, led to her expulsion from the Communist Party (270). In 1991 she spent over six months in prison for smuggling "secret documents"—likely her manuscripts—out of the country (270). Despite her release from prison, her novels are no longer published nor circulated in Viet Nam (Searle 226). Bao Ninh's The Sorrow of War was, at first, widely circulated in Viet Nam and is now "under a de-facto interdict—not officially proscribed, not reprintable" (Horner 51).

The Doi Moi period also afforded Vietnamese families the ability to reconcile with their "wandering soul" ancestors who, according to the Communist government, fought on the wrong side of the war, the American side. As anthropologist Heonik Kwon's Ghosts of the War in Vietnam (2008) illustrates, mourning these dead was not sanctioned by the state until this period when the government eased control over the culture of commemoration. Soon, families were employing the services of mediums help locate the remains of the missing and began conducting spiritual and religious ceremonies for the dead. As Kwon notes, this resulted in disintegrating the distance between the living and the dead, between different kinds of ghosts, and even between ancestral ghosts and foreign ghosts. Thus, the remains of French and American soldiers were integrated into the Vietnamese culture of commemoration. In a fascinating reconciliatory vein, Kwon also reports that mediums determined that the ghosts of the dead did not remember which side of the war they fought on. In response, Vietnamese built shrines to both ancestors and strangers, creating an equalizing attitude that far exceeded the binary first implemented by the Communist government that only recognized the deaths of Viet Cong and North Vietnamese soldiers.

It is this reconciliation between the living and the dead that Bao Ninh's *The Sorrow of War* champions instead of portraying reconciliation between former enemies or veterans and civilians, as O'Brien and Furie do. *The Sorrow of War* suggests that site-specific private memorial performances provide opportunity for reconciliation between the living and the dead. Bao Ninh thus posits the possibilities of communication with "wandering souls." As Kien, the main character, attempts to "put the dead to rest," he likewise hopes to bring closure to his survivor's guilt. Similarly, *Novel Without a Name*, although less reliant on place, depicts communion with the dead in an effort to encourage reconciliation between the living and the dead. Furthermore, Duong explicitly advances reconciliation between those who lived in the northern Democratic Republic of Viet Nam (DRVN) and the southern Republic of Viet Nam (RVN), and between the Vietnamese and Americans. In addition to representing relations between the living and the dead and promoting reconciliation, *The Sorrow of War* and *Novel Without a Name* serve as narrative memories of the war and thus provide the possibility for those with no direct experience in or connection to the war to form prosthetic memories of the war. Moreover, examining the work of those who fought against the United States and the RVN adds an interesting new perspective to a collected cultural memory of the war. Because the novels present the memories and perspectives of "enemy" PAVN soldiers, the potential for witnesses to form new memories not only reaches those with "no direct access" to the war but also includes American veterans of the war (Landsberg 2).

Bao Ninh's *The Sorrow of War* follows Kien, an PAVN infantry veteran who served from 1965 to 1975. Bao Ninh's narratological approach echoes O'Brien's metaficational play with character, memoir, and chronology. Like Bao Ninh, his novel's metafictional protagonist Kien fought with the "Lost Battalion" and lives as one of ten survivors of five hundred. The novel's nonlinear narrative comprises Kien's memories of his most recent ten years, remembrances of his prewar past and the war itself, his encounters with "wandering souls," and his disillusionment with the future for which he thought he was fighting.

Place is vital to memory in *The Sorrow of War* because it prompts spontaneous memories associated with the site and provides the locations of the living dead, souls that simultaneously occupy the past and present. The novel begins in 1975 while Kien works with a government group seeking the remains of soldiers missing in action (MIA) in the "Jungle of Screaming Souls," a site of memory "where his battalion met its tragic end" in 1969 (86). Since the battle, the area remained unchanged despite the typical vigor with which jungle foliage conceals scars on the land: "No jungle grew again in this clearing" (5). This site clearly displays topographical memory and is the dwelling for "numerous souls of ghosts and devils [who] were born in that deadly defeat. They were still loose, wandering... drifting... refusing to depart for the Other World" (6). Bao Ninh describes, and Kien holds, a generally indigenous, Animistic belief that multitudes of spirits inhabit the natural world (McLeod and Nguyen 43–44). Vietnamese Animism, also known as a "cult of spirits" and closely associated with ancestor worship, is a precolonial belief that, in its flexibility, often blends with and at a minimum coexists with other major religions in Viet Nam, including Taoism, Buddhism, Confucianism, and Catholicism (43). In a mid-1990s ethnographic study, sociologist Mai Lan Gustafsson ascertains that "many Vietnamese had not been permitted to forget the war because of an unforgiving presence in their lives: ghosts" (57). Vietnamese who die near home receive proper burial rites that thus transform the dead into linh hon, ancestral spirits regarded as part of the family for generations (62). If, however, someone dies a "bad" death, they become con ma, an angry ghost (63). "Con ma inhabit the Vietnamese version of hell," Gustafsson writes (63). It is "not a place, but a condition of homelessness and eternal hunger" (63). Because of their battlefield deaths, the spirits of Kien's fellow soldiers wander eternally through the jungle as con ma.

Kien's encounters with the con ma transport him to the past. When he returns to the "Jungle of Screaming Souls" on an MIA Remains Gathering mission, he hears an "echo from another world. The eerie sounds [that] come from somewhere in a remote past" (4). This is not his first return to this site. When Kien's regiment revisits the locale during the war in 1974, he and others erect an altar "honoring and recalling the wandering souls" (7). Kien conducts two memorial performances at this site, establishing an altar during the war and later returning with the MIA team to find and bury remains.

Although the Vietnamese government may intend to promote a national sense of closure through the burial of remains, for Kien, his obligation to appease the dead exposes him to the dangers of encountering the disembodied souls of the con ma. At the moment of burial "the final breath of [the] souls were released . . . penetrat[ing] Kien's mind . . . becoming a dark shadow overhanging his own soul" (25). Kien's second burial encounter with and imposed observances for the dead correlates with Durkheimian anthropologist Robert Hertz's demarcation of the two phases of death, which proffers an understanding of death not as a singular act or moment but as a lasting two-phase process that affects body, soul, and survivors (29). The first, intermediary phase of death is wet, biological, and the second phase of death is dry, spiritual (77). Hertz compares the wet temporary burial phase to mummification, embalming, and cremation and the dry phase to ceremony and final burial. Hertz's understanding of these two phases of death parallels Kien's burial of the MIA remains. For example, the final breaths that Kien witnesses when the souls of the dead are released at the moment of burial completes the first temporal disintegration of the material body, or corporeal soul, allowing for the release of another type of soul that Hertz identifies as the "essential element of the personality" (34). Ideally, in the Indonesian culture Hertz studied and in Vietnamese belief, the two souls converge again in the second burial and peacefully enter the land of the dead alongside ancestors (54).

However, for some souls "their death has no end" (85). Such is the case with the many "wandering souls" Kien encounters. According to the Vietnamese belief that Gustafsson outlines, the wandering souls of the con ma cannot transform into ancestral spirits because they are not buried at home alongside their ancestors. The "wandering souls" thus continue to trouble Kien just as the con ma haunt the "hundreds of people" Gustafsson encountered in Viet Nam, those who, despite erecting altars in or near the home or at the place of death, "suffered from a variety of ailments and attributed them to spirits on the basis of dreams, visions, episodes of dissociative speaking or writing, and auditory hallucinations" (61). Again, this psychosocial phenomenon is not singularly Vietnamese. Hertz, too, found that the "greatest calamity that can befall an individual is to die far away and thus be separated from his kin forever" (70). While this may no longer be of general social concern in America, it certainly holds sway during wartime. Promises of "leaving no man" behind pepper war literature, film, memorials, and political speeches and serve as the impetus behind the POW/MIA reclamation efforts in the United States.[11] Moreover, like Gustafson's study, Hertz determined that those who die violently become "unquiet and spiteful souls roam[ing] the earth forever" (85).

In addition to the presence of "wandering souls," the "Jungle of Screaming Souls" itself serves as a site of memory that holds the possibility for communication between the living and the dead. For example, the truck driver who accompanies Kien on the MIA gathering mission describes his uneasy encounters with spirits "who come out of their graves to talk to [him]. . . . You can look at each other, understand each other, but you can't do anything for each other" (41). Despite communion with the dead, there is no closure of the past. The spirits "will remain with Kien beyond all political consequences of the war" (63). And they do remain with him beyond the locale of their death, continuing to visit Kien during his postwar years in Viet Nam's capital, Hanoi. When they "reappeared before him in the room . . . the air vibrating with images of the past," his room becomes a liminal space between past and present (86). As with the American narratives addressed in the previous section, place in *The Sorrow of War* holds the possibility of transporting visitors to the past. Like Tim O'Brien's *The Things They Carried*, Bao Ninh's *The Sorrow of War* rejects a limiting discourse of sentimental closure, as exemplified in Sidney Furie's *Going Back*. Rather, Bao Ninh explores ongoing remembrance.

While *The Sorrow of War* shares similarities with American representations of memory, national reconciliation in the novel is not the generational or veteran-soldiers-with-civilians reconciliation of *The Things They Carried* and *Going Back*. For example, there are no civilian witnesses to Kien's private memorial performances. Thus, Bao Ninh does not directly stage the possibility for prosthetic memory or experiential reconciliation between soldiers and civilians at sites of memory or in private memorial enactments. However, Bao Ninh's critique of Communism as "more politics" and indoctrination implicitly encourages a unifying reconciliation between the formerly divided northern DRVN and southern RVN (8). For example, during a train ride home at the end of the war, Kien and his fellow soldiers, confronted with "loudspeakers blar[ing]. . . ironic teachings" against reconciliation between former enemies urging the PAVN veterans to "guard against the idea of the South having fought valiantly or been meritorious in any way," the soldiers "made fun of the loudspeaker's admonishments, turning their speeches into jokes, ridiculing them" (80). Moreover, Bao Ninh does depict South Viet Nam's Army of the Republic of Viet Nam (ARVN) as courageous, worthy opponents. For example, Kien's friend Phan recounts a story revealing the courage and strength of an ARVN commando whom Phan encounters on the battlefield. Phan explains that the ARVN soldier was gravely wounded, believing that "if it had been anyone else, not someone so strong and healthy, he would have died right then" (92). But the "Saigonese" did not die, and Phan went to find some bandages, not realizing until his return the impossibility of finding the wounded enemy in the dark, rainy night. The memory of his encounter with the ARVN soldier haunts Phan years later. Typically in war literature and film, this type of regret and survivor's guilt centers on the inability to save a comrade, not an enemy. He explains his sympathy for the ARVN soldier by saying, "no human being deserved the torture I left him to suffer" (94).

A more poignant example of the novel's encouragement of a unifying reconciliation between northern DRVN and southern RVN combatants occurs when Kien decides not to kill the enemy. Kien and his men discover that ARVN soldiers have raped and executed three farm girls who had romantic relationships with several of Kien's men. Despite the brutality of the enemy's attack on civilians and Kien's intense anger, he permits them to live after forcing them to dig their own graves. The memory of Phuong, Kien's boyhood love, serves as a moralizing influence in this moment. Kien's decision "was not because of their pleading, nor because of prompting from his colleagues. No, it was because Phuong's words had come to him like an inner voice: 'So you will kill lots of men? That'll make you a hero, I suppose?'" (140). Kien's compassion toward the enemy centers on his connection, through the memory of Phuong and thus love, to the civilian world. Phuong, as Kien's inner voice, functions as mediator between the civilian world and the realm of war. She fulfills a mediating, moralizing role similar to that of other women discussed in this chapter and in chapters 3 and 4. Kien's decision not to kill the "commandos" reflects the possibility of rejecting vengeance in favor of reconciliation between the DRVN and the RVN and between the realms of war and civilian life. Moreover, audiences in the United States, especially Vietnam veterans, will glimpse the humanity of a former enemy in Kien, a PAVN officer. The Sorrow of War thus implicitly encourages a unifying reconciliation between former enemies, especially the DRVN and the RVN.

Duong's Novel Without a Name is more explicit than The Sorrow of War in its political, national, and transnational reconciliatory aims. This novel, written more clearly for a broader audience that includes Americans, encourages reconciliation not only between the DRVN and the RVN, but also between the Vietnamese and Americans. However, Novel Without a Name, unlike The Sorrow of War, does not rely on or explore memory sites as the impetus for communion with the dead. Still, Duong does examine communication with the dead, specifically the spirit of an ancestor, interestingly as an influence of reconciliation.

Quan, the main character and narrator of Novel Without a Name, like Kien in The Sorrow of War, serves in the PAVN from 1965 to 1975. The central narrative follows Quan's journey home while on leave, his subsequent return to the front, and his experiences in the war through the fall of the RVN's capital,

Saigon, at the end of the war. Through Quan's prewar memories, dream sequences, and communication with the dead, the audience learns of important events in Quan's life: his prewar past; his undying love for his mother, who died when he was a boy; his boyhood love, Hoa; his initial enthusiasm for the revolution; the death of his brother in the war; and his strained relationship with his father, a veteran of the Viet Minh revolt against French colonial rule, who encouraged Quan's brother to join the PAVN. Again, like The Sorrow of War and many American narratives of the war, Novel Without a Name recounts a soldier's transformation from innocence to experience, from enthusiasm to disillusionment. Once an idealistic volunteer, Quan has comes to distrust the "Noble Mission," realizing that "lies are common currency" (85, 83).

Novel Without a Name draws on interconnected traditional Vietnamese conventions of storytelling that often include a close relationship between life and the other world seen in nature (Horner 51) and the Animistic belief that spirits inhabit the natural world, also evident in Bao Ninh's "Jungle of Screaming Souls." In Novel Without a Name, Duong constructs an Animistic landscape that joins the animate and inanimate through her portrayal of both nature and manmade objects as having something akin to souls. Moreover, like Bao Ninh's The Sorrow of War, Duong's Novel Without a Name depicts distinctions between life and death as indefinite. For example, the dedication in Novel Without a Name indicates that the dead reside in the memories of the living. The dedication reads, "For my friends who died, who live on in me." Corporeal memory is a recurrent theme throughout the novel, as is communication with the dead.

Strikingly similar to the opening of Bao Ninh's The Sorrow of War, Duong's Novel Without a Name commences in the "Gorge of Lost Souls." However, during war, not in the postwar years, Quan hears "endless moans punctuated by sobs . . . sweeping through the countryside in a macabre symphony of sound" (1). Quan often refers to spirits as "wandering souls," a direct translation from the Vietnamese vong hon, spirits of those who die far from home. Similar to the con ma—angry spirits of those who died and were buried apart from their ancestors—the vong hon may cause illness or accidents; therefore, the annual Vietnamese "Feast of Wandering Souls" includes offerings to appease the spirits (McLeod and Thi Dieu 45). Quan understands that the sounds of distress in the "Gorge of Lost Souls" originate from the souls of six young women who had been raped, mutilated, and killed and whose bodies he and his men had recently found and buried. Both novels refer to violent deaths of rural young women, and each depiction seems to represent the death of beauty, love, and innocence. In response to the presence of the wandering souls, Quan prays, "*Dear sisters, you who have lived and died here. . . Do not haunt us any longer. Protect us. . . When victory comes, when peace comes to our country, we will carry you back to the land of your ancestors*" (1–2). In an attempt to appease the spirits of the dead, Quan promises to return one day and complete funerary rites.

Quan not only encounters wandering souls but also is compelled to serve their needs. While on his journey home during a leave, Quan becomes lost and disoriented, and is near starvation, in the "Valley of Seven Innocents"— a valley so named when a group of soldiers discovered a lost soldier lying before a cave with seven skeletons. While also wandering lost in the valley, Quan determines that the valley's "haunted labyrinth" is "spirit-haunted" because there is an energy that will not permit him to leave (50). Quan then discovers the skeleton of an PAVN soldier suspended in a hammock. The soldier had created a temporary tomb for himself, replete with a tombstone. Quan presumes the man "must have made one final effort to preserve his body from the animals, to leave it intact, if only in the shape of some distant memory" (52). Similar to Robert Hertz's demarcation of two souls, the material and the spiritual, Animism delineates two types of souls, the *hon*, or spiritual, and the *via*, the material (McLeod and Thi Dieu 44). Thus, at death, the material *via* remains in the corpse's vicinity, and the spirit *hon* departs (45). Because "people's spirits survived the host body's death, they . . . were capable of acting in the world of the living. . . . they were asked for advice, protection, and material benefits" (45). The wandering soul of the dead soldier accordingly compels Quan to discover his entombed body. Quan reflects, "*So it was you, companion, who held me back here*" (51). Quan offers a prayer, but he still cannot leave, believing that "*there is still something more, some unfulfilled wish . . . surely [he] left behind a few relics*" (54). Under the tombstone Quan discovers the dead man's belongings: clothing, a flute, a diary, a photograph of a girl, a photograph of a young man in a PAVN uniform, and a note written by the young man requesting that whoever finds the belongings return them to his mother. These material memories—objects that come to signify individuals—may bring comfort to his family and will likely appease the wandering soul. Quan vows to fulfill the soldier's dying wish, promising, "*I'll bring your belongings to your mother. If by some misfortune she has left us, I'll visit her tomb, light incense, and read your diary to her from beginning to end. . . . At least her soul will taste this sweetness, this solace*" (58). Although he had no personal relationship with the man, Quan's actions and pledge reflect the importance of honoring the dead and the hope of healing and closure. He later fulfills his pledge and, in a scene reminiscent of those in the American films *Born on the Fourth of July* (Oliver Stone, 1989) and *We Were Soldiers* (Randall Wallace, 2002), returns the relics to the dead man's mother.

While Quan encounters wandering souls and thereby communicates with the dead, his contact with his ancestor spirit, a "wraith," connects Duong's two primary goals in the novel—exploration of memory and reconciliation. The wraith visits Quan, whose "*hatred has raised* [the wraith] *from the tomb*," so that he can communicate a "truth" to Quan (254–55). He warns Quan not to curse his ancestors, advising, "*No one can choose his own history*" (257). But Quan is angry and believes that the "triumphal arches" his ancestors left are worthless. He reflects, "*My poor ancestors. Wretched architects of glory*" (258). Yet when the wraith again visits Quan, the wraith is filled with sorrow because his generation "*fought to defend the altar of the ancestors, the future of the country . . . never fought for the cheers and applause of others*" (265). Quan thus comes to believe that the purpose of his war is corrupt, that soldiers fight for the applause of others under the name of a fabricated ideal.

Quan's realization that he is fighting for a false political ideal imparts the foundation for reconciliation between both the northern DRVN and southern RVN and between the Vietnamese and Americans in the novel. Quan continually questions the purpose of the war, examining the distinction between those who sacrifice and those who benefit from the war. One memorable scene critiquing the Vietnamese Communist Party so as to expose fabrication of political ideals depicts two party dignitaries aboard the same train on which Quan is traveling. He observes their demeanor: "like masters in the middle of the crowd," they came to "see with [their] own eyes" the common people (158). The dignitaries debate the progress of the revolution, the manipulation of power, and how best to satiate and persuade the "nation of imbeciles" while simultaneously mocking the political system they promote (167). For example, one of the dignitaries relishes the simplistic, purposeful manipulation of the people: "an ideal . . . the kids need it. And it's all we need to turn them into monks, soldiers, or cops. And it worked, whether it was the revolutionary uniform or the Nationalist police cap" (160). This attitude toward government posturing is not uncommon among American literary, cinematic, and popular-culture representations of the war. For example, the rock band Creedence Clearwater Revival's song "Fortunate Son" (1970) poses an argument akin to Duong's in its lyrics, which argue, "Some folks inherit star spangled eyes / Ooh, they send you down to war." Along with lines such as "I ain't no Senator's son" or "millionaire's son" or "military son," the song exposes contradictions in the American patriotic ideal just as Duong ultimately argues that the DRVN Communist Party is corrupt, incompetent, and avaricious.

In addition to critiquing the Communist Party as a means of promoting reconciliation between former enemies—the PAVN and southern ARVN and the PAVN and Americans—Duong is especially explicit in her endeavor to advance reconciliation between northern and southern soldiers. While holding prisoner ARVN soldiers, Quan asks one detainee about his reasons for fighting. Quan inquires, "'Why did you enlist?'. . . . [the captive responds] 'duty'. . . . 'the nationalist ideal'" (242). Quan then remembers the party dignitaries on the train and begins to provide answers to his questions. He lists, as questions, both his and his enemy's reasons for fighting: "'To defend the motherland?'. . . . 'To fulfill the patriot's duties. . . . ?'. . . . 'To serve the country, swearing to spill the last drop of your blood?'" (243). The prisoner answers yes to each question. Each man fights for the same reasons: "On both sides you screamed, you killed in mad, frenzied bursts, shrieking for joy when the blood gushed, the brains shattered; you went at one another like savages. . . . Then the survivors limped off the battlefields to swell the reserves, to join the ranks of future combatants. . . . On both sides you died believing that you had attained your ideal (247). Duong unequivocally critiques the bloodlust, the sentiments of sacrifice, and the myth of righteousness in the war.

While clearly promoting reconciliation between PAVN and ARVN soldiers and veterans, the novel also encourages reconciliation between the Vietnamese and Americans. Near the close of the novel, after the fall of Saigon, Quan's men bring him an American prisoner. Based on the man's appearance and gestures, Quan determines that he is not a soldier but a photographer. The American's "foreign features," however, "designated him as the target of . . . ancestral hatred [of] the foreign invader" (284). Surprising even to himself, Quan's hatred wanes, and he begins to imagine the man's life before the war, sharing similarities with Quan's own prewar, pastoral ideal. He "imagined a green hill, this young man embracing his lover. . . . Perhaps he too had stretched out beside a friend . . . and dreamed of the gods" as Quan and his boyhood friends had before the war (285). In The Great War and Modern Memory (1975), Paul Fussell keenly notes that wars take place within nature, and therefore representations of war are necessarily antipastoral (231). Invoking the prewar pastoral ideal and highlighting the antipastoral realities of war is a common theme in war literature. While his comrades encourage killing the prisoner, Quan reflects that the American may have "left it all behind to put on a soldier's uniform, to defend freedom. . . . He too must have been drunk on a vision of himself marching till dawn with his medals across his chest against a horizon of fire and flames" (285). Just as Quan, his comrades, and the ARVN soldiers fought for an "ideal," so too had the Americans. Here, as with the ARVN prisoners, Duong argues that both sides fought for an ideal, an ideal that leaves Quan disenchanted.

Through Quan's evenhanded treatment of the American prisoner of war, the novel responds to American cultural memory of the POW/MIA controversy that began with the signing of the Paris Peace agreements in 1973 and was later reinforced by the popular rescue-return films of the 1980s, such as *Rambo: First Blood, Part II* (George Cosmotos, 1985), *Missing in Action*, (Joseph Zito, 1984), and *Uncommon Valor* (Ted Kotcheff, 1983).[12] The POW/MIA mythology and disagreement continued to be a source of contention, especially among veterans and their families, concerning normalizing relations with Viet Nam in the 1990s. In the twenty-first century, cultural memory continues with representations such as the made-for-television film *The Veteran* (Sydney Furie, 2006) and the "inspired by a true story" POW escape film *Rescue Dawn* (Werner Herzog, 2006). Established in 2003, the Joint POW/MIA Accounting Command (JPAC) continues a global search for remains of POWs and MIAs and employs DNA identification in order to aid the U.S. Department of Defense account for personnel. With two of four permanent detachments in Viet Nam and Laos, the controversy continues to influence U.S.–Viet Nam relations. The novel comments on the issue when Quan refuses to allow the execution of the prisoner, explaining, "we're not in the jungle anymore. Anybody, including me, who doesn't respect the policy toward prisoners goes before court-martial" (286). Moreover, the men lead the American POW "off in silence, *gently*, trying to jostle him" (286, emphasis added). With Quan's words, the PAVN soldiers' adherence to POW policy, and the gentle treatment of the American POW, Duong tries to dispel the popular American belief that the Vietnamese mistreated American POWs in Viet Nam after the war's end. This further encourages reconciliation between the Vietnamese and Americans.

Novel Without a Name is a reconciliationist novel of the highest order. It not only explores communication with the dead as a means of promoting reconciliation but also attempts to destabilize the many cultural mythological remembrances of the war on behalf of former PAVN, ARVN, and American soldiers, as well as civilians in both countries. Her intrepid depiction of a failed "ideal," her critique the Communist Party, and her noncelebratory depiction of the fall of Saigon petition for reconciliation. Together Duong's position as a past member of the Vietnamese Communist Party and former participant in the PAVN who now criticizes the war form an appeal for former enemy audiences—members of the southern ARVN and the United States military. Yet Duong does not only criticize the ideal of the Communist revolution as misguided. She depicts the ideals of all who participated in the war—the DRVN, the RVN, and the United States—as flawed. The novel thus participates in a collected cultural memory—a culturally mediated collection of multifaceted memories—of the American War in Viet Nam that contests a singular, unified narrative or memory of the war.

The Vietnamese novels, especially *The Sorrow of War*, share similarities not only with the American narratives previously discussed but also with earlier traditional American narratives of the war of the 1970s and 1980s. For example, the novel's main character, Kien, moves from innocence to experience and from enthusiasm to disillusionment. According to William Searle, a literary scholar of the war, the novel parallels American narratives of the war in its "familiar litany of the horrors of war—disillusionment, drug use, racism, desertion, loss of moral compass, bloodlust, conflicts within ranks, soldiers cracking under stress, sexual assault, and a breakdown of discipline" (237). However, Searle posits a distinction between Vietnamese novels and their American counterparts concerning transnational reconciliation. He recognizes a promotion of reconciliation in the Vietnamese novels that he believes is absent in American novels. The turn-of-the-century American narratives of the war examined in this and in preceding chapters not only encourage reconciliation among Americans but also begin to seek reconciliation with the Vietnamese in their depictions of the psychological suffering of the Vietnamese, usually women.[13] Still, as Searle suggests, Bao Ninh's *The Sorrow of War* and Duong's *Novel Without a Name* certainly depict the suffering of Vietnamese women, as well as hopes for reconciliation between the DRVN and the RVN, and the Vietnamese and Americans (237).

The four reconciliatory narratives discussed in this chapter—Tim O'Brien's *The Things They Carried*, Sidney Furie's *Going Back*, Bao Ninh's *The Sorrow of War*, and Huong Thu Duong's *Novel Without a Name*—demarcate the possibilities that individual sites of memory and private memorial performances encompass for communication with the dead and reconciliation between opposing sides of the war. While the possibilities and limitations of memory, communication with the dead, and prosthetic memory vary, each narrative's characters encounter sites of memory where the dead reside. Tim in *The Things They Carried* returns to what appears to be an ordinary locale but one that possesses the memory of Kiowa's death. Moreover, this site of memory holds the possibility for memories acquired by individuals with no direct experience in the war. American veterans return to Viet Nam in *Going Back* seeking the truth beyond their mutable memories. While they visit several officially designated memorial sites, their search for truth, their private memorials, and their reenactment of the past takes place in what is now a common field but for them a private site of memory. In the Vietnamese novels, wandering souls haunt specific locales and by their absent presence obligate Kien's memorial performances in *The Sorrow of War*. Quan's communication with the dead in *Novel Without a Name* provides opportunities for him to encounter sites of memory that are not always part of his direct memory. However, Quan's communication with his ancestor's wraith provides the novel's impetus for reconciliation.

Furthermore, these narratives depict sites of memory as potential locations of reconciliation. In the American narratives, *The Things They Carried* and *Going Back*, observers with no direct access to memories of the war observe mediated representations of the war through the memorial performances war veterans enact. Civilian witnesses thus acquire prosthetic memories of the war, and their newly obtained memories refuse to relegate the war to the forgotten past. The Vietnamese narratives, *The Sorrow of War* and *Novel Without a Name*, are often more explicit and politically minded in encouraging reconciliation between the DRVN and RVN and between the Vietnamese and Americans. Because these two novels critique, whether implicitly or explicitly, the Vietnamese Communist Party, they refuse to portray postwar Viet Nam as a country that has recovered from the war, despite the official posturing in Viet Nam today that the war is over and belongs to the past. Regardless of the effort, official government policy in both countries cannot erase memories of the war or traditional religious understandings of life and death. While each narrative discussed in this chapter explores the possibilities of reconciliation between former foes, each also confronts the limits of sentimental, forgetful reconciliation. Neither memorial performance nor reconciliation creates assured closure; certainly, prosthetic memory denies closure in its unavoidable ongoing remembrance. Moreover, the narratives engage with American and Vietnamese cultural memory of the war, thus contributing to a multifaceted collected cultural memory of the American War in Viet Nam.

CHAPTER 6
• FORGETTING
THE AMERICAN WAR
IN VIET NAM

WE WERE SOLDIERS

American soldiers in battle don't fight for what some
president says on T.V.; they don't fight for mom, apple pie,
the American flag; they fight for one another.

—Harold Moore, in "Getting it Right," *We Were Soldiers* DVD

A collected cultural memory—a mediated gathering of multifaceted memories—of the American War in Viet Nam will inevitably include innumerable
attempts to reframe the war.[1] Although those who remember the war through
direct experience created many of the cinematic and textual narrative representations of the war produced during the 1990s, they began to explore
more broadly remembrances of the war by representing prosthetic memories
held by those with no direct connection to the war. Randall Wallace's film *We
Were Soldiers* (2002) might be called the seminal twenty-first-century depiction of the war. The film is an adaptation of the *New York Times* best seller *We
Were Soldiers Once . . . and Young* (1992) a memoir of the American War in Viet
Nam by retired Lieutenant General Harold Moore and photojournalist Joseph
Galloway. Like the memoir, one of the narrative's goals is to remind audiences
that, despite the narrative and cinematic tradition of portraying the war as
one fought against an invisible guerilla enemy, the war included actions such
as one particular early engagement—the initial 1965 battle of the Ia Drang
Valley—fought on conventional terms involving two standing armies. The
film explores only the memories of those with a direct connection to the
war: soldiers and their families. Although the book is more responsible and
even-toned, the film overlooks the cultural and political causes and consequences of the war, concentrating instead on representing the war as a fight

for survival among "brothers in arms." While many if not most films about the war also ignore the political causes of the war, Francis Ford Coppola's *Apocalypse Now Redux* (2001), discussed in chapter 7, does not. Further still, there are many films about the war that address the consequences of the war, such as the readjustment of American veterans to civilian life.

Moreover, Wallace's *We Were Soldiers* veils its revision and forgetfulness by attesting to its historical accuracy and the authenticity of experience. Although the film maintains its historical accuracy while representing a specific battle and its major players, and it does not aim to address the political causes and consequences of the American War in Viet Nam, it ultimately recasts memory of America's longest war as a sole three-day battle and thus delineates the war in terms of a micro-historical location of time and place. While the film does not aim to address the political causes and consequences of the American War in Viet Nam, *We Were Soldiers* ultimately recasts memory of the war within a framework of heroism and sacrifice. Thus *We Were Soldiers* remembers the war by forgetting it. However, Moore and Galloway's subsequent memoir *We Are Soldiers Still: A Journey Back to the Battlefields of Vietnam* (2008) serves as a significant addendum to Wallace's film. As a corrective to the film, *We Are Soldiers Still* rejects forgetfulness in favor of encouraging a postwar reconciliation based on mutual recognition between the Peoples Army of Viet Nam (PAVN) veterans and American veterans of the war. Besides encouraging twenty-first-century reconciliation, Moore and Galloway attempt to engage with and make peace with the past by exploring battlefield sites of memory. Finally, *We Are Soldiers Still* further clarifies the authors' negative assessment of the war as politically misguided, a parallel to their regard of the Iraq War. The book thus reclaims a twenty-first-century remembrance of the war's aftermath in the shadow of the film's forgetfulness.

However, long before Wallace's film, the 1993 ABC documentary, *They Were Young and Brave*, about Moore's first return visit to Viet Nam explains the trip as a "mission of healing." Although this documentary also accentuates the brothers-in-arms message of the book and Wallace's film, there is less emphasis on heroism. Indeed, the documentary stresses the great loss of life, discloses the errors of not one but two friendly-fire incidents, includes coverage of a second battle, and the horrors of killing the wounded. Significantly, the documentary highlights a hidden-story angle. In the aftermath of heavy losses—the greatest that American forces had suffered in a single engagement up to that point—military leaders called the battle a victory and used it as a means of justifying further participation in the war. Essentially, the documentary points out that the defeat of that day was buried until the release of this film. The documentary does what Wallace's film fails to do. It portrays Moore as a real man who suffered real losses and reveals the kill-ratio rationale that Westmoreland adopted in response to the devastating battle. Unfortunately, in many ways, Wallace's film tells a different story.

Circumventing American cultural remembrance of the war, *We Were Soldiers* reverts to the revisionism of President Ronald Reagan's 1980s declaration that the American War in Viet Nam was a "noble cause." Reagan further asserted that "for too long, we have lived with the 'Vietnam Syndrome'"—a misnomer for American postwar unwillingness to intervene militarily in the Third World. In a similar vein, in the post–Cold War American context of small-scale localized conflicts, President George H. W. Bush claimed during the Persian Gulf War (1990–91) that there would be "no more Vietnams" and declared, "We have finally kicked the Vietnam Syndrome." Thus Americans believed that they could now relegate the American War in Viet Nam to the forgotten past.

The turn of the millennium became a time in American cultural remembrance that favored remembering the "good war"—World War II—while ignoring the American War in Viet Nam. During this period, journalist Tom Brokaw coined the term "the Greatest Generation," using it as the title of his 1998 book containing personal accounts of American men and women, both soldiers and civilians, about their experiences and values during World War II. Thus America nostalgically turned to admire and to commemorate a pre–Viet Nam Generation. Shortly thereafter, construction began on the national World War II Memorial on the Mall in Washington, D.C., which was dedicated in 2005. Meanwhile, the Veterans History Project, established in 2002 and connected to the American Folklife Center in the Library of Congress, collected personal accounts from World War II veterans and civilians actively involved in the war effort. Further, the acclaimed historical film documentarian Ken Burns and his longtime colleague Lynn Novick recollected World War II in their epic PBS documentary series *The War* (2007), a title suggesting that there is only one war to remember. As a result of the renewed concern with preserving memories of the war, the resurrection of the World War II combat film was well underway. In 2003 historian Frank Wetta and film scholar Martin Bookli, suggested that the fiftieth anniversary celebrations in the 1990s of the war's events "provided a way to revive the notion of patriotism in public life, and as a natural consequence in films" and thus "Vietnam could be forgotten" (866).

Numerous films about World War II produced at the turn of the millennium attested to the resurgence of interest in remembering the war. They include but are not limited to *Memphis Belle* (Michael Caton-Jones, 1991), *A Midnight Clear* (Keith Gordon, 1992), *Schindler's List* (Steven Spielberg, 1993), *Stalingrad* (Joseph Vilsmaier, 1993), *Saving Private Ryan* (Steven Spielberg, 1998), *The Thin Red Line* (Terrence Malick, 1998), *U-571* (Jonathan Mostow, 2000), *Enemy at the Gates* (Jean-Jacques Annaud, 2001), *Hart's War* (Gregory Hoblit, 2001), *Pearl Harbor* (Michael Bay, 2001), Steven Spielberg and Tom Hanks's widely popular HBO miniseries *Band of Brothers* (2001), *Windtalkers* (John Woo, 2002), *Saints and Soldiers* (Ryan Little, 2003), *The Great Raid* (John Dahl, 2005), *Flags of Our Fathers* (Clint Eastwood, 2006), *Letters From Iwo Jima* (Clint Eastwood, 2006), *Valkyrie* (Bryan Singer, 2008), and *Inglourious Basterds* (Quentin Tarantino, 2009).

In response to the reemergence of World War II combat films, Jeanine Basinger, the leading authority on the combat genre, published a new edition of *The World War II Combat Film: Anatomy of a Genre* (2003); in it she notes that the "Vietnam combat film . . . had a desperation, an ambivalence, and a madness that suggested the last hurrah for the old combat format" (xi). Basinger attributes the regeneration of the combat genre to the box-office triumph of *Saving Private Ryan*. Film scholar Guy Westwell, interpreting the cultural impact of the combat film revival on contemporary war cinema (1989–2006), goes a step beyond Basinger. He claims that the resurgence chronicles a "shift in the cultural imagination of war" that has "fostered a sense of World War II as a 'just war' fought by a 'greatest generation,'" ultimately culminating in a "justification and endorsement of war" (84, 107).

Out of this cultural climate of sanctioning war and a resurgence in financing for combat films, likely a result of the success of *Saving Private Ryan*, Randall Wallace's film *We Were Soldiers* soared in popularity, becoming the twenty-first century's most prominent representation of the American War in Viet Nam. The film was not nearly as successful, grossing only $114,660,784 worldwide, compared to *Saving Private Ryan*, which reached $481,840,909 worldwide. However, one of the only other films about the American War in Viet Nam to appear at the beginning of the twenty-first century, *Tigerland* (Joel Schumacher, 2001) grossed only $139,692 in limited release. While Randall Wallace's sole previous film as a director was *The Man in the Iron Mask* (1998), he also wrote screenplays for *Pearl Harbor* (Michael Bay, 2001) and *Braveheart* (Mel Gibson, 1995). The latter two films serve as precursors for the revisionism and heroic action that Wallace employs in writing and directing *We Were Soldiers*.

Unfortunately, Wallace reframes and thereby disregards others' remembrances of the American War in Viet Nam by ignoring the political causes of the war. Rather, he focuses on courage, bravery, sacrifice, brotherhood, and victory over the enemy in a devastating battle. Wallace relies on historical specificity, the authenticity of experiences, and the conventions of the World War II combat film genre to recast the American War in Viet Nam as a "good war." The film thus represents "American military strategy in Viet Nam as credible, heroic, and morally right" (Westwell 107). It reverts to the themes of maps, tactics, and commanders common in World War II narratives wherein the troops, under the command of a heroic, competent leader, successfully accomplish a specific military mission.

We Were Soldiers recounts an early, singular, three-day battle in the Central Highlands of Viet Nam, specifically the Ia Drang Valley in 1965. The film's narrative chronicles the formation, training, and family life of the officers of the First Battalion, Seventh Cavalry, an air mobile division at Fort Benning, in Columbus, Georgia. During the war, General Westmoreland ordered the Seventh Calvary, under the Pleiku Campaign,[2] to "search and destroy" PAVN forces in the Ia Drang Valley, an area of about fifteen hundred squares miles (Moss 215–16). The book *We Were Soldiers* describes the battles at two sites in the Ia Drang Valley, "Landing Zone X-Ray" (LZ X-Ray) at the base of Chu Pong mountain and "Landing Zone Albany," two miles north of LZ X-Ray.

Wallace, however, does not include in the film the battle fought by the Second Battalion at LZ Albany that resulted in 151 American soldiers killed in action (KIA) and 130 wounded in action (WIA), a far greater loss of American life in a one-day battle than the 79 KIA and 121 WIA in the three-day battle at LZ-X Ray (Moore and Galloway, *We Are Soldiers Still* 206). It is cinematically understandable that Wallace chose not to incorporate the battle at LZ Albany in the film because of time constraints; however, his decision is ironic, considering that the U.S. military also chose to repress media coverage of the battle in favor of reporting the more "successful" battle at LZ X-Ray.[3] Together the estimated loss of life between the battles totaled 234 American soldiers KIA and 2,403 PAVN soldiers KIA, resulting in a so-called "favorable ratio of U.S. to enemy losses . . . fixed at 12:1" (Murray 40 and Moss 217). The perceived American military victory at LZ X-Ray greatly contributed to legitimizing a protracted strategy of attrition—a style of fighting wars based on material superiority, casualty rates, and a gradual reduction of enemy forces via constant harassment—employed by the United States military throughout the war.

Just as the battle erroneously bolstered a wartime strategy of attrition based on "kill ratios," the film seemingly seeks to shape twenty-first-century American attitudes in favor of the war. Moreover, the release of We Were Soldiers in March 2002 positions it as one among many films inexorably and symbolically linked to the attacks on September 11, 2001, and the ensuing "War on Terror." According to American studies scholar Christina Rickli, in the immediate aftermath of 9/11, Hollywood postponed the release of several films because of a perceived impropriety within the vengeance plots of Windtalkers (John Woo, 2002), Training Day (Antoine Fuqua, 2001), and Spygame (Tony Scott, 2001). Other films, however—including We Were Soldiers, Behind Enemy Lines (John Moore, 2001), and Black Hawk Down (Ridley Scott, 2001)—reached theaters ahead of schedule. Although they were likely conceived and shot before 9/11, it was probably no coincidence that each of these was a narrative about soldiers' survival (Lowenstein 178).

At the time of its release, We Were Soldiers culturally engaged a post-9/11 American audience whose country was embarking on a war in Afghanistan that had begun only five months earlier in October 2001 and that would, in the year following the film's release, unleash a preemptive war in Iraq. Some reviewers, however, contested that if "Hollywood intended We Were Soldiers to promote a prospective war of which it approves, the horror subverts that" (Coatney 313). Despite its gruesome portrayal of battle, many audiences would view the film, as Todd McCarthy of Variety claimed, "in the context of the current political climate as a coincidental but nonetheless remarkable symbol of we've-got-a-job-to-do-style patriotism" (69). The 2002 graduating class at West Point, for example, "had the highest number of infantry applications in many years after the film premiered there" (Coatney 313). The graduates' decisions to enter the infantry rather than combat-support branches or one of the other six combat-arms branches (such as armor, artillery, or the combat engineers), demonstrate the film's potential power to rally positive attitudes toward infantry service and the prospect of combat. Likely, more reasonable explanations for this increase include that the 2002 graduating class was the first post-9/11 graduating class eager to achieve combat badges in the War in Afghanistan, which began in 2001. However, it also seems clear that the film did not deter graduates from signing up for the infantry despite some critics' arguments that the horror of war portrayed in the film subverts the heroics. These choices may also indicate that audiences are most likely to remember the heroics and not the final words of the film.

The film's persuasion centers on Wallace's depiction of the valiant leadership of then Colonel (and soon-to-be General) Hal Moore. A West Point graduate, Moore commanded infantry units in the Korean War, and as the film portrays, the First Battalion, Seventh Calvary in Viet Nam, soon after which he became a general. The film's tagline honors Moore without naming him and imparts the film's emphasis on humanizing the soldiers. It reads:

Fathers, Brothers, Husbands & Sons.
We were . . . young, brave, husbands, wives, sons, mothers, daughters, soldiers.
400 U.S. paratroopers. 2000 Vietnamese soldiers. 12,000 miles away from home.
1 man led them into battle.

This movie advertisement introduces the film's primary concerns: the family, the challenging conditions of Americans outnumbered in battle, and the heroic father figure. The emphasis on family humanizes the American soldiers in the film and calls attention to the concern, worry, suffering, and loss that, indeed, over three million American families endured during the war. The description thus also acknowledges family members on the home front as part of the inner circle of the so-called Vietnam experience. Yet the film proffers a broader depiction of "family" than the traditional family to include the military family, especially "brothers in arms," with Moore as the father figure. Finally, the "1 man" is Colonel Hal Moore, played by Mel Gibson, who "has the closest thing to a John Wayne part that anyone's played since the Duke himself rode into the sunset" (McCarthy 69). As one of Moore's most famous lines from the film designates, he would valorously be the "first to set foot on the field, and . . . the last to step off." The film's narrative arc thus suggests that if every military leader were a tough, dedicated hero like Moore, America might have won the war.

Although the heroic character of Moore serves as the focus of the film, *We Were Soldiers* also participates in a collected cultural memory—a culturally mediated collection of multifaceted memories—of the American War in Viet Nam by way of its inclusive portrayal of civilian women on the American home front and more developed representation of the PAVN than nearly any other American narrative of the war. Thus, *We Were Soldiers* participates in a collected cultural memory of limited reconciliation between former foes via the recognition of mutual military competence and an acknowledgment of individual sorrow. Although the film limits representation to direct experience, it remains one of the more inclusive representations of the American

War in Viet Nam. Still, prosthetic memory is not proffered as a possibility in either Moore and Galloway's first book, We Were Soldiers Once . . . and Young, or Wallace's film. Primarily, the lack or impossibility of prosthetic memory stems from the narratives' emphasis on authenticity of experience. Despite reaching publication nearly twenty years after the war, and movie theaters over twenty-five years later, the book and film privilege only the memories of those directly connected to the war.

CONCESSION • REMEMBERING THE HOME FRONT

Although We Were Soldiers reframes the American War in Viet Nam as a "good war," it does present a fairly inclusive portrayal of the war because it represents the families of American soldiers fighting the war. Wallace treats distressing home-front experiences of confusion, anxiety, sorrow, and loss in more detail and with more sympathy and sentiment than Moore and Galloway's first book. For example, in the memoir We Were Soldiers Once . . . and Young, Moore's youngest daughter asks him, "'Daddy, what's a war?'" (Moore 25). His reply is stark; he recounts, "I tried my best to explain, but her look of bewilderment only grew" (25). In Wallace's film, Moore responds to his daughter by explaining, "It's something that shouldn't happen, but it does . . . when some people . . . try to take lives of other people . . . it's my job to go over there and stop 'em." His answer, and thereby the film's, repositions the war as a humanitarian mission with Moore figured as the hero. As opposed to the film, Moore and Galloway dedicate a single chapter of their book to the wives and families of the fallen soldiers entitled "'The Secretary of the Army Regrets . . .'" that consists of only 15 of the book's 372 pages.

Meanwhile, Wallace's film We Were Soldiers devotes a narrative thread of the home front, crosscut with battle scenes, that follows Moore's wife, Julia. She serves as the courageous female counterpart to her male hero husband. Just as her husband fearlessly leads his men in battle, Julia unflinchingly delivers telegrams to the wives on base informing them of their husbands' deaths. She distributes the death notices in an effort to correct the impersonal form of delivery by a stranger, a taxicab driver, imparting the announcements. Julia provides comfort for the women, and in effect, as the film suggests, she too endures her own battle on the home front; she confronts death while also fearing the prospect of her own husband's death. These scenes of Julia and the other wives mourning the loss of the men in battle impart sympathetic, cathartic moments for the film's audience.

Unlike the film, Moore and Galloway's book further depicts intergenerational psychological effects of the war on American children of veterans and those who died in the battle. For example, they include a quote from an interview with the daughter of one of the soldiers. She stresses the impersonality of taxi drivers delivering the notifications. She explains, "'today it almost sounds unbelievable. . . . The knock came at out door at 4 A.M. My Mom collapsed completely as this stranger handed the telegram to us. How cold and inhuman, I thought'" (Betty Jivens Mapson, qtd. in Moore 323). Moore and Galloway also include family members' accounts of the dead "in hopes that their words might somehow comfort other families who have lost loved ones in war" (326). While the book encourages healing, the varied collection of stories included in that chapter portray a range of emotions, from pride to sorrow and loss, and represent an assortment of attitudes toward the war, from questions and accusations to justifications about the war and the soldiers' deaths. Moore and Galloway's incorporation of intergenerational American narratives acknowledges the enduring psychological effects of loss on the home front. However, recognition of the war's effects on memory remains limited to those with a direct or hereditary "claim" to the so-called Vietnam experience. The possibility of prosthetic memory—memories acquired by individuals with no direct connection to the war—is nonexistent in the narratives of the book and film.

RECOGNIZING THE "ENEMY"

Just as Wallace's incorporation of American home-front experiences in *We Were Soldiers* is more inclusive than most American narratives of the war, so too is his demythologized rendering of PAVN soldiers. Wallace's portrayal of PAVN soldiers is threefold: it creates a more inclusive, less American-centered representation of the war; it emphasizes the perspectives of battlefield commanders; yet it further accentuates the limited authenticity of direct experience—the memory of the war that the film's narrative privileges. Despite the film's inclusionary depiction of PAVN soldiers, some reviewers and scholars have criticized the film, as Roger Ebert predicted, for representing the Vietnamese as "faceless, non-white enemies" ("A Soldier's Story" 29). Only two PAVN soldiers garner any specific attention from among the massive onslaught of PAVN troops. However, neither is typically vilified as the "enemy" usually is in combat films. The first and more developed Vietnamese character is Moore's counterpart, Vietnamese colonel An (Duong Don). Aligning Moore and An in the film serves to accentuate their leadership skills and militarily strategic prowess.

The film's second Vietnamese character is a silent, seemingly sensitive soldier (Lam Nguyen), designated as such by his costume and props. He wears eyeglasses, writes in a diary, and carries a photograph of a Vietnamese woman, presumably his wife, since the film's narrative constructs only marital relationships across genders. As with the American soldiers, audiences are supposed to identify and sympathize with the Vietnamese soldier. That he has a life beyond the battlefield is signified by the photograph he carries. Interestingly, the photograph of that Vietnamese woman strikingly resembles Moore's wife, Julia. Thus the film attempts to humanize America's former foes—if only fleetingly, compared to the development of American characters. Yet the PAVN soldier plays a further role in the film because he tries to kill Moore when, after running out of ammunition, he charges Moore with a bayonet, only to be shot by Moore at the last possible moment. The scene casts Moore as a reluctant warrior, one who takes action only to defend himself and others, and only when necessary.

Both the PAVN soldier's desperate charge at Moore and Colonel An's military proficiency contribute to Wallace's attempts and failures to portray the PAVN as a militarily worthy adversary. The scene represents the charging PAVN soldier as complicit in and even resigned to his death. Nonetheless, crosscut scenes between Moore and An illustrate a parallel PAVN and American proficiency with the use of maps and battle tactics. The film first introduces An in the ambush of French troops in the opening sequence and when Moore prepares for battle before leaving home; he studies the French failure and An's leadership capabilities. Moreover, in battle against Moore, An quickly and decisively evaluates and attacks the American troops. Equally resolute, Moore intuits An's tactics and orders counterattacks. The binary of Moore and An serves to further reinforce the view of the war from the commanders' positions; this is a perspective characteristic of World War II combat films but atypical among films about the American War in Viet Nam.

However, the commander's outlook is more common among memoirs of the war. Moore and Galloway invoke the determination of the PAVN in an attempt to assess the lessons of the war, an endeavor shared by several wartime officials, historians, and scholars of the war—efforts that include the memoirs of Robert McNamara, the Johnson administration's secretary of defense, and Errol Morris's more recent documentary *The Fog of War* (2004), wherein

McNamara outlines his eleven lessons of the war. In their assessment of the battle and its attendant lessons, Moore and Galloway determine that American troops "could stand against the finest light infantry troops in the world and hold [their] ground" (345). Although couched within congratulations for American troops and limited by the "light infantry" specification, the praise is atypical among American representations of the war. As American scholars of the war often remark, American representations of the war, both narrative and historical, habitually marginalize "'enemy' Vietnamese subject status in their own history" (Vlastos 54). However, the subject status of the Vietnamese is not clearly marginalized in the film because it is one of the first, if not the first, to depict the PAVN as a worthy foe rather than as an aggressive menace.

"GOOD WAR"

Despite creating a more inclusive representation of the American War in Viet Nam by portraying the wartime experiences of American families and the PAVN, Wallace's *We Were Soldiers* reframes and thus disregards the political and cultural causes and consequences of the American War in Viet Nam by drawing on the conventions of the World War II combat film genre and depicting it as a "good war." In doing so, Wallace purposely disregards the sociopolitical and cultural origins and consequences of the war as he reverts to the map and tactics of the World War II combat film genre. He further veils the narrative's forgetfulness in historical specificity and authentic military iconography.

The film portrays the war, and the battle, within Jeanine Basinger's framework for the World War II combat film. Basinger designates seventeen narrative elements of such films. They include the film's credits, "unfold[ing] against a military reference"; a statement or "dedication"; a group of men, led by a hero, "undertak[ing] a mission which will accomplish an important military objective"; the presence of an observer or commentator; a "hero [who] has leadership forced upon him in dire circumstances"; the "undertak[ing] of a military objective"; unfolding action; the enemy's presence; military iconography; conflict within the group; "rituals enacted from the past and present"; death; a climactic battle; utilization of the "tools of the cinema"; resolution of the situation; and an ending "roll call." Finally, the film should leave the audience feeling "ennobled" (67–69).

While the military leaders in this battle did naturally employ military tactics common during World War II, the narrative of *We Were Soldiers* correlates with and employs the cinematic expectations in Basinger's outline of the World War II combat genre almost perfectly. The air cavalry insignia seen during the title sequence accomplishes Basinger's "military reference" in the opening credits. Galloway's character, who also serves as Basinger's observer-commentator, narrates what Basinger would identify as the opening "dedication" that frames the film. In this statement Galloway grounds the narrative in historical specificity:

> these are the true events of November, 1965, the Ia Drang Valley of Vietnam, a place our country does not remember, in a war it does not understand. This story is a testament to the young Americans who died in the valley of death, and a tribute to the young men of the People's Army of Vietnam who died by our hand in that place. To tell this story, I must start at the beginning. But where does it begin? Maybe in June of 1954 when French Group Mobile 100 moved into the same Central Highlands of Vietnam where we would go 11 years later.

The film then illustrates Viet Minh soldiers ambushing French troops.[4] Thus the film seemingly endeavors to explore the causes of the American War in Viet Nam, yet ultimately glosses over the specific political history of the war, instead creating a historical narrative arc that focuses on loss. The film's invocation of loss through representations of the French battle and Custer's "last stand" at Little Bighorn, and Moore's studies of these events, creates a sense of impending doom by linking both place—the Central Highlands in Viet Nam—and name—"Seventh Cavalry," Custer's own regiment—with Moore and his troops.

While military historians may disagree about whether there was a clear military objective in the "search and destroy" tactics American troops in Viet Nam employed, the film fulfills Basinger's "definitive objectives" of the battle. The first military objective the film portrays is the military's assessment of the helicopter's efficacy in troop transport, medical evacuation, and resupply. The helicopter, while not entirely without its disadvantages, successfully transports rested troops to LZ X-Ray, as opposed to sending in march-weary soldiers. Moore and his men accomplish the second objective to "find and destroy" the "enemy" insofar as the American armed forces maintained the so-called positive kill ratio and overran the PAVN base.

Because Moore believes he is fulfilling his duty, Basinger's hero under duress might not be readily apparent in *We Were Soldiers*. However, as Basinger qualifies, "enforced responsibility, however willingly or unwillingly accepted," fulfills that category (68). As film reviewer Todd McCarthy notes, "since it's not Moore's job to question orders, only to 'find the enemy and kill him,' he does the best he can" (69). Although Moore questions the wisdom of the mission—fighting in unfamiliar terrain with inexperienced soldiers—Moore willingly accepts responsibility despite being understaffed and engaged with capable adversaries in overwhelming numbers.

Basinger's unfolding action transpires in several places: at LZ X-Ray, in the PAVN bunker complex, at the American base, and on the American home front. Although the home-front element is quite unusual for a combat film, We Were Soldiers otherwise steadily parallels Basinger's list. Her requirement of "enemy presence" is met in Wallace's film in overwhelming, endless, and often faceless waves of attack. Besides the helicopter discussed earlier, the M-16 rifle fulfills Basinger's "military iconography." The M-16 garners attention in the film that signifies long-held criticism of the weapon. Sergeant Plumley, doubtful of the M-16's reliability, describes it to Moore as "lotsa plastic. Feels like a BB gun."

One seeming exception from Basinger's list in We Were Soldiers concerns "conflict within the group"; however, a fight between helicopter pilots occurs, as does an ongoing conflict between Moore, who refuses to leave the battlefield, and the military intelligence officers back at his home base, who make several requests for his evacuation from the battlefield because, as one of them says, "I call losing a lot of draftees a bad week. Losing a colonel's a massacre."

Basinger's requirement of death certainly occurs in overwhelming numbers. The figures designate 79 American soldiers killed, 121 American soldiers wounded, and an estimated 1,215 PAVN soldiers killed in the battle (Moore and Galloway 199). Wallace's cinematic portrayal of death, while gruesome at times, serves to bolster the film's emphasis on noble sacrifice. For example, the first American soldier to die smiles and says, "I'm glad I could die for my country." The soldier's dying words direct audiences to regard American deaths in the battle not as senseless but rather as a noble sacrifice. In addition, the deaths provide an occasion for Moore, when he prays over the American dead, to enact Basinger's "ritual." Otherwise rituals are nonexistent on the battlefield because the soldiers have little time for repose or reflection. Moore, however, enacts other prewar prayer rituals with his family at home, with another soldier in the chapel at Fort Benning, and during a postwar ritual while visiting the Vietnam Veterans Memorial (VVM).

Much of the film, because it represents a single battle, fulfills Basinger's "climactic battle." The scene of Moore leading the final charge for the hill, developed in the following section, serves as the ultimate climax of the battle. Wallace employs Basinger's requirement of the "tools of the cinema" to "create and release tension" by crosscutting between battlefield scenes and the American home front, between PAVN Colonel An and Colonel Moore, and between PAVN encroachment and American response. Stylistically, Wallace further employs music, framing, acting, and lighting to emphasize tension and suspense.

A seeming victory in battle and Moore's return home provide Basinger's "resolution of the situation" for both the American soldiers and their wives on the home front. Images of Moore's character, his face reflected behind names on the wall at the VVM, invokes resolution and healing. The film then explicitly includes Basinger's "roll call" of those who actually died in the battle at LZ X-Ray by listing their names, hometowns, and states in a black and white aesthetic reminiscent of the names engraved on the VVM. A caption informs viewers of the exact location of the names on the memorial, Panel 3 East, where to "their left and right are the names of 58,000 of their brothers-in-arms." The film thereby encourages audiences to visit the VVM and view the names. In essence, the film's closing sequence positions the film as a celluloid memorial that may inspire viewers to engage further in remembering the American War in Viet Nam by visiting the VVM. While the narrative of the film privileges authenticity of experience and memories of the war on behalf of those who either directly experienced the war, or have a hereditary "claim" to that remembrance, the film's inclusion of the VVM encourages audiences to participate in a collected cultural memory of the war.

As with any combat film, it is difficult to determine if the audience acquires Basinger's "ennobled" feeling from their cinematic experience. However, *We Were Soldiers*, by reverting to the conventions of the World War II narrative, attempts to reshape the American War in Viet Nam as a "good war" fought between equally capable armies. Wallace portrays the American military leadership as some of the most proficient heroes the American military can produce. Thus the film holds the suggestive power of leaving American audiences feeling patriotic and exceptional.

In the director's commentary on the DVD about a deleted scene that would have come at the end of the film, Wallace defends his choice to circumvent the politics of the war. The cut scene, "Moore Debriefed by McNamara and

Westmoreland," represents a meeting in Saigon that actually occurred between Moore, Secretary of Defense Robert McNamara, and General Westmoreland, wherein the latter two convey that the American success in the Ia Drang valley "inspired" certain victory in the broader war. To convey the real-life McNamara's numbers-conscious, corporate strategy for war, his character boasts, "seventy-nine dead against 1,800–2,000, that's in the range of 22.8–26.2 to one." Westmoreland further discusses an escalation of American troops, and thereby the war, that he hopes will "run these little bastards back home." Moore tries to express their adversaries' patriotism by reading from the diary of the PAVN soldier who tried to bayonet him. He reads, "Oh my dear young wife, when the troops come home after the victory and you do not see me, please look at the proud colors, you will see me there." This selection demonstrates the patriotism of the PAVN soldier; he, like the first American to die in the film, is proud to die for his country. Moore then evaluates the battle as only a momentary success for the Americans, explaining, "We won. We slaughtered 'em [but] we won't 'run the little bastards back home,' sir. They are home." Although Wallace believes the real-life meeting holds historical significance, he explains his choice to cut the filmed scene as a consequence of his primary goal to humanize the soldiers:

> The movie is not about politics, I did not want to raise an intellectual issue at the end. I wanted this movie to say, ultimately, that soldiers are human beings no matter what we thought about the Vietnam War, no matter how it divided us. Those arguments over politics ultimately obscured for us a much more immediate reality which was the men who died on both sides of this conflict are human beings. . . this scene took us away from that moment, that reality, that truth. (Director's commentary, *We Were Soldiers* DVD)

Wallace aims to encourage a unifying reconciliation between those who supported and those who opposed the war, as well as between veterans and civilians. However, Wallace's evasion of politics, while not unique among combat films, ultimately creates a limited memory of the American War in Viet Nam as a noble cause fought valiantly on both sides.

Unfortunately, in cutting the meeting scene between Moore, Westmoreland, and McNamara, Wallace evades the historical and political consequences of the war and the battle at LZ X-Ray. For example, setting policy for the remainder of the war, the battle confirmed commander Westmoreland's commitment to "search and destroy" strategies, to the implementation of air mobility, and to conducting a war of attrition. Cutting the scene erases the historical fact that this was a war of attrition replete with kill-ratios and that this very strategy dehumanizes soldiers as they come to be regarded as numbers instead of as individuals. Despite efforts to avoid politics, Wallace unavoidably makes a political statement about the war by ignoring the battle's consequences—that is, further escalation and protraction of the war. Moreover, his efforts to create a historically accurate, mimetic rendering of the battle at LZ X-Ray could mislead audiences to believe that this accuracy extends to the broader war, including its causes and consequences. Thus the film as mediated representation encourages a limited, "brothers in arms," prosthetic memory of the war.

Wallace certainly seemed to hope that the audience would gain a sense of healing from the war by watching the film. Concerning audiences, Wallace said, "soldiers who came back from Viet Nam were never given gratitude and the respect that their country owed them. . . . We give that to them and then we've all moved toward being whole. . . . My hope is that the American family can heal the wounds that have been there since Viet Nam" (director's commentary, *We Were Soldiers* DVD). Thus Wallace determines that still, in the twenty-first century, there exists a need to salve old wounds from the country's division over the war. It is likely that Wallace successfully impresses upon audiences a sense of sympathy for American soldiers and thus their families. However, it is a strange, late time for Wallace to feel obligated to make an argument that humanizes American soldiers who participated in the war because they are no longer seriously stereotyped as brutal or alienated miscreants in the Rambo prototype of the 1970s and 1980s.[5] Rather, the repetitious stereotype of the alienated or violent American Vietnam veteran is a twenty-first-century cliché ripe for satire. For example, *Tropic Thunder* (Ben Stiller, 2008), a metafictional comedy about the filming of a movie about the war, employs several layers of stereotypical American soldiers in a farce so inconsequential that cliché itself becomes the memory of the war.

In addition to correlating with Basinger's listed elements of the World War II combat genre, *We Were Soldiers* dehistoricizes the American War in Viet Nam under the guise of historical specificity. Wallace endeavors to create a historical framework for the battle at LZ X-Ray in Galloway's opening narrative by invoking the context of the 1954 defeat of French troops at Dien Bien Phu in the same region. Yet the film otherwise broadly encompasses the battle at LZ X-Ray in transhistorical terms, evoking Custer's last stand in the regiment's shared history, rendering Moore's study of the massacre at Little Big Horn and illustrating Moore's self-comparison with Custer, which is finally put to rest when Sergeant Plumley reassures Moore, "Sir, Custer was a pussy. You ain't." Of course, Plumley's assessment of Custer as a coward conflicts with the bravado Custer was known for.[6] Finally, the film's soundtrack, specifically the mournful "Sgt. MacKenzie" played during battle scenes, further encourages a transhistorical view of the war. The song's lyrics about a Scottish soldier's courageous yet resigned attitude toward war and battle exude sentiments of sacrifice. The refrain, "lay me down, in the cold, cold, ground, wheretofore many men have gone. . . when they come, I'll stand my ground," is a fitting choice for the film's argument because it invokes a tradition of heroism, courage, and a willingness to die for country.

AMERICAN HERO

Besides these elements, Wallace primarily achieves his portrayal of the American War in Viet Nam as a noble cause in *We Were Soldiers* through the leadership of the battlefield commanders, especially Colonel Moore. Although Moore was likely an extraordinary military leader, and it may not have been unusual at this early stage in the war, it is quite unusual for a colonel, in the narrative and cinematic and narrative traditions of representing the American War in Viet Nam, to automatically garner the trust and respect of his men. *We Were Soldiers* thereby stands in opposition to most American narratives of the war because it portrays a colonel as a father figure, a leader with experience to be trusted. One of the hallmarks of American representations of the war is the turning away from official narratives of commanders toward depicting the experiences in war of common soldiers, or "grunts." Typically, in these narratives, a sergeant earns the confidence of his men over a lieutenant because of his battlefield experience or time spent "in country" in Viet Nam. Sergeants Burns and Elias in Oliver Stone's *Platoon* (1986) are among the most famous sergeants who fulfill the father-figure role and challenge the authority of their lieutenant, because his inexperience often requires that the battle-hardened sergeants lead and protect him. In narratives of the war, officers are nearly always suspect because they are most often products of the Reserve Officer Training Corps (ROTC). Their commission often creates a hierarchical divide between enlisted soldiers and officers, as well as between the uneducated and educated, thus calling into question the value of formal education as opposed to battlefield education.[7] Counter to negative portrayals of officers in other representations, Moore, at age forty-two, has a fourteen-month combat tour in Korea on his record and, before leaving for Viet Nam, studies the military history of the French War in Viet Nam (Moore and Galloway, *We Were Soldiers Once* 18). Moore's character and his rank as colonel deviate to a near polar opposite of this attitude and tradition, aligning more closely with the World War II combat narrative.

In the film, Moore's idealistic, rallying speech to his men just before their deployment to Viet Nam serves to highlight his leadership qualities and the film's themes of brotherhood, danger, and heroism:

> Look around you. In the Seventh Cavalry, we've got a captain from the Ukraine, another from Puerto Rico. We've got Japanese, Chinese, Blacks, Hispanics, Cherokee Indians. Jews and Gentiles. All Americans. Now here in the states, some of you in this unit may have experienced discrimination because of race or creed. But for you and me now, all that is gone. We're moving into the valley of the shadow of death, where you will watch the back of the man next to you, as he will watch yours. And you won't care what color he is, or by what name he calls God. They say we're leaving home. We're going to what home was always supposed to be. Now let us understand the situation. We are going into battle against a tough and determined enemy.
>
> [Pause]
>
> I can't promise you that I will bring you all home alive. But this I swear, before you and before almighty God, that when we go into battle, I will be the first to set foot on the field, and I will be the last to step off, and I will leave no one behind. Dead or alive, we will all come home together. So help me, God.

Moore's address emphasizes equality, democracy, and erasure of divisive difference. Noting the international and interracial composition of the group of officers, Moore declares that in battle differences in heritage, nationality, race, and religion disappear. He makes this claim despite the state of racial tensions on the home front during this period of the civil rights movement. He asserts that the men will achieve equality and will become "brothers in arms," fighting for each other, the film's ultimate message. In addition, Moore dedicates himself as the heroic leader promising to be the first and last on the battlefield. The final lines of his statement promising to "leave no man behind" may also remind contemporary audiences of the POW/MIA controversy that began with the signing of the Paris Peace Accords in 1973 between the United States and North Viet Nam.[8] American cultural contestation, later reinforced by the aforementioned rescue-return films of the 1980s, such as *Rambo: First Blood, Part II*, *Missing in Action*, and *Uncommon Valor*, endured as a source of contention among Vietnam veterans concerning normalizing relations with Viet

Nam in the 1990s. The debate persisted in influencing cinematic memory of the war in the 2006 POW escape film *Rescue Dawn*, and continued to influence U.S.-Vietnamese relations as recently as 2007 when the Pentagon sent MIA search teams to Southeast Asia (Weiner).

Again, deviating from typical narratives of the war that unflinchingly depict soldiers' fears in battle, Moore intrepidly fulfills his heroic promises on the battlefield. The film's iconic moments show Moore's combat boots, in slow motion, touching the battlefield first and leaving it last, as a visual frame to the combat. Throughout the three-day conflict, Moore fulfills his role as an audacious neo–John Wayne. While other soldiers duck and crouch amid incoming fire, Moore, appearing invincible, unflinchingly stands upright. He decisively directs his troops; he always correctly anticipates the PAVN's next mode of attack or retreat; he employs successful attacks and counterattacks; he refuses to leave the battlefield; and he has to be pulled back from firefights by his trusty Sergeant Plumley, who reminds him, "if you go down, we all go down." Finally, Moore implausibly turns at the last moment to shoot, point blank, the PAVN soldier who is about to bayonet him.

The film portrays Moore as the ultimate leader. He is fearless, unrelenting, and quick witted; he seems to be everywhere at once, directing and encouraging his troops. In the final charge up the hill, Moore, with one arm raised, leads his troops in a slow-motion battle charge, an image reminiscent of soldiers in World War I charging out of the trenches. Just as he is about to be shot by his enemies, a helicopter climactically swoops in to shoot the PAVN soldiers holding the hill, and with that support the Americans "win" the battle. Moore's heroism and courage, coupled with the casting of Mel Gibson, has not gone unnoticed by critics. For example, historian Michael Schaller views Moore as a "'new age' George Patton" and regards the film as reminiscent of "such 'classics' as *They Died with Their Boots On* (1941) and *Fort Apache* (1948)" (1173–74). Thus, a war once commonly depicted as rife with the confusion of youth and overwhelming violence, now becomes, through Wallace's lens and the specificity of an early single battle, a war fought between competent, capable, courageous military leaders.

AFTERMATH

After the battle, *We Were Soldiers* juxtaposes the media in two distinct fashions, thus reinforcing the authenticity of experience and contributing to the debate over the media's role in America's loss of the war in Viet Nam. The sympathetic portrayal of Joe Galloway, a United Press International reporter, stands in counter-distinction to the film's depiction of the mass of journalists who descend upon LZ X-Ray after the battle. The film dedicates a large role to Galloway, coauthor of the book *We Were Soldiers*. His character arrives on the battlefield early in the battle, and like Moore, he does not leave until the battle is over. When Moore asks Galloway why he is not a soldier, Galloway speaks of family tradition: "the Galloways have been in every war this country's ever fought." He further defends his noncombatant status, explaining, "I didn't think I could stop the war. . . . I just thought maybe I'd try to understand one, maybe help the folks back home understand. I just figured I could do that better shootin' a camera than I could shootin' a rifle." Despite Galloway's self-identification as a noncombatant, the coarse Sergeant Plumley toughly determines, after the battle becomes especially heated, "ain't no such thing today, son," and hands Galloway a rifle. With that Galloway transforms from a peaceful civilian into a proficient warrior.

Galloway's authenticity of experience, his incorporation into the battle as a combatant, heightens the film's theme of privileging direct memories. Not only does Galloway observe much of the battle, he also directly participates in the fighting, "only later returning to his camera and performing the function of witness for the audience" (Badsey 257). Because of his combative actions in battle, he can no longer be a detached, outside observer. Galloway eventually served four tours as a war correspondent in Viet Nam between 1965 and 1975. He continued his work as a war correspondent during the Gulf War of 1990–91, and in the Iraq War in 2003 and from 2005 to 2006, in addition to serving as a special consultant to General Colin Powell at the State Department from 2001 to 2002 (Moore and Galloway, *We Are Soldiers Still* xviii; www .huffingtonpost.com/joegalloway). Moreover, Galloway, the only American civilian awarded a medal of valor "for actions during the American War in Viet Nam," also received a Bronze Star Medal in 1998 for "rescuing wounded soldiers under fire in the Ia Drang Valley" (www.huffingtonpost.com/joe galloway). His editorial writing on war continues.

In the film, Galloway, distanced from other reporters by his battlefield experiences, will not or cannot answer their questions. They ask, "Joe, what happened here?" But Galloway does not reply, appearing contemptuous of their lack of experience. For example, when the other reporters crouch in fear at the thunder of artillery, Galloway, standing upright, clarifies that they hear "American artillery," adding, in military jargon, "friendly fire." His use of soldiers' language serves to create a distinction between himself and the other journalists. The journalists then turn to Moore, pummeling him with questions that begin with military strategy, asking him about the "key to victory" and his assessment of the PAVN's military prowess, and end with questions about the number of American casualties and whether families have been notified. Again, they get no response; Moore walks away. Here the film heightens the divide between those who were on the battlefield and those who were not. The film thus privileges the authenticity of experience, thereby rejecting the possibility of prosthetic memory—cultural memory held by those with no direct memory of, or access to, the war.

Although *We Were Soldiers* primarily focuses on the American soldiers' experiences in the battle at LZ X-Ray, Colonel An of the PAVN has the final word after the Americans leave the battlefield. As Roger Ebert notes in discussing the film's patriotism, when An approaches a small, battered American flag, "even. . . [he] looks at the stars and stripes with enigmatic thoughtfulness" ("A Soldier's Story" 29). An reflects, "such a tragedy. They will think it's their victory. So this will become an American war. And the end will be the same. . . except the numbers who will die before we get there." He then replaces the flag and walks away. Despite Wallace's choice to cut the scene of Moore's debriefing with McNamara and Westmoreland, Colonel An's comments reflect the false sense of American victory gleaned from the battle and alludes to the impending escalation and protraction of the war. Thus it becomes apparent why some might claim that *We Were Soldiers* is not a film about victory but about "survival"—as Hal Moore does in the "'Getting It Right': Behind the Scenes" special feature on the *We Were Soldiers* DVD.

While some might argue that the film does not glorify war or celebrate American military might because of its gruesome portrayal of battle or its depictions of sorrowful reactions to loss of life on the home front, or because of Colonel An's sobering reflection on the battle, the film unarguably dedicates most of its 128 minutes to valorizing the "reluctant warrior," especially Moore, his strategic prowess, and American military technology. Considering the film's rendering of Moore's character as a fearless, militarily superior, heroic leader, it becomes difficult to understand Colonel An's words about the ensuing protracted war and its attendant loss of life as the sacrificial message of the film.

BEYOND THE BATTLEFIELD

The post-battle, home-front scenes that close the film serve to reinforce the forgetful, "brothers in arms," "noble cause" focus of Wallace's *We Were Soldiers*.

Galloway narrates the veterans' homecoming experiences while simultaneously reinforcing the soldiers' apolitical positions in the war. He explains that
upon the soldiers' return to the United States, "some had families waiting.
For others, their only family would be the men they bled beside. There were
no bands, no flags, no Honor Guards to welcome them home. They went
to war because their country ordered them to. But in the end, they fought
not for their country or their flag, they fought for each other." Galloway's
account speaks to American cultural perception of the mistreatment of Vietnam veterans upon their return to the United States. The lack of a "Welcome
Home" celebration, coupled with veterans' accounts of being neglected by
the government and being despised by civilians of the antiwar movement,
left a generation of veterans feeling alienated from their country and their
fellow citizens.[9] Moreover, Galloway's commentary reinforces the film's evasion of the politics of the war by claiming that the soldiers did not fight, as
Moore reiterates, for "mom, apple pie, [or] the American flag," but rather "for
one another" ("Getting It Right"). Because of this shared message, film critics often compare We Were Soldiers to another twenty-first-century war film,
Black Hawk Down, about an attempted raid that turned into a rescue mission
during the battle of Mogadishu in Somalia in 1993 (Ridley Scott, 2001). Ebert,
writing about We Were Soldiers, explains, "The narration tells us, 'In the end,
they fought for each other.' This is an echo of the Black Hawk Down line, 'It's
about the men next to you. That's all it is'" ("A Soldier's Story" 29). In fact, the
similarities in message indicate a trend among twenty-first-century war films
to recast defeat, or at minimum military debacles, not as a fight against foes
but as a victory of solidarity among American soldiers. The trend of recasting
military purpose obscures—psychologically and culturally erases—the reasons
America entered the war in the first place.

Despite the film's revision of the war, postwar reflection in We Were Soldiers
possesses a positive value that contributes to an ever-broadening collected
cultural memory of the war. Besides direct commentary on the homecoming
experiences of Vietnam veterans, the film also addresses two women—one
American and the other, briefly, Vietnamese—whose husbands died in the
battle at LZ X-Ray. Moore's character narrates a letter to the American wife,
while Wallace crosscuts scenes of her reading the letter and clutching the
baby's name bracelet that her husband wore in battle with shots of a Vietnamese woman reading what appears to be a similar note that Moore inscribed at
the end of her husband's diary. Moore narrates:

Dear Barbara,

I have no words to express to you my sadness at the loss of Jack. The world is a lesser place without him. But I know he is with God and the angels and I know even Heaven is improved by his presence there. I know you too are sure of this and yet this knowledge can't diminish his loss and your grief.

With abiding respect and affection,

Hal Moore.

This scene correlates the loss of an American soldier with that of a PAVN soldier and indicates the significance of material memory—personal objects that, in this case, signify the dead and their prewar lives. It is the bracelet that brings Barbara to tears and the photograph in the diary that the Vietnamese woman handles most lovingly. Both objects—the baby's bracelet and the photograph of the wife—also signify the soldiers' love of family. Thus the film, like the Vietnam Veterans Memorial, reinforces the human loss as a consequence of the battle. It is possible, however, that as cinema scholar Guy Westwell asserts, the film employs family as a motivation for the war "in the contemporary war cinema's most simplistic articulation of war and war's purpose" (108). In addition, memory, specifically direct memory, gains final narrative attention in Galloway's concluding narration. While writing through his tears in a newsroom, Galloway explains in voice-over that "we who have seen war never stop seeing. In the sounds of the night we will always hear the screams. So this is our story, for we were soldiers once, and young." This final narration indicates the ongoing memory of war for those who participated in the fighting. While the allusion to posttraumatic stress is necessary and responsible, Wallace still only remembers and privileges the memories of those who fought, those who died, and their families, thereby recasting the war in terms of personal, rather than national, suffering, sacrifice, and loss.

SOLDIERS STILL

Six years after Wallace's *We Were Soldiers*, five years into the Iraq War, and on the eve of the historically momentous 2008 American presidential election, Harold G. Moore and Joseph L. Galloway's *We Are Soldiers Still: A Journey Back to the Battlefields of Vietnam* (2008) circulated. It offers a more ambiguous rendering of the war than their first, minutiae-laden book *We Were Soldiers Once . . . and Young*. As opposed to Wallace's film, *We Were Soldiers*, Moore and Galloway's subsequent *We Are Soldiers Still* extends a remembrance of the American War in Viet Nam that rejects the forgetfulness of "noble cause" revisionism. The book should be a corrective for audiences who believe that Wallace's film renders a false authenticity in its zealous portrayal of heroism and its failure to consider the cultural and political causes and effects of the war. The subtitle, A Journey Back to the Battlefields of Vietnam, suggests that We Are Soldiers Still accentuates an exploration of the memory of the war through return visits to specifically located private memory sites in Viet Nam. Through their journeys, Moore and Galloway experience and encourage postwar reconciliation between PAVN veterans and American veterans of the war. Moreover, the book further clarifies the authors' disapproval of the war as politically misguided, a belief that corresponds to their assessment of the Iraq War. We Are Soldiers Still thus reclaims a twenty-first-century remembrance of the war's aftermath in the shadow of the film's forgetfulness.

Writing of the "artistic license" in Wallace's We Were Soldiers, Moore and Galloway only explicitly clarify minor and specific points regarding the homefront experiences of the American wives of the soldiers. An appendix that serves in part as a tribute to Moore's deceased wife, Julia, describes her role in petitioning for changes to the film. For example, she influenced the choice of cast to include more racially diverse actresses to play the roles of the wives. However, she was unable to overturn decisions concerning the portrayal of military families' living conditions. When soldiers were deployed, their wives and families were ordered to vacate their living quarters on base. Yet the film "wrongly depicted all the wives and families of [Moore's] battalion living in ... nice two-story bungalows on Colonel's Row at Fort Benning" (Moore and Galloway, We Are Soldiers Still 218–19). Julia would have preferred that the film depict the reality of "women and children crammed into those little trailer houses" (222). While this is nearly all Moore and Galloway directly write about the film We Were Soldiers, the book We Are Soldiers Still serves as an implicit yet significant addendum to the "noble cause" memory of the war that the film promotes.

We Are Soldiers Still recounts and encourages postwar reconciliation via recognition among former foes. Reconciliation may, at first, appear too easily attained when Moore and Galloway recapitulate their discussions with the Vietnamese: the former Colonel, then General An—the PAVN battlefield commander at LZ X-Ray and LZ Albany—General Chu Huy Man—the division commander in the Central Highlands in 1965—Vietnamese military historians, and other PAVN veterans of the war (21). However, Moore and

Galloway are quick to clarify that the easy relationship evolved over several return visits to Viet Nam during a fifteen-year period, between 1990 and 2005. Nonetheless, it was no small feat that Moore and Galloway accomplished by meeting Generals An and Man in 1991, three years before the 1994 normalization of economic and diplomatic relations between the United States and Viet Nam.[10] In fact, Moore underscores that it had not been since World War II that Americans discussed any battles in detail with former enemies and that it was only possible then because German commanders were prisoners of war (20). In noting the rarity of detailed discussions between former wartime foes, Moore and Galloway can further emphasize the desire of both parties to reconcile with each other.

Moore and Galloway additionally explicate that the postwar reconciliation between Moore and An resulted from devastating loss of life on both sides, as well as their shared leadership qualities gained over the course of their respective lifetime military careers. Just as they recapitulate Moore's military career, Moore and Galloway also relate An's military experience, which began with his joining the Viet Minh guerrilla army in 1945 to fight against the French in Viet Nam (68). Ten years later, in 1954, An commanded a regiment in the battle of Dien Bien Phu, where the French surrendered and from that ended their war in and colonization of Viet Nam (68). Describing common experiences between PAVN and American soldiers and commanders, as well as Moore's and An's mutual respect for each other as opposing battlefield commanders, Moore and Galloway determine that "perhaps we have much more in common with such men as these, our old enemies, men like ourselves" than the average person (40). Here, they reinforce a "brothers in arms" message but expand it, as Galloway suggests, by regarding their former foes as "blood brothers" (40). In explaining their own sense of reconciliation with their past adversaries, Moore and Galloway implicitly encourage feelings of recognition and reconciliation toward the PAVN veterans among other American veterans of the war, a large part of their intended audience.

In addition to shared experiences, the passage of time eases Moore and An's reconciliation. For example, Moore believes that time created a mutual understanding between An and himself that "there were no victors in the battle—only the fortunate who had somehow survived" (99). Rather than recasting the war as a fight for survival only among American soldiers as Wallace's We Were Soldiers suggests, Moore conveys a mutual fight for survival for both the American and PAVN soldiers. Moreover, upon Moore and

Galloway's first meeting with General An, the Vietnamese officer stressed peace and forgetfulness, pronouncing that "there's no hatred between our two peoples. Let the past bury the past. Now we look to the future" (38). An voices the Vietnamese official policy that encourages forgetting the past; however, it seems by his choice of words, especially "hatred," that he is not posturing but is sincere.

As opposed to Moore and An achieving reconciliation via the passage of time, exploration of memory in We Are Soldiers Still centers on returning to the past by visiting particular sites of memory, specifically former battle-fields. Although Moore and Galloway faced diplomatic challenges in obtaining permission from Vietnamese authorities to visit their former battlefields, Moore and Galloway, along with General An and other American and PAVN veterans, finally achieved their goal. Near the end of their day at what was once LZ X-Ray and what the Vietnamese now call the "Forest of Screaming Souls,"[11] Moore gathered everyone into a circle (xix). As they stood with arms around each other and heads bowed, Moore offered an informal prayer in memory of all—Americans and Vietnamese—who died in the battle at LZ X-Ray. For years Moore hoped to spend a night at LZ X-Ray "to commune with fallen comrades so that they and [he] could finally be at peace" (102). Serendipity grants Moore that wish. After the first group of primarily Viet-namese veterans and officials leaves the former battlefield, an incoming storm prevents the return of the rented helicopter from extracting the remaining Americans and translators from the site. During the night, Moore walks the perimeter, explores his memories, and mourns the dead. Upon leaving his former battlefield, Moore optimistically believes that those who died "were finally at peace and this place . . . could at last be blessed with silence" and that the veterans "could go home with [their] own measure of peace as well" (111). Revisiting sites of memory in We Are Soldiers Still holds the possibility of healing psychological wounds.

Although the authors encourage reconciliation among former enemies, acknowledge gaining a sense of peace, and note the passage of forty-two years since their battles in the Ia Drang Valley, they reject forgetfulness. Moore and Galloway write: "If we had come here seeking closure, seeking to consign those memories to some hidden dustbin of history, we had failed. Some things are not meant to be forgotten or easily tucked away. . . . There is no such thing as closure for soldiers who have survived a war. They have an obligation, a sacred duty, to remember those who fell in battle beside them all their days and to bear witness to the insanity that is war" (155).

Clarifying that survival does not necessarily equal victimization, Moore and Galloway explain that survival, rather, carries with it an obligation to remember. Their book participates in bearing witness to the war as a reflection on memory that provides the possibility for their audiences to acquire individually felt prosthetic memories of the war. Moreover, the compulsion to remember and thus the impossibility of forgetting impel their desire to commemorate more publicly the war and the battles of the Ia Drang valley. For example, Moore and An planned to erect a "small monument" at LZ X-Ray in memory of both the American and Vietnamese soldiers who died there (149). Because General An would have been the primary Vietnamese advocate of the memorial, his death seems to have prevented that hope from becoming a reality. Still other memorial sites in Viet Nam attract Moore and Galloway's attention. For example, they make note of the many military cemeteries in Viet Nam; they discuss the rumor of one such cemetery being near LZ X-Ray; they describe, in detail, the family shrine for General An in his wife's home; and they visit the historic markers and memorials at Dien Bien Phu—the location of the last French battle in Viet Nam in 1954.

The French defeat at Dien Bien Phu and the broader French experience in fighting a war against the Viet Minh provide the impetus for Moore and Galloway to delineate lessons America failed to learn from the French and American Wars in Viet Nam that further translate, according to the authors, to the Iraq War. For example, the authors agree with the Vietnamese that if America had more closely considered the French War in Viet Nam, and specifically the French defeat at Dien Bien Phu, then America would have realized that the Vietnamese Communist war effort could outlast the inevitable weakening political motivation of another country over time.

Moore and Galloway also finally and openly critique the American War in Viet Nam. They begin by questioning the loss of life: "What did all of this mean? Was all this suffering and dying worth it? Even then [1965] . . . our political leadership could not explain coherently why we were fighting" (107–8). They further comment on Ronald Reagan's 1980 revision of the war as a "noble cause." They write, "he was wrong. There's never been a noble war except in the history books and propaganda movies" (108). Thus Moore and Galloway respond to the cultural revisions of the American War in Viet Nam that attempted to "cure" the "Vietnam Syndrome"—a misnomer for the national postwar unwillingness to intervene militarily in the Third-World. Truth and accuracy are always extremely important to Moore and Galloway in recounting the battles of the Ia Drang Valley in 1965. For example, in the prologue to their first book, *We Were Soldiers Once . . . and Young*, they write, "Hollywood got [the war] wrong every damned time" (xvi). This is the very same line that inspired Randall Wallace to create the film *We Were Soldiers*. Furthermore, in the DVD special feature, "'Getting it Right': Behind the Scenes," Moore attests to his belief that Wallace's film did accurately portray the American War in Viet Nam when he says, "the message of the movie [pause] hate war but love the American warrior. They finally got it right, they finally got it right." Yet, as an addendum to the film *We Were Soldiers*, Moore and Galloway finally seem to get it right themselves when, in the final chapter of *We Are Soldiers Still*, they explicitly denounce the American War in Viet Nam as "the wrong war, in the wrong place, against the wrong people" (193).

Although they critique the war and cultural revisions of the war, in *We Are Soldiers Still* Moore and Galloway also endeavor to explain the soldiers' perspective. They emphasize, "it wasn't [the soldiers'] place to question. We were soldiers and we followed their orders" (108). Finally, Moore and Galloway underscore, explain, and defend their previous "brothers in arms" message, which the film *We Were Soldiers* enthusiastically embraces: "in times and places like this, where the reasons for war are lacking, soldiers fight and die for each other" (108). The statement evokes Alfred Lord Tennyson's "Charge of the Light Brigade" (1854): "Someone had blunder'd: / Theirs not to make reply, / Theirs not to reason why, / Theirs but to do & die" (12–15). According to Moore's understanding, in dire political circumstances and essentially acting under orders they are not allowed to question, soldiers fight for what they can—in this case, each other.

Despite defending soldiers' apolitical position, Moore and Galloway fearlessly and explicitly critique "preemptive" war and thereby the Iraq War. They suggest that the Iraq War is a consequence of ignoring the lessons of the American War in Vietnam when they write that "a generation of political leaders who studiously avoided service in [the] war seemingly learned nothing from that history and thus consign a new generation of soldiers to 'preemptive' wars of choice. . . most wars are a confession of failure—the failure of diplomacy and negotiation and common sense, and in most cases, of leadership" (xx).

Clearly, they are addressing the Iraq War and the George W. Bush administration's preemptive-war strategy that came to be called the "Bush Doctrine." Developing a distinct argument specifically against the Iraq War, they deem the war an "unnecessary . . . misadventure," especially because they believe it diverted resources away from finding Osama bin Laden and dangerously depleted American military equipment and strategic reserves (194). Moreover, Moore and Galloway critically assess the military and foreign policy leadership of former president George W. Bush and his former defense secretary Donald Rumsfeld, comparing him to Johnson administration defense secretary Robert McNamara as others have, but further claiming that McNamara "look[s] good" by comparison (196). Concerning Bush, they scathingly suggest that he should have "these words from Erasmus: *Dulce bellum inexpertis* (War is delightful to those who have no experience of it) . . . carved over the entrance to the planned $500 million George Walker Bush Presidential Library in Dallas" (195). The actual cost of the George W. Bush Presidential Library and Museum dedicated in April 2013 on the campus of Southern Methodist University in Dallas, Texas, was $250 million, compared to $165 million for the William J. Clinton Presidential Center. Bush's library is the largest presidential library to date, boasting 226,560 square feet.

CONTINUED REMEMBRANCE

Both of Moore and Galloway's books and Wallace's film contribute to a collected cultural memory of the American War in Viet Nam even among and between the multifaceted memories of the war with which each narrative engages. The film is certainly one of the most inclusive representations of the war in its depictions of the home front, PAVN soldiers, journalists, range of ranks, and allusions to a prewar historical context. Unlike earlier narrative films about the war, the film encompasses American civilian women's military-base and home-front experiences. It also deviates from typical representations that vilify the Vietnamese. The variety of perspectives contributes to an ongoing collected cultural memory of the war.

Regrettably, despite being one of the most inclusive representations of the war, the film remains distinct from other remembrances of the war when it reverts to the genre conventions of World War II combat films and attempts to authentically recast the war as a noble cause. Thereby, it evades the sociopolitical causes, complications, and consequences of the war in favor of directing cultural and prosthetic memory of the war toward those moments that demonstrate courage, bravery, sacrifice, brotherhood, and victory over the enemy in a singular battle. It reverts to the maps-tactics-commanders focus common in World War II narratives wherein the troops, under the command of a heroic, competent leader, successfully accomplish a specific mission. Consequently, the film falls into a category of twenty-first-century combat films that, in Guy Westwell's words, promotes "a myopic view of the past—predicated on . . . nostalgia for a mythologized version of World War II—[that] has become justification for war in the present" and thus ultimately forgets the broader political issues of the American War in Viet Nam (115).

Conversely, *We Are Soldiers Still* serves as a response to revisionary narratives by elucidating contemporary cultural, political, and military implications of forgetting the American War in Viet Nam in Moore and Galloway's explicit critique of both the American War in Viet Nam and the Iraq War. *We Are Soldiers Still* clarifies the "artistic license" and potential audience interpretation of Randall Wallace's film *We Were Soldiers* insofar as the book critiques the glorification of war, illuminates the authors' views on the wrongs of "preemptive" war, especially in Iraq, and both develops and encourages reconciliation between former enemies, a reconciliation only obliquely implied in Wallace's film.

Both Wallace's film and Moore and Galloway's two books participate in a broader remembrance of the American War in Viet Nam that includes representations of American civilian women and Vietnamese soldiers. Inclusiveness of remembrance will expand further into the Philippines as the following chapter seeks to demonstrate by examining Jessica Hagedorn's *Dream Jungle* (2003). In addition, *We Are Soldiers Still* will likely serve as a precursor to imaginative representations of the American War in Viet Nam that create parallels with the Iraq War, one of the issues the concluding chapter will explore.

CHAPTER 7
• UNFINISHED REMEMBRANCE

BEYOND THE UNITED STATES AND VIET NAM—
JESSICA HAGEDORN'S *DREAM JUNGLE* AND FRANCIS
FORD COPPOLA'S *APOCALYPSE NOW REDUX*

Often American and Vietnamese narratives of the war promote postwar reconciliation between former foes in addition to exploring, demonstrating, and encouraging prosthetic memories However, memories of the American War in Viet Nam do not solely affect Americans and the Vietnamese but also the culture, politics, and citizens of other countries. Moreover, direct and prosthetic memories of the war surface beyond the literal and figurative battlefields of Viet Nam and the United States. For example, South Korean and Australian military personnel directly participated in the war. After the United States military, South Korean soldiers constituted the second largest military contingent during the war with 50,000 troops in 1968 alone and over 260,000 troops in Viet Nam between 1964 and 1970 (Larsen and Collins 23). The War Memorial of Korea in Seoul, dedicated in 1994, includes monuments inscribed with the names of Korean soldiers who died in Viet Nam. According to the Australian Department of Veterans Affairs, approximately 61,000 Australians served in the war between 1962 and 1975 (Australian Government). The Australians experienced mounting antiwar protests during the war, have since conducted studies on the postwar physical and psychological effects of the war on veterans, and have also memorialized those who died in the war at the Australian War Memorial.

Furthermore, memories of the war materialize in the Philippines, a country not typically associated with remembrance of the American War in Viet Nam. However, during the war, the United States maintained its two largest overseas military bases in the Philippines—Clark Air Base and Subic Bay Naval Complex—under President Ferdinand Marcos (1965–1986). Although the Philippines was an American colony for forty-seven years (1899–1946),

American "national ignorance of the Philippines" renders the two countries' entangled colonial history a forgotten memory (Kirk v). Yet the history of the Philippines encompasses Spanish and American colonialism, numerous rebellions, and the protracted presence of United States military installations that resulted not in a postcolonial but rather a complex neocolonial relationship between the Philippines and the United States.

Engaging with the memories of the American War in Viet Nam, Jessica Hagedorn's novel Dream Jungle (2003) addresses neocolonialism in the 1970s Philippines. Hagedorn writes out of a transnational perspective; she is a Filipina American who moved, with her family, to the United States in 1963 at age fourteen. Dream Jungle begins in 1971, before the end of the American War in Viet Nam, and concludes in 2000. Hagedorn's fragmented narrative, intended to be "epic" (Hagedorn, qtd. in Aguilar-San Juan 6), intertwines two actual occurrences in the Philippines in the 1970s: the filming of Francis Ford Coppola's own war epic, Apocalypse Now (1979), and Manuel Elizalde Jr.'s 1971 discovery of a primitive tribe, the Tasaday, subsequently alleged to be a hoax. Hagedorn's novel appeared in the early twenty-first century after the death of Elizalde and after Coppola released a reworking of the 1979 film, Apocalypse Now Redux (2001). In her fictional account of these events, Napalm Sunset denotes Coppola's Apocalypse Now; Tony Pierce represents Coppola; Zamora López de Lagazpi, a descendant of Spanish colonialists, stands in for Manuel Elizalde Jr.; and the "lost" mountain tribe, the Taobo, represents the Tasaday. Discussing her combination of the filming of Napalm Sunset with the controversy over Zamora's "discovery" of the Taobo, Hagedorn explains, "as legend goes, the filming of Apocalypse Now was a grueling, crazy process that had an impact on the Philippine landscape and on the filmmakers themselves. A conquistador like Magellan or the fictional Zamora has to be obsessed in order to do what he does. The same goes for a genius director like Coppola or my fictional Tony Pierce" (Hagedorn, "A Conversation"). The pairing highlights the novel's central themes: "Discovery and Conquest," the title of part 1; and "cultural mythmaking" (Hagedorn, "A Conversation").

Reworking the American and Philippine cultural mythology of the Apocalypse Now filming and the controversy over the Tasaday tribe discovery, Hagedorn weaves an intertextual story of colonial memory blending Coppola's Apocalypse Now and Apocalypse Now Redux, about American militarism in Viet Nam, and her own Dream Jungle, about neocolonialism in the Philippines. Hagedorn's contribution to a collected cultural memory of the war transports Coppola's films, and thus memories of the American War in Viet Nam, intertextually into the twenty-first century. The intertextuality echoes Coppola's invocation of Joseph Conrad's *Heart of Darkness* (1899), about Belgian imperialism in the African Congo, Sir James Frazer's *The Golden Bough* (1922), and T. S. Eliot's "The Waste Land" (1922) and "The Hollow Men" (1925) to create a narrative that moves metaphorically into the late-nineteenth- and early-twentieth-century past. Beginning in 1960s Saigon, the capital of South Viet Nam's Republic of Viet Nam (RVN), Coppola's characters travel upriver and, illegally, into Cambodia toward the ancient temple at Kurtz's compound. As Coppola reflects on the prewar past, the narrative simultaneously progresses forward, up the river to Kurtz, and further still into the 1970s by the creation of the film in the Philippines. Yet another retelling, *Hearts of Darkness: A Film-maker's Apocalypse* (1991), compiles Eleanor Coppola's documentary movie footage, photographs, and a diary that describe the making of *Apocalypse Now* in 1976 and 1977. The 1991 release of the documentary reinvigorated the legends and controversies surrounding Coppola's filming.

Further revitalizing these controversies and memories of the American War in Viet Nam, Hagedorn's twenty-first-century novel invokes Coppola's film and thereby Conrad, the making of the film, American militarism and neocolonialism, and the American and Spanish colonizations of the Philippines. Both Hagedorn's and Coppola's allusions and adaptations represent "colonialism [as] a movable horror prone to displacement and repetition" (Norris 735). Hagedorn's narrative primarily addresses the colonial legacy of the Philippines, wherein the memory of the American War in Viet Nam, via the filming *Napalm Sunset*, encroaches on the Philippines as an act of neocolonialism. Hagedorn creates a mediated representation of the war that depicts prosthetic memory of the war in the filming of *Napalm Sunset* and her novel. Memory of the war thus extends far beyond the literal and cultural battlefields of Viet Nam and the United States.

COLONIAL CONTEXTS

Reminding audiences of the colonial context out of which she writes, Hagedorn begins *Dream Jungle* with a passage from Antonio Pigafetta's journal about Magellan's 1521 travels in the Philippines under the Spanish monarchy. Magellan's arrival in the Philippines brought with it requirements for baptism in the Catholic Church, demands for tribute to the Spanish monarchy, the first armed resistance to Spanish control in the Philippines, and Magellan's death in the battle of Mactan (Nadeau 24–26).[1] Subsequent Spanish expeditions, throughout the following fifty years, culminated in Miguel Lopez de Legazpi's 1565 settlement expedition of and dominion over the island of Cebu (26). Hagedorn interweaves this colonial history into *Dream Jungle* to demonstrate the active vestiges of colonialism at work in the Philippine archipelago. For example, Zamora, a fictional descendant of Miguel Lopez de Legazpi, maintains a colonial hierarchy at his compound through the subservience of his hired help. He also revives and relives his ancestors' colonial discovery and conquest in his relationships with the Taobo.

Spain's official colonial rule in the Philippines endured from 1565 to 1899 while the concept of Filipino nationalism continued to evolve, manifesting in protests and rebellions punctuating the eighteenth and nineteenth centuries (39, 45). The growing revolutionary movement between 1896 and 1898, coupled with American support during the Spanish-American War, resulted in Filipino control of much of the country just before the United States took Manila during the Spanish-American War (43). Despite a Filipino proclamation of independence, the establishment of the First Philippine Republic, and revolutionary liberation of much of the country, Spanish surrender to the United States in Manila translated into American control of the Philippines (43). Thus the Philippine revolution against Spain became a revolution against the United States that continued from the Philippine declaration of war in 1899 through the 1901 capture of Emilio Aguinaldo, president of the First Philippine Republic, the surrender of General Miguel Malvar in 1902, and President Roosevelt's declaration of an end to the war (111, 44, xix). Nevertheless, Filipino resistance continued throughout American colonization.

American colonization of the Philippines persisted from 1899 to 1946. In addition, the Philippines became a Japanese-occupied battleground during World War II. Finally, in 1946 the United States relinquished colonial power, granting the Philippines independence by officially recognizing the Republic of the Philippines. Yet military and economic associations with the United States persisted. The United States military maintained large military bases in the Philippines that played a vital, strategic role throughout the American War in Viet Nam. In fact, the bases were well established until a breakdown occurred in the political agreement within and between the Philippine and the United States governments concerning lease renewals for the bases; the United States withdrew in 1991 (Kirk 8–10). Nonetheless, military exercises in the Philippines between the United States and Philippine militaries continue into the twenty-first century. More recently, in 2003 the Philippines, the so-called "Second Front" in the "War on Terror," joined the George W. Bush administration's "Coalition of the Willing" in the Iraq War (Tyner 9). In a speech at the White House in 2003, Philippine President Gloria Macapagal-Arroyo solidified the Philippine-American alliance when she spoke of unwavering Philippine commitment (1). However, in 2004, the Philippines withdrew from the war under the demands of a hostage agreement (1).[2] Hagedorn calls attention to this colonial, postcolonial, and neocolonial Philippines that resides "at a geo-political and cultural juncture between East and West" (Bankoff and Weekley 6).

Hagedorn employs the experiences of Vincent Moody, an American actor cast in *Napalm Sunset* and a substantial character in *Dream Jungle*, to accentuate the Philippines as a juncture between East and West. Moody encounters a Philippines reminiscent of American cinematic representations of Viet Nam during the war. Upon his arrival at the Manila airport, Filipino children surround Moody, asking, "*Carry your bags, Joe?*" His interaction with the children parallels that of many, although certainly not all, cinematic representations of American soldiers in Viet Nam.[3] He "marveled at the children—stunning in their sad-eyed beauty, skinny, anxious, hungry. Little hands flapped in his face. Moody gave the children money. They demanded more, shoving and pushing to get closer to him. "*Me, me, gimme Joe!*" (133). The children, too, correlate with their counterpart representations in American films of the war; they are desperate, hungry, crowding, and demanding.

This scene not only suggests the poor economic conditions in the Philippines and Filipino reactions to Western visitors but also alludes to American soldiers' interactions with Vietnamese children who, during the war, surrounded the soldiers seeking to sell black-market cigarettes, alcohol, and other sundries. Moreover, the thriving American-run black market depicted in *Apocalypse Now*, at the munitions depot where the United Service Organization (USO)[4] *Playboy* Playmate scene takes place, suggests that war profiteering "align[s] the ideologies of anti-Communist war with those of colonialism" (Norris 738). Thus both Hagedorn and Coppola expose U.S. cultural imperialism's "importation of Western values and habits into Eastern colonial contexts" of the Philippines and Viet Nam respectively (739).

In addition to reminding audiences of Philippine colonial history and incorporating subtle reminders of the American War in Viet Nam, *Dream Jungle* also calls attention to the ongoing United States military presence in the Philippines. In 1971, when Moody arrives in the Philippines, United States military bases were still central to the geopolitics of Southeast Asia and the war in Viet Nam. Again, in Dream Jungle, Moody reminds audiences of the American military presence in the Philippines. In another moment reminiscent of American cinematic representations of the war in Viet Nam, Moody encounters "rowdy American soldiers on leave, strolling with their girls" (139). Further still, Moody sees a sunburned man, likely a western tourist, wearing a T-shirt imprinted with the words "MISSING IN ACTION" (134). Here, Hagedorn cleverly alludes to the POW/MIA controversy that took hold with the signing of the 1973 Paris Peace Accords between the United States and Viet Nam.[5] As noted earlier, cultural memory of the POW/MIA cinematic mythology reached American audiences most broadly in the 1980s with such films as Rambo: First Blood, Part II, Uncommon Valor, and Missing in Action. The debate continues to plague twenty-first-century American cultural memory of the war. Yet Hagedorn also capitalizes on the transformation of that memory in the popular-culture adaptation of the phrase that has come to identify the pleasures of vacationing or an anti-intellectual celebration of empty-headedness. Hagedorn thus aligns United States militarism, neocolonialism, and the ongoing westernization of the Philippines.

HAGEDORN'S (NEO)COLONIAL ARC

Hagedorn's Dream Jungle examines a transnational colonial trajectory by creating distinct parallels between the portrayals in Joseph Conrad's Heart of Darkness and Francis Ford Coppola's Apocalypse Now of the renegade colonizer, Kurtz, with her colonial and neocolonial characters—Zamora, Pierce, and the corrupt government officials, ranging from the president to the local mayor. Hagedorn constructs an argument quite like the one literary scholar Margot Norris identifies in Conrad's and Coppola's narratives. As Norris understands it, "the folly both Conrad and Coppola underline in their criticism of colonial adventurism . . . is the senseless brutality, waste, and destructiveness of enterprises with misguided and hypocritical goals and inept and ill-conceived strategies" (741). Hagedorn composes the very same critique by recasting Zamora and Pierce as Kurtz figures.

Hagedorn's Zamora and Pierce, like Conrad's and Coppola's Kurtzes, take on a commanding presence. They position themselves in a symbolic station as colonial "fathers" in order to create a following among tribal peoples.

Resembling the earlier Kurtzes, Zamora positions himself as a father figure by identifying himself to the Taobo as "Amo Dato" or "Spirit Father" (52). He also "adopts" a Taobo boy, Bobadil, who comes to live with Zamora; however, "the boss's pet" stays in one of the outbuildings near the dog kennel (32). By comparison, Pierce does not appear as subjugating; however, he too constructs his own following among the cast and crew of *Napalm Sunset*. Each colonizing character controls an enclosed environment that functions for his pleasure. Pierce and Zamora incessantly talk about themselves and desire attentive, admiring audiences, as evidenced by each man's large dinner parties, their acceptance of interview offers during periods of success, and their refusal of interviews during times of failure.

Hagedorn seems to have taken her inspiration for the unsympathetic Pierce character from the following excerpt in Eleanor Coppola's diary entry about her husband. In it, Eleanor Coppola perceives a direct parallel between Francis Ford Coppola's proceedings in the Philippines and the American corruption of Viet Nam. She wrote of her husband, "he was setting up his own Vietnam with his supply lines of wine and steaks and air conditioners. Creating the very situation he went there to expose . . . with his staff of hundreds of people carrying out his every request, he was turning into Kurtz—going too far" (Eleanor Coppola 177). Reflecting both Kurtz's and Coppola's exclusivity, Pierce's establishment of a private lunch tent, where cast and crew may dine by invitation only, exudes the extravagance of his "own cook and a personal waiter" (Hagedorn 179). Inviting a cast member to "partake of [his] sumptuous bounty," Pierce boasts of his "chef who travels with [him] everywhere" (182). In fact, when the Coppolas arrived in the Philippines in 1976, a housekeeper and a nanny attended them; in addition, the Marcos government immediately appointed Coppola a bodyguard (Cowie 49).

Hagedorn portrays Pierce's excessiveness as a means of revealing his neo-colonial interactions with the people and government of the Philippines. He hires locals to provide food service for his cast and crew; in his own words, they offer "cheap labor" (Hagedorn 247). Even Hagedorn's Billy Hernandez, an American actor cast in *Napalm Sunset*, complains, "You see the way the cast and crew walk around here like they own the place? Pierce is the worst. Thinks this country's nothing but a backdrop for his movie. The people don't matter, except when they service him and his family" (179). Hagedorn's examination of Pierce's acts of neocolonialism reveals a further truth in a Coppola statement at the 1979 Cannes film festival wherein he said, "My film is not a movie; it's not about Vietnam. It *is* Vietnam. It's what it was really like; it was crazy" (qtd. in Goodwin and Wise 263). Hagedorn's *Dream Jungle* suggests that like the war in Viet Nam, the filming of *Napalm Sunset*, and by association *Apocalypse Now*, further exports American cultural imperialism into the Philippines. The films, according to *Dream Jungle*, re-create in the Philippines the neocolonial conditions of Viet Nam during the war.

Pierce, Hagedorn's fictional mirror of Coppola, bribes Philippine government officials and thereby contributes to the corruption of those in power. For example, an interviewer suggests, to no response, that the local mayor is Pierce's "protector, [his] fixer, [his] landlord, [his] biggest fan" (247). More important, Pierce has no qualms about paying the government large sums of money for the use of helicopters, a direct parallel to Coppola's payment of thousands of dollars a day to the Marcos government for their use (Cowie 49). Pierce refuses to recognize his implicit participation in funding the government's suppression of political uprising. Hagedorn, however, does not ignore Pierce's passive participation. She employs actor Vincent Moody as her critical voice during one of Pierce's dinner parties with the local mayor in attendance. Moody questions Pierce and the mayor about the helicopters being called away from filming by the military because of "guerilla sightings" (Hagedorn 202). Moody unabashedly asks, to no avail, "'How many people were killed?'" (202). Again, Hagedorn took her inspiration from Coppola's dealings with Marcos's authoritarian regime. In her diary, Eleanor Coppola comments on the uprising during the filming of *Apocalypse Now*. She calls the incident part of a "civil war" but explains, "It is hard to know what is going on. There is no news of the war in the government-controlled press"; however, a Filipino crewman told her that the predominantly Muslim southern islands "are fighting for independence" (Coppola 26).

Francis Coppola's transactions did not go unnoticed by critics who believed he was essentially underwriting the Marcos regime and thereby endorsing the government's corruption, human rights violations, cronyism, and repressive martial law that continued from 1972 until 1981 (Nadeau 90). Some critics found Coppola's dealings with Marcos more reprehensible than the United States' endorsement of corrupt South Vietnamese governments. For example, cinema scholar Jeffery Chown, author of *Hollywood Auteur: Francis Coppola* deems that "in paying the Marcos government for use of its military equipment, Coppola was supporting a government possibly more repressive than the South Vietnamese government of Diem" (126). Ngo Dinh Diem, president of the southern Republic of Viet Nam, consolidated his rule, with public support from the United States, when he rejected national elections as prescribed in the 1954 Geneva agreement.[6] While Diem did employ a ruthless response to antigovernment protests led by Buddhist monks, the Buddhist motivations were far more complicated than they once seemed, as historian Edward Miller's *Misalliance: Ngo Dinh Diem, the United States, and the Fate of South Vietnam* (2013) illustrates. Still, Diem's response to those protests prompted President John F. Kennedy to encourage the coup, but not necessarily the assassination, of Diem. In 1963 Diem was overthrown and killed by his own generals. Yet Coppola, his critics, and Hagedorn alike attempt to expose the repetition of entangled corruption. Coppola parallels the Belgian colonialism in Conrad's *Heart of Darkness* to the United States' militarism in Viet Nam. Coppola's critics have perceived the same errors the U.S. military engaged in during the war in Viet Nam repeated in the Philippines. Hagedorn coalesces recurrent colonial, military, and neocolonial corruptions in her Zamora and Pierce characters.

While Pierce's and Coppola's dealings with the Marcos government and Filipino people generally merit these critiques, Coppola's decisions should be taken in context. According to the documentary *Machete Maidens Unleashed!* (2010), between the end of World War II and up through the 1980s, the Filipino exploitation film industry exploded, producing about 350 titles a year. According to the official Dark Sky Films synopsis, "Boasting cheap labour, exotic scenery and non-existent health and safety regulations, the Philippines was a dreamland for exploitation filmmakers whose renegade productions were soon engulfing drive-in screens around the globe like a tidal shock-wave!" Typically these American productions were Western-style, low-budget, second-run films. One interviewee described them as having three essential elements: "blood, breasts, and beasts." Seeking locations where it was least expensive to make films, the companies found in the Philippines the allure of the "Wild East," with its lush jungles, cheap labor, ready-made studios, and a cooperative government. Just as he did for Coppola, Marcos provided military equipment and personnel to stage battle scenes for numerous films. Eventually, however, the political climate became too risky for American companies to insure U.S. companies in the Philippines. Injuries were high and accidental deaths among the Filipino crew members were not uncommon. Because of the general lawlessness before martial law, interviewees in *Machete Maidens Unleashed!* reiterated that "life was cheap" in the dangerous, gun-happy Philippines.

Within this framework, Coppola's fifteen-month production provided much needed, although temporary, employment for thousands of Filipinos and infused the national economy with the millions of dollars he spent in the islands (Cowie 47). Nonetheless, such spending was not without consequences. For example, *Newsweek's* film critic, Maureen Orth, charged Coppola of corrupting Filipinos with his disproportionate spending. She wrote, "although the local wage was less than $10 a week, for nine months the company had been spending $100,000 a week" (qtd. in Goodwin and Wise 226). However, local Philippine dignitaries felt differently. During a farewell party hosted by Coppola, they said "the millions of dollars [the production] brought to the local economy were more help to them than any government economic aid program had ever been" (qtd. in Eleanor Coppola 200).

Still, Coppola believed that he had no choice. The U.S. Department of Defense (DOD) refused to support the film because, they alleged, the film's narrative did not depict the American War in Viet Nam accurately and maintained that the loan of U.S. military aircraft would be denied unless there were changes in the script (Cowie 49). Coppola took issue with the DOD's decisions and voiced them in a cable sent to then Secretary of Defense Donald Rumsfeld. Coppola wrote that since the DOD had assisted John Wayne's *The Green Berets* (1968), yet refused to assist *Apocalypse Now*, he could "only assume that the military uses its control of these aircraft as a means of dictating which films can be made and which films cannot be made. Perhaps this is the reason there has been no motion picture dealing with the subject of Vietnam" (qtd. in Cowie 50). In her dairy, Eleanor commiserates, adding, "a film about World War II gets all sorts of cooperation" (35). The DOD does in fact have a long history of assisting, requiring changes in scripts, and denying assistance to war film productions.[7]

Although Coppola may have had better intentions than critics concede, Hagedorn's title for the film, *Napalm Sunset*, calls attention to the destruction of the environment and landscape occasioned by the filming of *Apocalypse Now*. For example, the opening sequence of *Apocalypse Now* revels in the devastation of napalm on the jungle. In slow motion helicopters move across the screen as a palm-tree lined horizon explodes in an overwhelming cacophony of flames devouring the foliage. Later in the film, the caricature Kilgore professes his "love [for] the smell of napalm in the morning," a frequently repeated line on rock radio stations and among college students in the 1990s. However, *Dream Jungle* eradicates all the romanticism and awe of destruction. Hagedorn's

Filipina-American character, Paz Marlowe, reflects on "the stink of dying fish washed ashore, stunned by all the explosives. . . . They were always blowing things up. Building elaborate sets only to blow them all up. . . . coconut trees on the shoreline of Lake Ramayyah ablaze with fire and smoke. The noise had been deafening. . . . The older townspeople . . . kept their distance" (219). Francis Coppola, also aware but appearing unconcerned about the environmental impact, commented, "There aren't too many places in the world you could even do it; they'd never let you in the United States. The environmentalists would kill you," yet ironically added, "But in a war, it's okay" (Eleanor Coppola 189). In the Philippines, Coppola and Pierce replicate the U.S. military's destruction of the land in Viet Nam with bomb craters, napalm, and defoliating agents. Thus the American War in Viet Nam holds not only the capacity to return to the United States via violence, the memories of veterans, and Vietnamese refugees and immigrants, but is also revisited upon the Philippines.

Hagedorn pairs the destruction of the landscape with Pierce's and other colonizing figures' attempts to control nature. In a chapter entitled "The Tiger," Hagedorn further portrays Pierce's attempts to reveal the power of, yet simultaneously to control, nature. Here, Hagedorn reimagines the filming of the tiger scene in Coppola's *Apocalypse Now*. In the film's only jungle sequence, Captain Willard, accompanied by "Chef," forays into the wilderness in search of mangoes. The tiger springs at them, and although it is not the suspected Vietnamese "enemy," the tiger represents the dangerous unpredictability of the jungle. The sympathetic "Chef," a reluctant draftee and would-be saucier from New Orleans, runs in terror back to the boat, repeatedly screaming, "never get out of the boat." Chef offers yet another repeated line from the film, one with continued popularity on YouTube in the twenty-first century. The tiger signifies the unknown danger in nature; the land itself, Viet Nam, is a hazard. Coppola's cinematographer, Vittorio Storaro, understood the tiger as "the symbol of nature, an unconscious fear" (qtd. in Cowie 61).

Hagedorn, too, regards the tiger as emblematic of an unconscious fear that holds the possibilities of "ferocious beauty and power" (Hagedorn 263). Rather than adopting the tiger's actual name, Gambi (Cowie 61), Hagedorn renames the tiger Shiva after the "Hindu god of destruction" (Hagedorn 263). The creature "assume[s] supernatural powers and dimensions" especially for Lina,[8] Hagedorn's central Filipina character (263). Lina's fascination with the tiger commences before its arrival in her repetitive dreams. After filming the tiger scene, Lina "stared at the tiger, riveted. She was looking for a sign" to help her decide whether or not she would leave the Philippines (270). She believes the tiger's roar provides her answer. Even after she sees it, the tiger continues to hold a mystical power over Lina, "disturb[ing] every waking moment, every attempt at sleep. In her dreams his scowling face peered out at her" (271). Obsessed, Lina repeatedly draws the tiger and cannot escape "its multiplying visions . . . her nightmare of tigers" (272).

Lina eventually leaves the Philippines to live in the United States and once there seems to have gained an independence from her colonial and neocolonial past. Perhaps Lina's renunciation of the nightmare jungle of her youth is the only possible answer to recurrent colonialism. However, Lina's lover Vincent Moody remains in the Philippines instead of returning to the United States. Hagedorn renders an ambiguous dream jungle that Eleanor Coppola's reflections might best explain. She writes, "many unreasonable things have happened to me since I have been in the Philippines, I no longer try to make them all fit a reasonable linear context. . . . Here, the waking world and the dream world have many things in common. The line between the two is not abrupt and definitive" (132). This is true of both Hagedorn's *Dream Jungle* and Coppola's *Apocalypse Now*.

In addition to figuring the filming of *Napalm Sunset* as an act of neocolonialism, *Dream Jungle* interrogates the meaning of *Apocalypse Now* and thereby questions the American War in Viet Nam. While participating in one of the "read-throughs of the ever-evolving script" for *Napalm Sunset*, Moody reflects, "What, ultimately, was this damn movie about? That war made men crazy?" (177). An interviewer directly asks Pierce why he chose to make a film about the war. He begins with a vague explanation, "Because war fascinates me. And this particular war . . . well, it's so very intimate and ambiguous" (214). However, his response evolves during the interview, and he later explains, "'The Vietnam War makes us uneasy. It's a dirty little war, full of dirty little secrets. . . . This particular war is not heroic, not simple, and that's why I'm obsessed by it'" (215).

Hagedorn's Pierce reflects the answers one might expect from Coppola based on his film's portrayal of the "dirty little secrets" of the war and his avoidance of rendering the war as a noble cause. Some of Coppola's critics believed that he produced an apolitical, ahistorical account of the war. For example, Joel Zuker contended, "the matters of American colonialism in a war we could never win are passed over" (31). Hagedorn, seemingly aware of that general critical consensus, has her Pierce insist that he has no "'political agenda" (215). Cinematographer Vittorio Storaro, however, maintained that Coppola "wanted to express the main idea of Joseph Conrad, which is the imposition of one culture on top of another culture" (qtd. in Cowie 133).

The ambiguity of political message in *Apocalypse Now* renders the film open for contending interpretations that often depend on audience. Coppola's brash, gung-ho Kilgore character, who "loves the smell of napalm in the morning," will lead some audiences and scholars to believe that the film relishes the reckless destruction of war. Still others will view Kilgore as satirical hyperbole. For example, his cavalry hat and his name, a conflation of "kill-gore," calls attention to the exaggerations of character. So, too, a Vietnamese woman tossing a grenade into an American helicopter may direct viewers to deem the film an examination of a devious, unpredictable "enemy." Simultaneously, however, Coppola depicts the chaos and destruction that the United States military thrust upon the people and landscape of Viet Nam. In addition, Willard's voice-over narration relays that the narrative is a "confession" of his own "sins" and "like Kurtz's extremism, they are product, effect, and confession of the American corporate violence [neocolonialism] that was Vietnam" (Norris 757). While the political message in the film may remain uncertain, Viet Nam's historical colonial context, as portrayed in Coppola's *Apocalypse Now Redux*, helps to clarify Coppola's intentions.

REDUX

Hagedorn is not alone in her persistent memory of the intertextual colonial context of contemporary neocolonialism. Still, in the twenty-first century, Francis Ford Coppola is unable to forget *Apocalypse Now* and thereby the American War in Viet Nam as evidenced by his reimagining of the original film in *Apocalypse Now Redux* (2001). Twenty-one years after *Apocalypse Now*, Coppola felt compelled to retell the story, thus inducing audiences to revisit the war. More than a simple director's cut, Coppola and his editor Walter Murch "re-edited the film from the original unedited raw footage—the dailies" (Murch, qtd. in Ebert "Rev. of *Apocalypse Now Redux*"). *Redux* includes an additional forty-nine minutes, twenty-five of those devoted to a scene on a French plantation in Viet Nam.

Coppola's inclusion of the French colonialists creates a more historically responsible narrative framework for the American War in Viet Nam and counters critics who deemed the original film recklessly ahistorical and apolitical.[9]

The French Plantation scene did not appear in the 1979 theatrical release of *Apocalypse Now*; it was cut rather late in post-production editing, in the spring of 1979, because Coppola and Murch believed it slowed the narrative momentum of the journey upriver to Kurtz (Cowie 111). Nonetheless, the intention of the scene was, according to Murch, to construct "an interlude to give [audiences] some emotional, political background as to why the Americans were there in Vietnam. . . . Because the French had been there before and had come to this tragic end" (qtd. in Cowie 110).

Thus, the reinsertion of the French Plantation sequences into *Redux* provides colonial context and reinvigorates the film's intertextual rendering of imperialist recurrence. In addition, the release of *Redux* in 2001, like Hagedorn's *Dream Jungle*, visited intertextual imperialist repetition on the twenty-first century. Hagedorn reminds audiences of the Spanish colonization of the Philippines that preceded American colonization, thus to reveal the neocolonialism at work in the filming of *Napalm Sunset*; correspondingly, Coppola recalls French colonization of Viet Nam before American militarism in Viet Nam.

Historians such as Mark Atwood Lawrence in his *The Vietnam War: A Concise International History* (2008), David L Anderson in his *The Columbia Guide to the Vietnam War* (2002), and George Donelson Moss in his *Vietnam: an American Ordeal* (2002) note the significance of French colonial influence on Viet Nam, which came as early as 1627 when French missionaries populated Viet Nam, making commercial and trade privileges possible for France. As the French presence in Viet Nam increased to include troops, eventual conflicts arose between French forces and the Vietnamese. By 1861 French forces controlled Saigon in South Viet Nam, and by 1863 their control extended into Cambodia. Establishing a French civilian government in 1879, the French solidified control over Viet Nam, Cambodia, and Laos with the 1887 formation of what the French called Indochina. French colonialism profoundly altered Vietnamese culture, society, politics, and economics. In addition to replacing Vietnamese political leadership, colonization stifled the literature, culture, religions, and peasant sustainability in Viet Nam. The French plantation economy resulted in economic exploitation that could not, however, subdue the Vietnamese resistance that evolved throughout the nineteenth and twentieth centuries. Revolution eventually defeated the French, who withdrew from Viet Nam in 1954 after the infamous battle of Dien Bien Phu.

Coppola's *Redux* reminds audiences of the French colonization of Viet Nam when Willard and his crew encounter a vestige of that history at a French plantation. Here, they experience temporal disruption wherein time seems to have stopped during the French colonial rule in Viet Nam of the 1950s. For the dinner scene, Coppola insisted on a cinematic verisimilitude that invokes the nostalgia of his French characters for colonial "civilization." He adamantly selected actors from Paris, the furnishings exude authenticity, and his set dressers assembled detailed props, such as the food and wine, with precision (Cowie 73–74). In the documentary film *Hearts of Darkness: A Film-maker's Apocalypse*, Coppola tells the cast and crew that he wants even French audiences to wonder, "My God, how did they do that?"

Enclosed in familiar yet surreal Western surroundings of the past, Willard is subjected to an impassioned debate in answer to his inquiries. He asks, "how long can you possibly stay here? . . . When will you go back to France, to your home?" The French respond with laughter over the word "home," and the men, representing three generations, proceed to explain to Willard their political, economical, and emotional positions. They begin and end by reproaching the Americans. First, these French colonial characters recount the historical context of the Japanese occupation of Viet Nam during World War II and the initial U.S. military support of the Viet Minh, which declared independence in 1945. The Viet Minh, otherwise known as the Vietnamese League for Independence, formed in 1941 under the leadership of Ho Chi Minh. Their anticolonial movement gained momentum throughout the Japanese occupation of Viet Nam during World War II.

Similar to occurrences in the Philippines during the Spanish-American War, the Viet Minh declared independence when the Japanese surrendered to the United States in 1945 and established the Democratic Republic of Viet Nam (Moss 21–28). Despite support from United States military personnel and advisors in Viet Nam and Southeast Asia, leaders in Washington, D.C., were more concerned with maintaining alliances with France and thus supported reinstating French colonial rule in Indochina (Moss 29–30). The Viet Minh eventually became part of the National Liberation Front (NLF)—a South Vietnamese resistance to American military forces throughout the American War in Viet Nam (Moss 106–7). Because of this history, the French men in Coppola's dinner scene accuse the Americans of "inventing" the "Viet Cong"— a derogatory term for the Vietnamese Communists who fought in South Viet Nam against the South Vietnamese government and the U.S. military. While Coppola's Philippe De Marais, the spokesman for the French family, might be right in accusing the Americans of "inventing the Viet Cong," their predecessors, the Viet Minh, successfully revolted against and ousted French colonial rule.

In further response to Willard's inquiries, Marais vehemently defends his family's right to stay in Viet Nam, explaining that

> we lose in Dien Bien Phu, we lose in Indochina. In Algeria, we lose . . . we do not lose here, never. This small piece of earth, we do not lose. . . . When my grandfather came here, there was nothing—the Vietnamese were nothing. We work hard, we bring the rubber from Brazil, and implant it here . . . and we make something. . . . We stay because this is ours; it belongs to us. We fight to keep what is ours. You Americans fight for the biggest nothing in history.

At the end of Marais's colonialist tirade, audiences hear a representational French critique of the American War in Viet Nam as a senseless war. However, Marais begins by recounting the military losses France has experienced, including their protracted war in Algeria, often ironically referred to as France's equivalent of America's War in Viet Nam. France's invasion of Algeria in the 1830s led to colonial rule and an eventual war for Algerian independence that lasted from 1954—the same year as French defeat in Viet Nam at the battle of Dien Bien Phu—to 1962. Despite devastating losses, Marais's "dismissal of the Vietnamese as 'nothing' before the [arrival of the] French" demonstrates that he endorses imperialists' beliefs (Demory 347); he regards the French colonizers as intrinsically more intelligent and cultured than the "natives" they "civilize"—that is, colonize. Unsurprisingly, Marais also invokes ownership. Despite his imperialist rant, the French, too, seem near victims of colonialism.

While the French men speak, Willard passively listens, providing no narrative voice-over as he does through most of the film. The lack of Willard's interpretive narrative voice-over heightens the scene's surrealism. As Coppola suggested, the French resemble ghosts (Ebert, "Rev. of *Apocalypse Now Redux*"). Like Hagedorn's Zamora, the French live in a sheltered time capsule of colonialism; they are the vestige specters and spectacles of the colonial past.

Coppola's characters, on their journey toward and encounter with Kurtz, experience a wondrous, surreal, and nightmarish dream jungle much like the characters of Hagedorn's novel. Both Coppola's *Apocalypse Now Redux* and Hagedorn's *Dream Jungle* figure characters entwined in a complicated, intertextual, colonial, and neocolonial history. Resembling Conrad, Marlow, Coppola, and Willard, Hagedorn feels compelled to retell the story. Hagedorn concludes her novel with an epilogue set in 2000 wherein the now dead Zamora narrates from the confines of his funeral urn. Like the ending of T. S. Eliot's "The Hollow Men" that Coppola's Kurtz reads, each narrative—Coppola's and Hagedorn's—ends "not with a bang, but a whimper." Hagedorn parallels the final words of *Apocalypse Now*, Kurtz whispering, "the horror . . . the horror," with Zamora's ghostly voice from beyond the grave mourning an end to his colonial era: "not once does my name come up. Not once" (325).

Hagedorn tranhistoricizes yet simultaneously repoliticizes as neocolonial Philippine memory the imperialist trajectory in Viet Nam that critics accused Coppola of dehistoricizing and thus depoliticizing. Her *Dream Jungle*, like the *Hearts of Darkness* documentary, reveals that "the habits of imperialism are so ingrained that they extend beyond governments to civilian organizations—to individuals" (Demory 348). The cyclic telling and retelling of colonial and neocolonial corruption reveals that the memory of the American War in Viet Nam exists in the Philippines. These two twenty-first-century narratives engage with the enduring memory of the American War in Viet Nam and thereby contribute to a continuous and continual collected cultural memory of the war. Coppola's *Apocalypse Now*, his *Redux*, the texts surrounding the film, and especially Hagedorn's *Dream Jungle* call attention to the multifaceted memories of the American War in Viet Nam that exist well beyond the literal and cultural battlefields of Viet Nam and the United States.

CHAPTER 8
‧ VIETNAMESE
AMERICAN DIASPORA

IDENTITY, MEMORY, AND REPETITION

Just as American social conflicts, and cultural imperialism were exported to Viet Nam during the war, so too the trauma of war transferred back to the United States via American veterans, as discussed in chapter 4. The war was also transported to the Philippines via the American military presence and the filming of *Apocalypse Now* as outlined in chapter 7. Yet the narrative is incomplete without considering the Vietnamese American perspectives because they contribute to a collected cultural memory of the war and its aftermath. Although chapter 4 examines Le Ly Hayslip's experience during the war and, later, as a Vietnamese American, the majority of that representation is mediated through Oliver Stone's film, *Heaven and Earth* (1993), based on Hayslip's memoir. Moreover, Hayslip's experience is that of a first-generation, first-wave immigrant, whereas most Vietnamese diasporic literature produced during the turn of the millennium emanates from Vietnamese American authors of the 1.5 and second-generations. An ambiguous but intriguing term, the 1.5 generation refers to people who immigrate to another country in their childhood or early teens. This literature also often focuses on identity, interactions with American veterans of the war, repetition, and prosthetic memory.

Common subjects in Vietnamese American literature produced since 1990 include family, inheritance, ancestors, obligation, respect, and honor—the Confucian tradition. The literature also engages with legends—the mythological, the historical—and a hybrid of the two, such as the legend of the Trung sisters in Vietnamese American author Lan Cao's *Monkey Bridge* (1997), which takes on an imaginative twist, or fairytales that end in sorrow, which Vietnamese American writer Andrew Lam also reflects on in his writing. Parents tend to maintain these traditions and cultural beliefs, but their children do not. Parents share lessons about family, war, history, and the attitudes of Vietnamese exiles toward the war, particularly in regard to the loss and attendant humiliation, in addition to their anticommunist attitudes, which grow once they become exiles. The literature also accentuates tension over who has access and authority, who is an insider or outsider, when it comes to memories of Viet Nam and the war. These common topics and themes are nearly always entangled in the Vietnamese diaspora and its attendant questions of identity. Although the Vietnamese diaspora is a global issue, South Vietnamese veterans and Vietnamese exiles and immigrants came to America in significant numbers. According to Andrew Lam, four million Vietnamese have "fled or migrated" to five continents, half of them to North America, resulting in around one million Vietnamese in America; about half of them reside in California (*East Eats West* 128).

A large population of Vietnamese refugees came to the United States during and for decades after the fall of Saigon in 1975. In the first book-length study of Vietnamese American literature, Asian American scholar Isabelle Thuy Pelaud's *This is All I Choose to Tell: History and Hybridity in Vietnamese American Literature* (2011) outlines the historical context of Vietnamese immigration to the United States as a complex nonlinear narrative. However, social scientists attempt to delineate a general chronology by designating three waves of Vietnamese immigration. While these are not all-encompassing or free from debate, the general distinction between groups includes the first wave, 1975–78, consisting of those who had close ties to the United States military and personnel; the second wave, 1978–80, comprising "boat people"; and the third wave, 1980–1995, including those who were part of the Orderly Departure Program, a problematic program that attempted to determine if the Vietnamese were refugees or immigrants.[1] Many among this last group had been in reeducation camps in Viet Nam, and they believed that being sent back to Viet Nam meant certain death.[2] In 1989 the United Nations no longer regarded Vietnamese as political refugees and closed refugee camps in 1996. Of course, these waves of immigration changed drastically when the United States and Viet Nam agreed to normalize relations in 1994, the U.S. Congress lifted the trade embargo with Viet Nam, and in 1995 Viet Nam reinstated the United States embassy in Ho Chi Minh City. However, there were still refugees in the Philippines, and they were admitted into the United States under a refugee resettlement program as late as 2005.[3]

The Vietnamese diaspora, like other diasporas, includes affective dimensions such as homesickness, memory, nostalgia, and melancholy. For example, cultural theorist Stuart Hall, contests that members of diasporic communities "confront the fragmented and pathological ways in which [their] experience has been reconstructed within the dominant regimes of cinematic and visual representation of the West" (394). However, the diasporic response of "imposing an imaginary coherence on the experience of dispersal and fragmentation, which is the history of all enforced diasporas," may be a solution (395).[4] As Hall understands it, this "imaginary coherence" is not inherently negative but rather a method of resisting narratives imposed on diasporic groups by the pervasive cinema of the West. These narratives can govern prosthetic memories by the very influence of their mediated representations. However, voices among the Vietnamese diaspora also create mediated representations of the diasporic experience. Because such voices have been marginalized, particularly in American representations of the war, the surge in literature from the diasporic perspective serves as a welcome addition to a collected cultural memory of the war.

Isabelle Thuy Pelaud outlines the publication history of Vietnamese American literature in *This Is All I Choose to Tell*, noting common themes such as those addressed in the coming pages, particularly identity. As Pelaud observes, the most popular Vietnamese American literature at the turn of the twenty-first century is that written by members of the 1.5 generation, authors "who combine memories of Viet Nam with discussions of racial and ethnic identity" (36). Three of the most widely read 1.5 generation and second-generation Vietnamese American authors who illustrate issues of identity, interactions with American veterans of the war, prosthetic memory, and repetition include Lan Cao in her *Monkey Bridge* (1997); Andrew Lam in his three books, *Perfume Dreams: Reflections of the Vietnamese Diaspora* (2005), *East Eats West* (2010), and *Birds of Paradise Lost* (2013); and GB Tran in his *Vietnamerica: A Family's Journey* (2010).

Law professor Lan Cao coauthored *Everything You Need to Know about Asian American History* (1996) with Himilce Novas and wrote a novel about the Vietnamese diaspora, *Monkey Bridge*. Cao's family fled Viet Nam just before the fall of Saigon, when she was thirteen. *Monkey Bridge*, dedicated to Cao's mother, who passed away in 1992, explores the experiences of her primary narrator, Mai, a Vietnamese American girl in high school. Mai's mother, Thanh, provides secondary narration in the novel through her journals and through a letter she addresses to Mai that appears at the end of the novel. While *Monkey Bridge*, a coming-of-age story, addresses issues such as truth, fiction, and family legend, it significantly represents diasporic identity, interactions with American veterans of the American War in Viet Nam, memory, and a repetitive fascination with the fall of Saigon.

Andrew Lam, journalist, essayist, and short-story writer, is a popular Vietnamese American author who is part of the so-called first wave of Vietnamese American immigrants. He often distinguishes his privileged position as first wave, as the son of a French-educated general in the South Vietnamese army, the ARVN. Lam's texts provide a more intimate portrayal of the Vietnamese diaspora in his essay collections, *Perfume Dreams: Reflections of the Vietnamese Diaspora* and *East Eats West*, in addition to his collection of fictional stories, *Birds of Paradise Lost*. His three books, combined, serve as fairly representative of the 1.5 generation. Although he gives voice to loss associated with diaspora, Lam clearly celebrates his cosmopolitan, global villager identity. In addition, Lam not only portrays interactions among Vietnamese Americans and American veterans of the war but also participates in repetition and revision in his fiction.

GB Tran, author and illustrator of the graphic novel *Vietnamerica: A Family's Journey*, writes in the graphic memoir tradition of Art Spiegelman's *Maus* (1986), awarded a Pulitzer Prize for its nuanced representation of the Holocaust, and Marjane Satrapi's *Persepolis* (2000), about life in Iran in the wake of the Islamic revolution. Tran is a second-generation Vietnamese American, born in South Carolina. His parents fled Viet Nam during the fall of Saigon. *Vietnamerica* is a story of a family, a journey through the family's history, and an account of GB's experiences as a second-generation Vietnamese American who visits Viet Nam with his family to learn about his family's history and about Viet Nam's cultural history through the perspectives of his extended family and their friends in Viet Nam. Tran's illustrations create a hybrid diasporic aesthetic of identity. GB confronts a complex geopolitical family history and confronts his position as an outsider in the Vietnamese culture.

Together, these three authors of the Vietnamese American 1.5 and second generations tell complex narratives of diaspora and its attendant tension between loss and identity. As they contemplate identity, they also reflect on their position in relation to Viet Nam, the American War in Viet Nam, and American veterans of the war. Moreover, their applications of repetition, revision, and prosthetic memory serve as ethical means of bearing witness to their experiences.

DIASPORIC IDENTITIES

Concerning identity, these authors provide a multifaceted rendering of hybrid identity, including both an inability and an ability to move between nations, depending on the author, character, and time period. While Lan Cao's main narrator, Mai, seems ambivalent about her identity, Andrew Lam is among the most celebratory of this group, and GB Tran regards Viet Nam and the war as part of his hitherto unknown family and cultural history. Because he is second generation, he has no direct memories of Viet Nam or the war; thus, his identity is American.

These issues of identity, entangled with diaspora, pervade Lan Cao's *Monkey Bridge* as well, and the characters' identities are frequently framed in response to American attitudes, whether perceived or real. For example, Mai believes that being Vietnamese is "troublesome," compounding the usual difficulties facing immigrants, because "in America, Vietnam meant war, antipathies" and Mai "didn't want to parade an unpleasant American experience in America" (42). This desire to dissociate from Viet Nam, and thus the war, is not uncommon in Vietnamese American literature. For example, in *Catfish and Mandala* (1999), a travel memoir about his bicycle expedition around the Pacific Rim to Viet Nam in the wake of his sister's suicide, Andrew X. Pham writes about his animosity toward questions about his identity. He formulates a "prepared invention" that he is a "mixed-race Asian," wherein he lists several countries of origin but consciously avoids any reference to his Vietnamese ethnicity (6). He does not want to call attention to his past or the war and its attendant anxieties. More important, he regards himself as an American, and questions such as these call that identity into question. Like Andrew Pham, Lan Cao's Mai does not want to be associated with the war. Yet these beliefs are not unfounded. Having read in the papers that refugees are a burden on the economy, Mai describes the Vietnamese community as "a ragtag accumulation of unwanted, an awkward reminder of a war the whole country was trying to forget" (15). Mai and Pham posit their identities as unpleasant memories of war. However, their very existence resists forgetfulness.

Mai's fear of American reprisal comes to a crisis when she drives to the Canadian border, intending to cross so that she can make a telephone call to Viet Nam. This scene occurs before the United States and Viet Nam normalized relations in the 1990s. Rumors about not being permitted back into the United States are only heightened by her mother, who believes that the Americans would "jump at the chance to send [them] all back. Nomads, that's what [they've] become" (15). This fear of deportation ultimately paralyzes Mai; she cannot cross into Canada despite the urgency she feels to contact her grandfather in order to convince him to come to the United States. She sees the Canadian border through her mother's eyes and can see only danger; the border "contained the unthinkable, more ominous with its terrifying nakedness" than war itself (20). The Canadian border is "uncrossable" (29). Unlike Pham, Lam, and Tran, Mai lives in a time and place where movement and communication across borders seems unattainable. This contributes to Mai feeling like a homeless outsider.

Mai's mother, Thanh, also experiences a sense of being not only an outsider but a lesser citizen. For example, she complains that "even the store clerks look down" on them. Mai reflects on this as a "lesson in what was required to sustain a new identity . . . adopt a different posture, to reach deep enough into the folds of the earth to relocate one's roots and bend one's body in a new direction, pretending" that the world has not changed (40). However, she explains that new identity holds positive possibilities because it is also entwined with the "Vietnamese version of the American Dream," wherein the immigrant, looking to the future, could become anything in America and "change what [they] had once been in Viet Nam (40–41). She describes it as "re-birthing the past" (41). Always negotiating between the past, present, and future, many Vietnamese Americans in Mai's community embrace forming new identities. Some believe they can forget the past, while others maintain a complex relationship with the past, a significant issue in diasporic communities that Andrew Lam will further illuminate.

Yet Mai also shares an uncanny sense of prosthetic memory in relation to the Vietnamese diaspora. She compares the experience of those in her Little Saigon community with someone who has had an amputation. She explains that some members of her community feel their former lives, and country, as an amputee might feel a phantom limb; a part of their being and identity is "exiled into a space that could not be reached" (255). Phantom limb syndrome—the perception of feeling, often pain or discomfort, in the absent amputated limb—gives the impression that the limb still exists.[5] Thus, Mai perceives diasporic pain and loss akin to bodily amputation for some in diasporic communities. Mai, too, deals with absence in her struggle to understand her identity as a Vietnamese American.

While the novel opens with the dilemma of Mai's inability to cross the Canadian border, another crisis recurs throughout the novel that reveals Mai's sense of no longer being Vietnamese. When she reflects on memory and time, Mai believes that "Bona fide Vietnamese" regard "life in terms of centuries, millennia" (60). Note the word choice here: Mai doesn't regard herself as fully Vietnamese; she is not "bona fide." The most poignant moment of this identity crisis does not deal with public perception but Mai's sense of being an outsider among others who experienced the war and Viet Nam as adults. Mai's mother, Thanh, and her close Vietnamese friend, Mrs. Bay, work in a Vietnamese grocery store. Here, Mrs. Bay forms supportive friendships with American veterans of the war, chiefly one named Bill. One day, while Mrs. Bay, Mai, Thanh, and Bill are standing in a circle regarding a new lifeline that Thanh said appeared on her palm, Mai reflects on the others' "common contagion of nostalgia" (212). At this moment, Mai believes she sees in her mother's eyes that Bill is not the outsider here, but Mai herself. This sense of limbo between cultures, this lack of a sense of belonging is not unique in the immigrant experience. However, that Mai believes an American veteran has more standing in her own community is heartbreaking. Readers will encounter this attitude again in Andrew Lam's writing, particularly in his fiction.

Compared with Lan Cao's narrator, Mai, Andrew Lam is more celebratory of his hybrid sense of identity. Concerning the widely varying experiences of Vietnamese immigrants and Vietnamese Americans, Lam acknowledges that he did not have to risk crossing the ocean as a "boat person." However, his migration was not without pain and suffering. He spent time in a refugee camp, and he witnessed the downtrodden defeat and disillusionment his parents initially experienced in America. He also depicts his childhood assimilation as one that occurred with relative ease. Hitting puberty when he was learning English, his voice broke and he became a new person—an American. However, his American experience was not as smooth as he might portray it. This privilege that he sometimes claims he or his family had is always relative, always written with the awareness of someone who has observed and once lived in a more daunting position as compared with the life at the moment he is writing. His seemingly easy assimilation came with a price. For example, he sacrificed filial obligations—he spoke English in the home, he Americanized his name, and he did not go to medical school as his parents wished. He became the "selfish" one in the family and solidified this identity by becoming a writer instead of a doctor. He also solidified his identity as an American when he changed his name to Andrew; indeed, sometimes his parents refer to him as "Andrew Lam," as he explains in *East Eats West*.

Yet Lam celebrates his hybrid identity, explaining that he has one foot in diaspora, the other in the global village. Despite his independence and self-proclaimed hybridity, in a chapter entitled "Trash," from *East Eats West*, Lam experiences a sense of guilt for throwing out paper and bottles because he has forgotten the old ways of poverty and thrift and feels as if Vietnamese Americans, like himself, have "carelessly tossed away [their] memories" as they have gained material success (110). For Lam, Cao, and Tran, identity and memory are conjoined; thus, resistance against forgetfulness becomes integral to identity.

However, it is far more common for Lam to extol his position as a voice of hybridity and his identity as global citizen. In *East Eats West* he reveres the Obama presidency as an end to colonialism. Entitled "Our Man Obama: The Post-Imperial Presidency," the chapter delineates Obama's presidency as "the beginning of the end of a . . . colonial curse" (115). Lam argues that because Obama is president Americans can now fully acknowledge, embrace, and celebrate multiple narratives and identities (119).

GB Tran, in the graphic-memoir *Vietnamerica* (2010), also explores a hybrid identity consisting of multiple narratives. A second-generation Vietnamese American, Tran has no direct memories of Viet Nam because he was born in the United States. His attitude toward identity accentuates his distance from Viet Nam, from his family, from his extended family, and from the wars in Viet Nam. The book opens with GB traveling with his parents to Viet Nam.

A two-page spread appearing very early in the novel, when GB and his parents land in Viet Nam, calls attention to the title, *Vietnamerica*, which also stresses GB's identity. The spread consists of a pastiche of images that blend Viet Nam and America. The Golden Gate Bridge straddles a river that does not predictably separate Viet Nam on one side and America on the other. Instead, each side of Vietnamerica, as portrayed in these images includes both Vietnamese and American architectural landmarks. For example, there is a city skyline with what appears to be the twin towers on one side of the river and, on the other side, a building that looks like the Empire State building. There are also palm trees, a pagoda, and a Washington Monument–type obelisk with a Communist star, which readers will see again in the Communist Veteran's Cemetery in Viet Nam when GB and his father visit GB's grandfather's grave. These aesthetic choices serve to emphasize GB's sense of hybrid identity—he is Vietnamerican.

Like Lam, GB changed his name. While he does not choose an entirely new, American name, as Lam did, he did choose to change GiaBao to GB because he wants to fit in at school and in America. Yet the aesthetic qualities of the graphic-memoir tell a more complex version of this decision. Tran provides an illustrated cast of characters on the flyleaf of the book that looks like head-shot photographs of the main characters, each holding a nameplate.

GB, however, is not depicted in this manner. Instead, he is outside of these mock-photo panels holding several other nameplates that are slipping out from under his arm. While he still holds the "G.B." nameplate, the "Gia-Bao" nameplate is falling just out of the reach of his outstretched arm. As his hand grasps for this falling nameplate, it is as though he is chasing his Vietnamese name, pursuing his identity, history, and prosthetic memories.

GB's continual grasping for his identity is the primary theme of the novel. After the introduction and two-page Vietnamerica spread, readers see a book opened to the inscription from father to son with a Confucian quote: "A man without history is a tree without roots." Readers later learn that this book, about the American War in Viet Nam, was a high school graduation gift from GB's father. The appearance of the inscription and book this early in *Vietnamerica* further stresses GB's search for his identity via family and history. The bulk of the novel follows GB as he learns about his family's history and his county's history by visiting Viet Nam. While there, he hears about the end of the war and its aftermath, but also about the earlier days of World War II, the French War, and the influx of Americans through stories shared by his parents, siblings, extended family, and friends. For example, he discovers that his paternal grandfather left his family to fight with the Viet Minh and that his paternal grandmother eventually married a French colonel and had a child with him. He also comes to realize that his siblings are not his mother's children, but that their mother was a French woman who left his father and her children because of the dangers of war.

These discoveries reveal a complex, geopolitical family history that GB translates onto the American landscape via another interesting aesthetic choice. A map of the United States appears in the novel wherein readers see a "Parent's Republic of Vietnam" in red; they are living in the past. Yet their children live in the "Federation of Free States"—New York, Florida, and California, seemingly free from familial, historical, and cultural obligations. The rest of the country, consisting of "The Great Generational Divide" in brown, serves to magnify this gulf. However, the "Sea of Cultural Loss" surrounds the United States. This map underscores a generational divide that Lam, too, often writes about, wherein the parents consider themselves temporary exiles who will one day return to a non-Communist Viet Nam to live. The children, however, desire to be free from their familial duties and obligations to the past, to Viet Nam. Still, the "Sea of Cultural Loss" denotes the loss and sorrow of diaspora. His parents' generation, the 1.5 generation of his siblings, and his second generation are all surrounded by this "Sea of Cultural Loss."

The "Sea of Cultural Loss" also signifies GB's outsider position in relation to Viet Nam and Vietnamese culture. When he first arrives in Viet Nam he experiences culture shock. He is overwhelmed by the noise, the food, the crowds, and size of his extended family. He flips the immigrant experience wherein the immigrant feels unsettled in a new country, their new home. GB is disoriented in the country of his family, his history, and their memories. While such moments make GB want to flee, he also acquires a greater understanding not only of the wars and his family's history but also of Vietnamese traditions. For example, he learns about Vietnamese attitudes toward death and funerary traditions such as white serving as the color of mourning. However, this is not a welcome, easy lesson for GB. Instead, it highlights the rift between his parents and himself. For example, when GB wears black to the cemetery, he complains and asks his father why he did not tell him about this tradition. This is one of those indicative moments in which GB demonstrates his ignorance of the Vietnamese culture, but it also demonstrates that his parents did not share their cultural heritage with him.

Thus, GB's parents hold some responsibility for GB's identity being detached from his Vietnamese heritage and family history. Despite their participation in GB's identity formation, they are critical of him. For example, when GB questions his father for knowing so much about GB's grandfather, despite not having any contact with him for fifty years, his father responds, "You can't look at our family in a vacuum and apply your myopic contemporary western filter to them" (11). Like Lam's parents, who sometimes call him "Andrew Lam," and Mai's mother in *Monkey Bridge*, who worries about her daughter's too-easy adoption of American customs and values, GB's parents also criticize him for being too Western. Thus, the generational divide contributes to the complex identities of these Vietnamese American characters and authors.

Although GB Tran does not include any representations of American veterans of the war in *Vietnamerica*, the other authors do; however, Lam only does so in his fictional *Birds of Paradise Lost*. Typically referred to as "American GIs" in Vietnamese American literature, American veterans, in Pham's *Catfish and Mandala* and in Lan Cao's *Monkey Bridge*, function in relation to the identity issues discussed above.

AMERICAN GI

American veterans of the American War in Viet Nam play a complex role in their positioning in relation to the Vietnamese American communities and in relation to the obligation the veterans' very presence demands. For example, in Catfish and Mandala, Pham encounters an American veteran, Tyle, in Mexico. Upon hearing Tyle say "I was in Nam," Pham reflects on the broad-ranging implicit meanings of this phrase, which take on a range of emotions depending on the tone of the speaker (8). Always, though, Pham feels the urge to apologize to these veterans. However, when they ask for forgiveness, as Tyle does, Pham suffers under the obligation. These moments highlight the binary and hybrid position that Pham's diaspora takes on. He cannot forgive someone when, according to his own narration, Pham himself has benefited from the suffering of others. Yet he is also obliged to hear the veterans' sorrows and "carry [their] secrets" forever (9). In this interaction with Tyle, Pham grants a "fraudulent" pardon to help ease the sorrow and the obligation (9). Here, the refugee is not debt-ridden; the veteran is.

In Monkey Bridge, it is Thanh's good friend, Mrs. Bay, who interacts the most with American veterans of the war and embraces this obligation of forgiveness. She serves as the "keeper of the Old World" and "represent[s] the hidden part" of the veterans' lives (64). Mai reflects on the connections between American veterans and the Vietnamese in America, writing, "in some ways, like us, they were custodians of a loss everyone knew about but refused to acknowledge" (64). Thus, Mai recognizes issues of identity placed on both the Vietnamese and the America veterans by other Americans who prefer to forget the war. Mrs. Bay concludes that "as long as America hated its own soldiers, [the Vietnamese] would never be welcome" in the United States (65). Mai describes the affinity some Vietnamese and American veterans had for one another, explaining, "Those who had been in Vietnam, the vets and us, were forever set apart from everyone else who hadn't" (65). She believes that their fate was intertwined with the fate of the American veterans. These veterans, like the Vietnamese Americans, "had been trained to decipher in strangers' eyes the silent fact that they had failed to produce a victory. Viet Nam had been their life, and now it must become nothing" (64). Like the Vietnamese in American, the veterans' very presence makes other Americans confront their desire to forget and the impossibility of doing so. Still, Little Saigon becomes a source of consolation and familiarity for the "former GIs," just as it is for the Vietnamese (64). Unlike Pham's sympathetic reaction of obligation under duress in Catfish and Mandala, Lan Cao provides a more empathetic portrayal of American veterans.

One veteran, Bill, is a regular at the Vietnamese grocery and a friend to Mrs. Bay, who "ministers to his memories" (208). Bill "did not subscribe to

President Ford's proclamation that the end of the war 'closes the chapter in the American experience'" (207). Bill understands that Americans have not kicked the Vietnam Syndrome because, according to Mai, the "debris of Vietnam remained" in the way Bill was cautious, cynical, and suspicious (207).[6] Vestiges of the war and of the country cling to American veterans in this novel in the same way they cleave to the Vietnamese characters. During one of his visits with Mrs. Bay, Bill is pleased to share a story about waiting in line for gasoline when a man in another car cut in front of him. As Bill approached this man's car to ask him to move to the back of the line, the man fearfully recognized Bill's "Vietnam Veteran" insignia pin. Once Bill realizes that the man is afraid of him, he accentuates it, frightening the man with threats to his life. Mai reflects that Americans do not bother to question whether or not veterans are crazy; they simply "believe that men who returned from the original sin and primordial evil of Vietnam had a natural predisposition toward madness" (209). Notice, though, that Cao's narrator is making a greater commentary on public thoughts and beliefs about Viet Nam than a simplistic stereotype that trauma begets violence. Instead, Mai emphasizes what Viet Nam must mean to the American public. She provides a commentary on the oriental otherness of the country that these veteran characters often believe transfers onto their identity as well.

In his fictional *Birds of Paradise Lost*, Lam's representations of American veterans of the war also struggle with and influence identity. The short story "Slingshot" is among the most memorable because of the distinctive voice of the narrator, Tammy, who is an audacious teenage girl, replete with slang straight out of the turn of the century. She feels no sympathy or connection with the American veteran, "Uncle Steve," who is a regular at her mother's restaurant. Unlike her mother or sister, Tammy refuses to call him that, addressing him as "U.S." instead. This seems fitting and good; however, she not only denies him a privileged position in her world, but she is also cruel to him. She is annoyed because he often speaks to her mother about Viet Nam, calls Tammy and her sister his "favorite Mekong Delta girls," and claims, in Vietnamese, to the reassurance of her mother, that he is "also Vietnamese!" (40). As he inserts himself into their family and identities, Tammy worries and fantasizes that he will marry her mother, who lost her husband in the war.

Although neither Tammy nor Steve is particularly likeable, the story shifts after Tammy berates Steve. Tammy's world is put back in order when one of the women hints that Steve should leave until the situation settles; he does not return to the restaurant. Without telling the family, Steve returns to Viet Nam "to look at the past" and comes back to California with Tammy's father's ashes (47). However, while Tammy and her boyfriend get stoned on the roof of her mother's restaurant and use her slingshot and jawbreakers to deface a Disney billboard—an iconic image of American mythological happiness— they see Steve approaching. Tammy determines, with the encouragement of her boyfriend, to hit Steve and she is successful. Upon being hit, Steve drops and breaks a vase containing her father's ashes. Steve had no intentions of disrupting Tammy's family; instead, he hoped to bring them peace, but her fear results in the permanent destruction of that reassurance, that connection with her father. Perhaps, Tammy, like Mai in *Monkey Bridge*, feels that she is an outsider and that U.S. has usurped an insider identity in her family and Vietnamese community. Metaphorically, Uncle Steve, is the United States, U.S., and Tammy perceives him as representative of a Western power reconstructing the Vietnamese experience, just as, in Stuart Hall's explanation, "cinematic and visual representation of the West" have commandeered many other marginalized experiences (394). Tammy does not want Uncle Steve, or U.S., to hold any position or regard in her family, not just because of the impossible threat that he might replace her father but because he may have been closer to her mother than Tammy could have been in regard to their memories of Viet Nam. She fears his privileged position may reposition her as an outsider in her own community.

REPETITION, REVISION, AND PROSTHESIS

In addition to identity and its association in relation to American veterans of the war, Lan Cao and Andrew Lam often employ repetition, and Lam revision, as a primary means of representing and bearing witness to trauma. In Cao's *Monkey Bridge*, repetition centers on the very public fall of Saigon and, for Mai, the equally private mystery of her missing grandfather. Not only does Cao pose this historical moment as a repetitive obsession for Mai, but it is inexorably linked to Mai's sense of identity.

During the fall of Saigon, Mai was living with "Uncle Michael," an American soldier who became good friends with her father during the war. Mai left Viet Nam with Uncle Michael in 1975, two months before the fall of Saigon. Her mother said it would only be for a few weeks or a month, but Saigon fell and her mother evacuated to the United States as well. While she is living with

Uncle Michael and his wife, Mai watches events unfold on television and reads about them in the newspapers (42–44). For example, she sees the felling of the tamarind tree at the U.S. Embassy, which had become a symbol of American protection; cutting it down would cause "national panic" (44), as noted in the PBS documentary *Last Days in Vietnam* (2014). The story was "Already . . . being repeated as standard history" (44). Public and private intermingle, and Mai comes to realize that she, other Vietnamese Americans, American veterans, and the Vietnamese now belong to "an inescapable history that continues to be dissected and remodeled" by "experts" and "commentators" in the months following the fall of Saigon (42). Like Lam's identity, as discussed in the following pages, Mai's identity is inexorably linked to this historical moment both publicly and privately.

The fall of Saigon as a private moment for Mai serves as the origin of a family mystery, the question about what happened to her grandfather when he failed to meet her mother as part of their evacuation plan. They were supposed to meet across from the National Assembly in Saigon, at the statue of three South Vietnamese soldiers, poised for attack, guns aimed directly at the "heart and brain" of the South Vietnamese government (23). About this, Mai's mother, Thanh, often commented, "Who needs enemies when your own guns are pointed at your head?" (23). Thanh believes it is a bad omen. Indeed, Mai explains, a South Vietnamese colonel shot himself at that war memorial during the fall of Saigon.

Consumed with the news about the fall of Saigon, Mai experiences prosthetic memories of the evacuation. She does not experience these moments first-hand, but comes to form memories of these events as mediated through media coverage. One of her responses is that she "slips into the ancient frontier of dreams," and "In this imaginary world, a helicopter skittered on the edge of the U.S. embassy, breathless under the weight of several Vietnamese hanging from the closing doors" (99). She envisions the sound and wind of the helicopters blades and the masses of people pressed up against the embassy fence. The repetitive image of the helicopter, which came to symbolize the war and the end of the war, becomes a symbol for Mai's attitude toward the end of American involvement in Viet Nam as well.[7] Mai reads that tear gas had been dropped as marines got into the last helicopter out of Viet Nam. Clouds of the gas were sucked up into the air, and "it appeared that the United States had flown its last flight out of Viet Nam with visibility completely obscured" (152). The fog of war becomes one that physiologically causes tears. Mai also reiterates a description of a helicopter being pushed overboard so that more could land on a destroyer escort. This is a significant moment in the collected cultural memory of the war that symbolizes the waste associated with the war.[8]

Mai is also obsessed with the events of the fall of Saigon because they were interconnected to the "endless possibilities" of what could have happened to her grandfather (165). She describes it as a day "still packed with the tight, coiled force of the unknown, a force with sufficient potency to blow the daily routine off its hinges" (166). Although the fall of Saigon occurred a few years earlier, Mai's fixation never ceases and is only inflamed again as she fixates on the fate of her grandfather. Although Mai's mother, Thanh, frequently relays the day's events to Mai, she asks about them again. She repeatedly asks about her grandfather because "like the detective who believed a rehearsal of the same facts would in time reveal a detail that had previously been missed, [Mai] continued [her] desire to probe for a loose memory" (195). The fall of Saigon signifies her missing grandfather, and Mai seeks answers to this current condition through family history, just as GB does in Vietnamerica. Yet, like GB, Mai also connects family secrets with unknowable history.

Mai wonders whether her grandfather observes first-hand what she views on television; had he "witnessed these unbreathable sights?" (165). Notice the word choice; she says they are "unbreathable" as if they are unspeakable: don't breathe a word. However, these moments are also "unbreathable" because they have come to signify the unrepresentable trauma of the war, of the Vietnamese diaspora, and of the fates of so many Vietnamese that could not ever, or immediately, flee the country, but were instead sent to labor or reeducation camps, or were relocated under the Communist government's agricultural plans that, combined with embargos, resulted in starvation for many in the country.

Instead of speaking about the fall of Saigon, Mai marks it with a material memory object.[9] She places a 1975 penny under the carpet at Uncle Michael's house. When she visits later in 1979, she feels for the penny, and it is still there she reflects "that terrible year, was still as present, and still as inevitable, as ever" (93). The penny serves as an archeological, material memory object. Buried under the carpet, easily and repeatedly retrievable, Mai has created her own memorial. It is an American penny, engraved with that significant date, symbolizing the moment she left Viet Nam, the moment her country and family changed, and the moment she entered diaspora. Like the Vietnam Veterans Memorial discussed in chapter 1, the penny is also a tactile memory object. Touch is important here, because she only touches the penny; she does not retrieve it and look at it. It is something she can feel but not something she shows others; it is a private memorial. Although material memory objects left at the Viet Nam Veterans Memorial enable visitors to transcend personal memory in a public space, Mai's memory object is private; only she knows that the penny is buried under the carpet.

Secrecy, mystery, and burial play a significant role in *Monkey Bridge*; the fate of Mai's grandfather is also "unbreathable." As readers learn at the end of the novel, Mai's mother and grandfather never made plans to meet and flee the country together. Although Mai had been reading her mother's journals without permission throughout the novel, she finds, in the second-to-last chapter, a letter from her mother, Thanh, addressed to her explaining that these journals were meant for Mai to find and read. They tell a revised family history that softens the horrors of war and hide the fact that Mai's grandmother was the landlord's concubine, that her grandfather was an angry drunk and a Communist who killed her biological father, the landlord, while Thanh looked on unseen. Her father, face painted red, killed her biological father as a result of "slow-burning rage" and in the name of revolution (249).

Although Thanh is shocked that her father did this, particularly on "sacred earth, [the] village burial ground," she explains that she understood a raw truth in that moment, the culminating rage and revenge within her father (249). With that realization, she also lost a part of herself that "died forever" in that moment (250). She explains that she never recovered, never fully returned from that limbo moment, that intimate encounter with death. Thus, Mai's private, mysterious family history associated with the fall of Saigon was a fabrication. Her grandfather was never missing; her mother never searched for him. Just as American veterans of the war believe a part of them died in the war, a part of Thanh died in Viet Nam, while another part of her drowns in diaspora, and she ultimately commits suicide.[10]

While repetition in Lan Cao's *Monkey Bridge* centers on Mai's obsession with the fall of Saigon and her missing grandfather, Andrew Lam's repetition takes on revision in addition to repetition, and this occurs across his three books, in both his nonfiction and fiction. He retells many stories, including accounts of the day he left Viet Nam, his father's escape from Viet Nam, his descriptions of photographs on the family alter, and the end of his grandmother's life. However, his revised retelling of his sympathies with refugees and immigrants of other wars takes on additional poignancy because they are updated to reflect wars at the turn of the twenty-first century. Two other repetitive revisions—stories about the influence of his first teacher in America and stories about the realizations he came to when he visited Waterloo with his father—significantly reappear in both nonfiction and fictional versions.

In the "Letter to a Young Refugee" (dated April 1999) from *Perfume Dreams* (2005), Lam writes to a young Albanian boy he saw on the television news, whereas in "Letter to a Young Iraqi Refugee to America" from *East Eats West* (2010), he writes to an Iraqi refugee he saw on the Internet. He encounters images of both by chance and via mediated representations. Each of these encounters remind him of himself when he was an immigrant-refugee. In the letter to the Albanian refugee, Lam admits that he doesn't know much about the historical or individual circumstances, yet he "think[s] [he] knows what [the boy] is going through" (*Perfume Dreams* 19). However, he softens the certitude in his letter to the Iraqi immigrant, writing that he "has an idea of what the [Iraqi] is going through" (*East Eats West* 129). Although the Iraqi immigrant and Lam share more similarities, Lam tempers his tone in the five years between publications.

In this second letter, he lists the many similarities between the American War in Viet Nam and the Iraq War, such as parallels between the Gulf of Tonkin incident and the insistence that there were weapons of mass destruction (WMDs) in Iraq. He notes the resemblances between My Lai and Haditha, Hearts and Minds and Operation Iraqi Freedom, in addition to Vietnamization and Iraqization.[11] While the second letter echoes the first and seems like an updated and more intimate revision, each has a distinct purpose. The first letter provides advice about how to survive a refugee camp, while the second offers guidance about living in America and dealing with American ironies and revisions of the war. He warns that "the American experience in Iraq will, in time, be reconstructed—through books, movies, and songs—into a mythic reality around which the nation flagellates itself and reexamines what now seems its routine loss of innocence," while the experiences of Iraqis, like those of the Vietnamese, become marginalized footnotes (130). Here, Lam reminds audiences of the risks inherent in mediated representations that can create new, prosthetic memories of these wars. Again, like his character Tammy in "Sling Shot," Lam is weary of the Western appropriation that Stuart Hall responds to in the opening pages of this chapter. Although, as a writer of nonfiction and fiction, Lam also contributes to these mediated representations, his motivation is to give voice to the marginalized experiences of refugee-immigrants so as to counterbalance the American exceptionalism inherent in many American cultural reproductions of these wars.

Although Lam takes on a more critical tone about America in the second letter, he advises both the Albanian refugee and the Iraqi immigrant not to "give into hatred" because it only leads to further grief (Perfume Dreams 21; East Eats West 131). Finally, he shares what seems to be his most important message about accepting tragedy when he writes of it as an inheritance in both letters. What is this inheritance? In the Perfume Dreams "Letter to a Young Refugee," Lam describes it as the suffering of the refugee and that of "those who suffered along with" him (22). In the East Eats West "Letter to a Young Iraqi Refugee to America," this inheritance, he explains, does not mean that "the past owns" Lam; instead, he has "learned to appropriate it" (131). This inheritance is also inexorably linked to the obligation to remember and to bear witness. Lam implores, in both letters, that the recipient "commit everything . . . to memory" because their stories of suffering and triumph matter (Perfume Dreams 22; East Eats West 132–33). Thus, the inherent obligation results in repetition.

Concerning his repetition, revision, and retelling, Lam offers a poignant moment of self-consciousness about rewriting these letters when he describes how he repeatedly returns to the past, "find[ing] new points of articulation" (East Eats West 131). Of all the times Lam revisits, rewrites, revises, and retells stories, this is the only moment at which he consciously acknowledges it in his texts.

The story of Lam's first teacher in America is one of his more well-known stories, and he relays it in both nonfiction and fictional forms. It appears in "My Teacher, My Friend" from East Eats West and "Show and Tell" in the fictional Birds of Paradise Lost (2013). The "Show and Tell" version echoes references in Lam's earlier writing to the boy of his childhood drawing pictures on the board in Perfume Dreams. In the fictional version of Birds of Paradise Lost, a seventh-grade refugee from Viet Nam deals with Billy, a bully whose father is a Vietnam veteran, who during his show-and-tell session shows images of atrocities that occurred during the war. The immigrant, Cao, cries at seeing these pictures, and then draws his story on the board. Because he cannot speak much English, his new-found friend, Robert, explains. In his fictional revisions, Lam does not explicitly create the meta-narrative that Tim O'Brien is known for in The Things They Carried, wherein he names his fictional character Tim.[12] Instead, Lam renames his characters. The Vietnamese refugee in this fictional version is named Cao, not Andrew.

Although Lam had already renamed himself Andrew when he was young, he also renames himself in each of the stories, wherein one of his nonfictional stories makes a reappearance in his fictional *Birds of Paradise Lost*. The first, nonfictional version of the story about Lam and his father visiting Waterloo appeared in *East Eats West*. In the fictional version from *Birds of Paradise Lost*, the narrator is Ethan, not Andrew. Both Andrew and Ethan had heard the story of Napoleon's defeat from their fathers many times; Napoleon is their fathers' hero. In this story Ethan and Andrew make the same choices, have the same attitude, and they both experience a moment of overwhelming emotions as they feel pity for their fathers. They mourn their fathers' losses.

The crux of this emotion, however, rests on prosthetic memory. As Lam and Ethan contemplate their fathers' losses, each is transported to the past as they each formulate memories to which they have no immediate access. They remember their fathers fleeing Viet Nam and resigning themselves to new lives in which they are no longer generals in the South Vietnamese Army. In *Birds of Paradise Lost* Ethan describes it as such: "this was how he looked on that naval ship as they headed . . . from Vietnam at the end of the war. I imagined him staring at his gun for a long, long time before he tossed it into the sea" (160). In the nonfictional *East Eats West*, Lam describes this as an ordinary, if solemn, moment. He describes his father "fold[ing] away his army uniform, chang[ing] into a pair of jeans and a T-shirt, and toss[ing] his gun into the sea" (36). Yet in his first nonfictional rendition of this moment in *Perfume Dreams*, Lam explains that although he "did not bear witness to [his] Father's gesture, [he] can see it clearly, having imagined it over the years. [He] sees his [father's] hand trembling before he flung the gun out in an arc over the sea, which rises to swallow it. [He] sees his eyes looking to the water as he thinks about an uncertain future" (25). Why is this such an important moment that recurs in all three of Lam's books? It ultimately becomes a memory within a memory. As he explains it in his first book, *Perfume Dreams*, he has "come to regard [it] as a major turning point in [his] own story. That gun, rusting at the bottom of the sea, serves as a kind of marker. It spelled the end of [his] childhood mythology" (25).

Like Mai's penny in Lan Cao's *Monkey Bridge*, the gun serves as a material memory object. In this case, the gun is more like a lost artifact, because unlike Mai's penny it cannot be physically retrieved; it is, after all, a signifier of his father's martial identity and an end to his war. Yet both the gun and the penny come to signify a specific historical moment—Mai and Lam's break with Viet Nam. These objects symbolize the origin of their diaspora. Lam reflects on the fall of Saigon as a specific historical moment that marks his changed identity. For example, in *East Eats West*, Lam writes that his "childhood end[ed] so precisely on a historical marker" that he was "sent into exile" and "quickly transformed into someone else entirely" (163). Mai and Lam's obsession with the fall of Saigon is not simply a result of a break with Viet Nam but is central to their very identities.

What is distinct about Lam's fiction, compared with his nonfiction, is the variety of narrative voices. They cross genders and generations. Not only are his narrators young men and women in their teens and twenties, but they also span the waves of immigration to include first-wave exiles and their children, the 1.5 generation and second generation. The result is hybridity, which reflects his politics and embraces globalization, or as he often refers to it, the positioning of himself as a cosmopolitan world citizen.[13]

Issues of diasporic identity, family history, and Vietnamese Americans' relationships with Viet Nam and the war connect to American issues of identity, memory, and history. Yet they contribute voices to those narratives and memories that have been and, for some, continue to be marginalized. In addition, the texts discussed here have more to offer, such as stories about Vietnamese Americans returning to Viet Nam, as briefly noted in chapter 5.[14] They also offer stories more closely related to first-generation Vietnamese American attitudes, identities, and memories. However, questions of identity, interactions with American veterans of the war, repetition, revision, and prosthetic memory speak to the enduring connections between Viet Nam and America at the turn of the century. They contribute to a collected cultural memory of the war that is becoming a transnational global memory, one that is rife with the possibilities of prosthetic memories that refuse to relegate the war, its aftermath, and Vietnamese American diasporic experiences to the forgotten past.

CHAPTER 9
· EXIT STRATEGY

THE NEW VIETNAM SYNDROME

Three decades later there is a legitimate debate about how
we got into the Vietnam War and how we left . . . one
unmistakable legacy of Vietnam is that the price of America's
withdrawal was paid by millions of innocent citizens whose
agonies would add to our vocabulary new terms like "boat
people," "re-education camps," and "killing fields." There was
another price to our withdrawal from Vietnam, and we can
hear it in the words of the enemy we face in today's struggle.

—President George W. Bush at the
Veterans of Foreign Wars Convention, August 18, 2007

The American War in Viet Nam remains a specter in the debate over American
withdrawal from protracted twenty-first-century wars. As President George W.
Bush defended his administration's refusal to withdraw from the Iraq War
three decades after the war in Viet Nam, he invoked the "legacy" of the American War in Viet Nam as one of disaster for Vietnamese and Cambodian civilians.[1] He further connected the outcome of the war to bolstering terrorism
in the twenty-first century. Bush cited Osama bin Laden's and "his number
two man, Zawahiri['s]" references to the American War in Viet Nam as de-
monstrative of a credibility problem. According to Bush, bin Laden pointed to
American antiwar movements and lack of political will to sustain a protracted
war when he said, "the American people had risen against their government's
war in Vietnam. And they must do the same today." In addition, Bush quotes
Zawahiri summoning the outcome of the American War in Viet Nam when
he wrote of "the aftermath of the collapse of the American power in Vietnam and how they ran and left their agents." Thus, Bush contended that U.S.
withdrawal from the war in Viet Nam continues to damage American military

credibility. In doing so, Bush invoked the "shame" and "guilt" that former President Ronald Reagan associated with the "Vietnam Syndrome" in his 1980 Veterans of Foreign War Convention speech. Bush not only employed the memory of the American War in Viet Nam as a reason to continue the Iraq War, but he also believed that America's withdrawal from Viet Nam emboldened enemy resistance. Ultimately, he argued that withdrawing from the American War in Viet Nam was a mistake.

In the 1990s, the Persian Gulf War (1990–91) seemed to place a bookend on America's "shame" associated with the "Vietnam Syndrome," when, upon achieving military objective in the Persian Gulf, President George H. W. Bush declared that Americans had finally "kicked the Vietnam Syndrome." However, the twenty-first-century "War on Terror," especially the Iraq War, renewed American political remembrance of the war in Viet Nam. This book is a product of that remembrance among other cultural and more personal memories of the war's aftermath. This study explores the range of public and private memories of the American War in Viet Nam, between the Persian Gulf War and the "War on Terror" that began in 2001, to demonstrate that the war in Viet Nam has not and cannot be relegated to the forgotten past.

A multifaceted and ongoing collected cultural memory of the American War in Viet Nam rests at the center of the memorial, poetic, cinematic, and prose narratives examined herein. Although direct memories continue to inspire representations of the war, memories of the war are no longer solely the domain of those who directly participated in the war, nor do they belong only to the so-called Vietnam Generation, nor are they limited to direct intergenerational memories held by those descending from participants in the war; instead, memories of the war have taken on a transgenerational, transnational prosthetic value. They are moveable and supplemental additions to direct, experiential memories of the war. Prosthetic memories unbind memory and make remembrance viable for those who have no direct experience with or connection to the events remembered. Tensions among and the multiplicity of official, public, direct, private, material, and performative commemorations existent in collected cultural and prosthetic memories expand insight into twenty-first-century modes of remembrance.

The Vietnam Veterans Memorial (VVM) in Washington, D.C., serves as an impetus to these multifaceted, turn-of-the-century remembrances of the American War in Viet Nam. The memorial design incited controversy over how Americans would memorialize and thereby remember the war. The memorial encourages a collected cultural memory of the war in the public and private memorial performances in addition to the material memories deposited at the memorial. The VVM became a democratic space of multifaceted memories that inspires and encourages further remembrance. For example, poetic responses to and representations of remembrance at the VVM illustrate means of interacting with the memorial. Although the poems often originate from the direct memories of the war that the Vietnam veteran poets hold, the poems also explore the possibilities and limitations of prosthetic memories in their representations of nonveteran visitors to the memorial.

In the shadow of the VVM's dedication, new voices of direct memory had yet to be heard. Thus, servicewomen who participated in the war initiated a women's memorial fund. With the dedication of the national Vietnam Women's Memorial (VWM) in 1993, a new moment of more inclusively remembering the American War in Viet Nam began. The VWM attempts to memorialize women's vital participation in the war. Its narrative representation of that service in the sculpted figures legitimizes women's service in the war. Unfortunately, the project of legitimation succumbs to patriarchal, mimetic modes of representation. Importantly, the VWM contributes new perspectives and memories to a collected cultural memory of the war. The VWM serves as a significant representation of American women's direct experiences in and memories of the war. American cinematic and literary narratives broaden this spectrum to include American and Vietnamese civilian women's war and postwar direct and prosthetic memories. These narratives represent a reality that wives of Vietnam veterans also often acquire proximity-induced posttraumatic stress disorder. Wives of Vietnam veterans remain underrepresented in cultural memories of the war. Perhaps humanities and psychological scholars will now reconsider the importance of women's and spouses' experiences for memory, cultural, political, historical, and military studies, especially in the context of twenty-first-century wars and the 2013 lifting of the ban on women holding combat positions in the U.S. military.

These new memories, contending with a desire to forget the misnamed "Vietnam Syndrome," seek recognition of service at the VWM and reconciliation between former foes—both veteran and civilian, Americans and Vietnamese, in American and Vietnamese narratives. Thus, Vietnamese literature, beyond that of the state-sanctioned celebratory patriotism, arrived in English translation in the 1990s. Finally, American memories of the war began to include the direct memories of the Vietnamese, specifically those of America's and the southern Republic of Viet Nam's (RVN) past adversaries—veterans of the northern People's Army of the Republic of Viet Nam (PAVN), also known as the North Vietnamese Army (NVA). Imaginative representations of the war written by America's former foes broaden a collected cultural memory of the war and make possible further prosthetic memories of the war. Moreover, these works encourage Vietnamese unity beyond official propaganda and reconciliation efforts between Vietnamese and American veterans of the war. The study of Vietnamese imaginative representations of the war is the newest burgeoning area of interest in the field of Vietnam War studies.

Viet Nam is evolving in the American imagination into a country rather than a war. Twenty-first-century American narratives explore returning to Viet Nam as a means of demarcating the country from veterans' memories of the war. Place, in these narratives, becomes vital for private memorial performance as it does in other literatures. The simultaneity of past and present at private sites of memory holds the potential for the living to confront the present absence of the dead.

Despite women's and Vietnamese voices broadening representations and memories of the war, American turn-of-the-century remembrances of war have preferred to recall, reenact, and memorialize the "good war," World War II, fought by the "Greatest Generation." Thus, twenty-first-century responses to the "Vietnam Syndrome" in the aftershocks of attacks on the World Trade Center and the Pentagon on September 11, 2001, resulted in the popular reception of Randall Wallace's *We Were Soldiers* (2002). The film returns to direct memories of the American male soldier in Viet Nam. More important, however, the film reverts to the generic conventions of World War II combat films in part to reframe the American War in Viet Nam as Reagan's "noble cause." As one of the most recent and more frequently recalled narrative films about the American War in Viet Nam, *We Were Soldiers* influences some audiences to regard favorably the prospect of war.

Yet in the twenty-first century, Viet Nam and the United States are not the only places of remembrance. Memories of the American War in Viet Nam haunt such locations as the Philippines. The Philippines as a site for prosthetic memories of the American War in Viet Nam, as depicted in Jessica Hagedorn's *Dream Jungle* (2003), reveals the recurrence of colonialism and neocolonialism. The novel also demonstrates transnational memories of the war that may be found elsewhere, such as in South Korea and Australia—two countries that contributed the greatest ground-troop support to the U.S. military during the war.

A NEW "VIETNAM SYNDROME"

The specter of the American War in Vietnam continues to haunt twenty-first-century American consciousness, militarism, politics, and foreign policy. It remains necessary to confront fully the effects of fighting a war of counter-insurgency and sectarian violence on a nation's ideology and the disillusionment of those who participate in war. However, American attitudes toward the Iraq War are further entangled with the legacies of the American War in Viet Nam, resulting in what I define as a New Vietnam Syndrome—the seeming impossibility of withdrawal or formulating an exit strategy in the midst of war. The New Vietnam Syndrome, particularly when it is espoused by neoconservatives, reliant on cultural memories about the end of the American War in Viet Nam, entails a reluctance to withdraw troops from Iraq and Afghanistan before achieving elusive "victory." The partial American-perceived necessity of continuing to wage these wars is born from fears of repeating the failures of the war in Viet Nam and its aftermath, particularly the defeat and chaos associated with the 1975 fall of South Viet Nam's capital, Saigon, after American troop withdrawal from Viet Nam.

The New Vietnam Syndrome first surfaced within the context of the Iraq War. At the core of the New Vietnam Syndrome, unwillingness on the part of American neoconservatives to determine terms of "victory" and to create a regional diplomatic solution, along with a refusal to withdraw troops from Iraq, reverberated with fears of reenacting the war in Viet Nam. Moreover, the syndrome accompanied rhetorical debates that framed the Iraq War as a good war synonymous with World War II, or a bad war similar to the American War in Viet Nam. Ironically, the New Vietnam Syndrome requires a poignant remembrance of the "shame" and "guilt" at the core of Reagan's understanding of the "Vietnam Syndrome" and President George W. Bush's 2007 Veterans of Foreign Wars convention speech quoted at the opening of this chapter. It also insists on amnesia concerning America's conduct during the war in Viet Nam. America's response to guerilla warfare and sectarian hostility in Viet Nam entailed violence against civilians and a continuous escalation of American troop levels. Concerning the Iraq War, withdrawal, in the dominant rhetorical strategy during the George W. Bush administration (2000–2008), would cause defeat, and defeat would signify "another Vietnam."

Withdrawing troops from Iraq threatened George H. W. Bush's 1990 promise of "no more Vietnams." If the "Vietnam Syndrome" of the 1970s, indicating a reluctance to engage militarily in international affairs, accused those who were against war of being isolationist, the New Vietnam Syndrome of the twenty-first century requires that the United States maintain a military presence in protracted wars. In other words, the argument was that America must not withdraw troops from Iraq. The echo of failure, defeat, and guilt in Iraq reminds some Americans of an unbearable reenactment of the American War in Viet Nam. Still, Americans continue to wage war in the name of an old myth—an American historical destiny of exceptionalist benevolence. America, in the Iraq War, has imported American myths of progress, technological superiority, and moral legitimacy into a new desert frontier and a ravaged urban jungle, Baghdad. And yet the United States was caught in a bind reminiscent of the American War in Viet Nam.

Although 9/11 and the wars in Iraq and Afghanistan garnered most Americans' attention in the early twenty-first century, American antiwar movements against the Iraq War harkened back to the antiwar movement of the 1960s. Some of the faces of the earlier antiwar movement reappeared in the media, and the antiwar movement had learned a very crucial lesson, as Harold G. Moore would have them think of the American War in Viet Nam: "hate war but love the American warrior."[2] In order to avoid the negative connotations associated with the 1960s antiwar movement, members of the more recent antiwar movement very carefully reminded the public that they were supporting the soldiers in their call to end the Iraq War.

Some Americans called into question the purpose of the Iraq War. They questioned the misinformation presented to the world at the outset of the war; they questioned motives for continuing to fight a war that seemed to have no good cause. As the Iraq War protracted into a war longer than World War II, with little improvement militarily, politically, or physically for the lives of Iraqis, the antiwar movement continued to be concerned that Americans and Iraqis would persistently be embroiled in violence for years to come.

However, with the 2008 election of President Barack Obama, the antiwar movement seemed to dissipate. For example, in September 2007 an estimated one hundred thousand protesters marched in Washington, D.C., whereas in March 2010 only an estimated several thousand marched there to mark the seventh anniversary of the U.S. invasion of Iraq. In March 2011 a few hundred protestors gathered outside the White House and over one hundred were arrested for refusing to disperse. These examples provide just a sampling of the decreased interest signified by diminishing numbers. However, a study conducted by Michael T. Heaney, a professor of organizational studies and political science, and Fabio Rojas, a professor of sociology, found that the antiwar movement's dissipation with the election of President Obama was due to a misperception of him as an antiwar candidate despite his aggressive military policies. Even though many among the young generation know someone who is serving in the War on Terror, a collective amnesia, or at least inattention, likely brought on by fatigue and the lack of a draft has set in. Political scientist Andrew Bacevich has identified this as apathy in his *Breach of Trust: How Americans Failed Their Soldiers and Their Country* (2013), which scrutinizes an American public's distancing from our current wars as we have shifted to a professional army instead of a citizen army since the end of the American War in Viet Nam. Like the amnesia that occurred after the 1973 Paris Peace Accords and ensuing prolonged withdrawal of U.S. troops from Viet Nam, American citizens are reexperiencing cultural forgetfulness.

Besides fatigue, the eventual withdrawal of troops from Iraq contributed to this collective inattention. As President Obama promised, the withdrawal began in June 2009 and was completed on December 18, 2011. In a speech given at Camp Lejeune, North Carolina, on February 27, 2009, Obama recognized the continuing debate about whether or not the United States should pull out of Iraq but noted a decline in violence compared to 2006 and 2007. Arguing that the "long-term solution in Iraq must be political—not military," Obama shifted focus to Iraqi accountability for Iraq's future. In response to those who were still reluctant to withdraw from Iraq, Obama reminded them that we cannot "let the pursuit of the perfect stand in the way of achievable goals."

Emphasizing honor and reconciliation, likely a lesson learned from the American War in Viet Nam, Obama vowed that "we will bring our troops home with the honor that they have earned." Unlike the American War in Viet Nam, the United States has an influence on reconciliation and recovery in Iraq, and Obama focused on resettling refugees back in Iraq as key to these concerns. In an effort to promote reconciliation between the United States and Iraq, Obama directly addressed Iraqis, saying, "Our nations have known difficult times together. But ours is a bond forged by shared bloodshed, and countless friendships among our people. . . . We respect your sovereignty and the tremendous sacrifices you have made for your country." Reminiscent of the rhetoric shared between the United States and Viet Nam at the turn of the millennium, recognition of shared suffering attempted to promote reconciliation. For example, reunions between former American and Vietnamese foes in memoirs and fictional narratives discussed in the preceding chapters rely on the notion that everyone—winners and losers—suffer in war. This acknowledgment often encourages reconciliation.

Acknowledging the need to care for veterans is another lesson learned from the American War in Viet Nam. Along these lines, Obama invoked the so-called Greatest Generation and the post–World War II G.I. Bill when he said, "We will also heed the lesson of history—that those who fight in battle can form the backbone of our middle class—by implementing a 21st century GI Bill to help our veterans live their dreams." In reference to the specter of the American War in Viet Nam, he emphasized accomplishment and closure: "We sent our troops to Iraq to do away with Saddam Hussein's regime—and you *got the job done*. We kept our troops in Iraq to help establish a sovereign government—and you *got the job done*. And we will leave the Iraqi people with a hard-earned opportunity to live a better life—that is your achievement; that is the prospect that you have made possible" (emphasis added).

Several themes in this speech echo President Richard Nixon's January 23, 1973, "Peace with Honor" speech, wherein he announced the conclusion of the Paris Peace Agreement and plans for U.S. troop withdrawal from Viet Nam. For example, Nixon noted the accomplishment of peace when he said, "The important thing was not to talk about peace, but to get peace and to get the right kind of peace. *This we have done*" (emphasis added). He also addressed all parties involved in the conflict, and as Obama said to the Iraqis, Nixon noted the "courage" and "sacrifice" of the South Vietnamese. Reconciliation is another common thread that both presidents spoke of in relation to peace. So, too, both presidents mentioned the selflessness of military personnel serving with honor.

Obama promised that the fallen would not be forgotten, as he reminded Americans of the immediate memorialization already underway in the United States: "Their names are written into bridges and town squares. They are etched into stones at Arlington, and in quiet places of rest across our land." He also spoke of the Iraq War as part of our broader military history, referencing World War II, the Korean War, and contemporary conflicts but made no reference associated with Viet Nam. He said that the Iraq War "is now a part of the history of the United States of America—a nation that exists only because free men and women have bled for it from the beaches of Normandy to the deserts of Anbar; from the mountains of Korea to the streets of Kandahar."

So, just as he attempted to right the wrongs of the past, he avoided raising the specter of the American War in Viet Nam at a time when he was discussing withdrawal from a contemporary war.

Since the withdrawal of U.S. troops from Iraq, however, the country continues to endure coordinated bombings and attacks in addition to more traditional military fighting. For example, in April of 2013 over forty people were killed in Mosul during fighting, and in May 2013 a series of car bombings inundated Shiite Muslim neighborhoods in and around Baghdad, killing over sixty people. There are numerous examples of this type of violence, both localized and widespread.

Just a year later in 2014, the Islamic State (IS), also known at ISIS (the Islamic State of Iraq and Syria) or ISIL (the Islamic State of Iraq and the Levant), seized swaths of land and military equipment in Iraq, including Mosul, Iraq's second-largest city, in addition to Tikrit and Ramadi, among other cities and towns. The Islamic State currently has a presence ranging from southern Baghdad to Syria's Mediterranean coast. After six months and over two thousand U.S.-led coalition airstrikes, Obama made a formal request to Congress in February 2015 seeking "Authorization of Force Against ISIL." While airstrikes continue and a U.S. military presence advises Iraqi and Kurdish forces, the resolution "is not the authorization of another ground war"; it is a three-year authorization, and it strikingly "repeals the 2002 authorization of force for the invasion of Iraq." Of course, this last element is the most controversial and will likely be revised as the resolution moves through committees and hearings. Still, the call for the resolution emphasizes lessons learned from the American War in Viet Nam and the early years of the Iraq War. For example, Obama said that "we owe [U.S. troops] a clear strategy and the support they need to get the job done."

Although the United States withdrew troops from Iraq and is now fighting in a conflict that better fits the "War on Terror" phraseology, focus shifted to Afghanistan at the official end of combat in Iraq and continues to once again as we attempt to secure Iraq from the Islamic State. Focus began shifting toward Afghanistan as early as 2009. In a speech given at Camp Lejeune, North Carolina, on February 27, 2009, President Obama announced his plan for withdrawal from Iraq and in the following month called for an additional seventeen thousand troops for the War in Afghanistan, a 50 percent increase. In this speech Obama emphasized lessons learned from Iraq and from the American War in Viet Nam. He said, "We have learned that America must go to war with clearly defined goals, which is why I've ordered a review of our policy in Afghanistan." He announced, in March 2009, a new strategy of counterinsurgency and civilian support for economic development.

"OBAMA'S WAR"

Politically and militarily, the American War in Viet Nam also unavoidably haunts the War in Afghanistan. Soon after President Obama's inauguration, *Newsweek* dubbed the war "Obama's Vietnam" in its February 9, 2009, cover story, and Bob Woodward published *Obama's Wars* in 2010. President Obama's inheritance of protracted wars recalled Presidents Lyndon Johnson's and Richard Nixon's inheriting the American War in Viet Nam. The October 2009 PBS *Frontline* documentary "Obama's War" examined the challenges in Afghanistan, including local and international mistrust of then President Hamid Karzai's government in addition to cultural and communication barriers faced by troops trying to appear as protectors rather than as invaders to the local populace. Eight years into the conflict, the documentary highlights frustrations reminiscent of the American War in Viet Nam such as taking control of an area like the Helmand Province, only to discover later that it was not secure after all and having to refight for control and security there. Other similarities with the American War in Viet Nam have included accusations of a corrupt leadership and tainted elections.

In his December 2009 Address to the Nation, "On the Way Forward in Afghanistan and Pakistan" at West Point Military Academy, President Obama directly addressed comparisons between the American War in Viet Nam with the War in Afghanistan. Speaking of "those who suggest that Afghanistan is another Vietnam," President Obama emphasized their call for withdrawal, explaining,

> They argue that [Afghanistan] cannot be stabilized and we're better off cutting our losses and rapidly withdrawing. I believe this argument depends on a false reading of history. Unlike Vietnam, we are joined by a broad coalition of 43 nations that recognizes the legitimacy of our action. Unlike Vietnam, we are not facing a broad-based popular insurgency. And most importantly, unlike Vietnam, the American people were viciously attacked from Afghanistan, and remain a target.

Unlike his negative assessment of the U.S. military invasion of Iraq, President Obama differentiated the War in Afghanistan as a necessary war. Unfortunately, his distinctions between the American War in Viet Nam and the War in Afghanistan depend on that "false reading of history" he accuses opponents of the war of employing. In fact, during the American War in Viet Nam, the United States garnered a coalition of seven countries that supplied ground troops and thirty-nine nations that provided nonmilitary aid to Viet Nam.[3] Certainly both wars share counterinsurgency military tactics. Just how "broad-based" the insurgency in Afghanistan is rests at the center of many debates about the war and remains to be seen.

Two years after the Iraq withdrawal speech, the killing of Osama bin Laden in May 2011 may have provided some closure in relation to 9/11 and a sense of accomplishment in relation to the War in Afghanistan. Announcing bin Laden's death at the hands of U.S. Navy SEALS on May 2, 2011, Obama said, "The death of bin Laden marks the most significant achievement to date in our nation's effort to defeat al Qaeda." Despite claiming that "Justice has been done" and reminding audiences that the Taliban government no longer controlled Afghanistan, he also warned that this would not end our war in Afghanistan when he said, "Yet his death does not mark the end of our effort." George W. Bush reiterated the message in one of the few public statements he has made since the end of his presidency. His statement ended with, "The fight against terror goes on, but tonight America has sent an unmistakable message: No matter how long it takes, justice will be done." Again, both presidents claim justice but no conclusion to the war in Afghanistan and the inevitably never-ending War on Terror.

Of course, conspiracy theories arose concerning whether or not bin Laden was actually captured or killed and how he was killed, whether by special forces, or by suicide. Seymour Hersh's 2015 article "The Killing of Osama bin Laden" essentially accuses the Obama administration of lying about how closely it worked with the Pakistanis, about an original plan to report that bin Laden had been killed in a drone attack, and about the burial at sea that Hersh claims did not occur. Much of the broader controversy resulted from bin Laden's burial at sea and the lack of photographic or DNA evidence released to the public. The lack of a burial on land seemingly averted a memorial shrine or place of pilgrimage for bin Laden's followers; however, the house where he was killed in Abbottabad, Pakistan, became a macabre destination of interest until the compound was razed a few months before the one-year anniversary of bin Laden's death. Still, the moment is memorialized in celluloid and memoirs that focus on the manpower that went into finding bin Laden. For example, Kathryn Bigelow's controversial *Zero Dark Thirty* (2012), a fictional rendering of the search for and killing of Bin Laden, and Greg Barker's

HBO documentary *Manhunt* (2013), based on journalist Peter Bergen's book by the same name (2012), join a rash of memoirs, each claiming to provide the inside story about the decade-long search.

Despite the potential for closure, the war was not over and the theater of war continued to broaden as the administration discussed Afghanistan and Pakistan as part of the same theater. In his March 2009 speech, Obama said he was "announcing a comprehensive, new strategy for Afghanistan and Pakistan." He described the "situation" as "increasingly perilous." Prospects of broadening the "War on Terror" in Pakistan, Yemen, and Syria seem to exhaust an American public and military.

Despite a broadening drone war and an increased number of "advisors" sent to Afghanistan and now Iraq, the combat mission in Afghanistan "officially" ended in December 2015. However, that formal end of combat operations does not clearly result in an end to further military deployments and redeployments. As Obama noted in a December 2014 statement, "our combat mission [in Afghanistan] is *ending*" (emphasis added). America's longest war is not over; the country remains "a dangerous place." The approximately ten thousand U.S. troops will continue to train Afghan troops and to conduct "counterterrorism missions" in Afghanistan through—but as hoped by the White House, not *beyond*—2016. Repeatedly, Obama and White House representatives have emphasized that the war is "coming to a responsible conclusion." This emphasis on reasonability goes beyond Nixon's "peace with honor" in an effort to avoid withdrawing from a country in the midst of a war we created. The government and military policies seem to indicate a desire to prevent another "fall of Saigon," or the growth of ISIS in Iraq. Indeed, in his last State of the Union Address (2016), Obama argued that the United States should not move forward with a policy of rebuilding nations in crisis because this results in "quagmire" and that "It's the lesson of Vietnam; it's the lesson of Iraq—and we should have learned it by now."

Still, the rise of ISIS in the region speaks to those "perilous" conditions Obama recognized in 2009. Despite the impetus for the U.S. military to maintain a presence in Afghanistan, Iraq, and the broader region, the United States is war weary. As wounded soldiers return from wars in the Middle East with amputations, brain injuries, and posttraumatic stress, the United States and much of the world encounters new vestiges of war resulting from the wars in Afghanistan and Iraq that George W. Bush initiated, and these vestiges echo those of the American War in Viet Nam.

So, too, do twenty-first-century memorials to war echo memorials recognizing the American War in Viet Nam, particularly the Vietnam Veterans
Memorial (VVM). Since its dedication in 1982 the Vietnam Veterans Memorial
continues to influence modes of memorialization for other wars. For example,
black granite is no longer taboo in war memorials. In addition, memorials
proliferate that name or enumerate loss of life. Other war memorials emphasize loss of life by either listing the names as the VVM does, or by means of
gold stars as seen in the World War II memorial, or by using combat boots to
represent the number of dead as the antiwar *Eyes Wide Open* traveling memorial project did for the Iraq War. This memorial, in particular, employed the
absent body as the primary means of memorialization. The present absence
located in the empty combat boots attempts to communicate simultaneously
individual and mass loss of life. Many towns are erecting their own memorials to the "Global War on Terror." In fact, the War on Terror Foundation in
Hermitage, Pennsylvania, has already built a memorial listing the names of
those who died in the war since 1975. Yes, they begin in 1975. The memorial
lists the names of the dead, etched in dark glass reminiscent of the Vietnam
Veterans Memorial. The memorial includes over four hundred American
flags, a circular fountain, and a circular layout of glass panels. Of course, the
memorial also includes the names of women and provides space for more
glass panels as the list of the dead grows. While in the twentieth century we
waited to memorialize those who died in war, it is now an ongoing process
that begins almost immediately in keeping with the nearly immediate onset
of cultural amnesia.

If Americans have already forgotten the War on Terror while still in it, what
does this mean for our memories about the American War in Viet Nam? It
may seem for the moment that the war in Viet Nam is now ancient history;
however, considering the collective amnesia that set in after the 1973 Paris
Peace accords and before the fall of Saigon in 1975, we are again reenacting
much of what we experienced at the end of the American War in Viet Nam.
Yes, there are lessons learned about providing services to military veterans,
but we have yet to fully understand the consequences that ongoing twenty-
first-century wars will have on our collected cultural and prosthetic memories
of these wars. Certainly, in the coming years, there will be a resurgent interest
in remembering the American War in Viet Nam, just as there was for World
War II. Those cultural memories will likely further evolve to include more
prosthetic memories that refuse to relegate the war to the forgotten past.

AFTERWORD

Whenever acquaintances ask what this book is about, I tell them that I am writing about the way "we" remember the American War in Viet Nam since 1990, between the Persian Gulf War and the "War on Terror." Their initial response is silence, quickly followed by a variety of reactions that range from "that was a bad war," to some quasi-personal story about someone they knew who was drafted or who luckily missed the draft for a variety of reasons, to blaming Jane Fonda for losing the war. The recall of Jane Fonda exposes continuing contestation over the war's outcome and thereby memories of the war. If the silent response lasts a beat too long, I further explain that twenty-first-century remembrance of the war differs greatly from the 1980s Ramboesque version of the war. To this everyone agrees, discussing the way we regard war as heroic, the way we think about military service as one of sacrifice, and how we now treat military veterans with more care. Thus, they turn their attention to the "War on Terror." In the twenty-first century, the American War in Viet Nam becomes the specter of protracted war, counter-insurgency, and loss of life.

While the war may become "ancient history" for many of my future students, I have also recently taught students whose fathers participated in the war. Still, most students hold prosthetic memories of the war based on either their interest in the 1960s generation and the antiwar movement, or their memories of watching movies about the war, or further still from cultural sound bites played on the airwaves from *Apocalypse Now*. They all seem to know that Coppola's Colonel Kilgore "love[s] the smell of napalm in the morning." Still other students have an interest in studying the American War in Viet Nam in the context of twenty-first-century wars.

The inspiration for the preceding chapters stems from personal, intergenerational, cultural memories of the war, and prosthetic memories of the war. The memory of the American War in Viet Nam has been an integral part of my identity since childhood. How could someone born the year after the fall of Saigon hold memories of the war? By and large, my memories of the war are cultural memories; they are American memories; and they are the memories of a Vietnam veteran's daughter. They are memories of American cultural and familial legend and mythology. They are memories of Sylvester Stallone as John Rambo in First Blood—they are echoes of family members reciting Rambo's famous "one man dead, not my fault" line. They are memories of my little sister and me crawling through the woods playing Rambo. They are memories of acting tough and playing at survival. They are memories of Chuck Norris as Colonel James Braddock going back to Viet Nam long after the war was over to rescue American POWs in Missing in Action. My memories of the war intermingled with Platoon and later Full Metal Jacket, from which I acquired one of my nicknames—Jelly—from my brother and his best friend; they called the tall, gangly, "too skinny" girl that I was "Jelly Doughnut," or "Jelly" for short.

The war was also a mystery, an inaccessible secret. I remember sitting on the living room floor watching my father looking at his photo albums, which had the gold outline of the borders of Viet Nam embossed on the cover. But Viet Nam was not then a country for me; it was a war; it was a disaster; it was something we could have won; it was my father. I wondered why or how a war could have stolen the man who I thought my father might have been without it. "Vietnam" was a reason and an excuse.

Later, while attending college, I took a course called "Art and Disaster." Under the guidance of my professor, Bruno Chaouat, I discovered that I could, after all, write about the war. Since then, my memories of the war have evolved from equating the word Vietnam with war, disaster, loss, and lingering emotional consequences to regarding Viet Nam as a country where the United States engaged in a war. Yes, that war still haunts my family and my country. Today, memories of the American War in Viet Nam continue to be of loss, failure, and disappointment; however, these memories expressed in American cinema, literature, and memorials have transformed into a broader reflection on memory and memorialization. Thus, the modes of memory and means of memorialization over forty years after the end of the war becomes the focus of the preceding. What was once a private memory is now also a prosthetic, public, intergenerational, and transnational memory.

NOTES

PREFACE

1. While the name Robin is more commonly a female name, perhaps it was my desire to read the name of a woman (there are only eight listed on the memorial) that prompted this interpretation. However, this Robin was not a woman after all, because there is no Robin in the list of American military women who died in Vietnam.

INTRODUCTION

1. Although the dates of the war are debatable, I defer to the dates of the first and last American deaths, as noted on the Vietnam Veterans Memorial in Washington, D.C.

2. The Gulf of Tonkin incident began on August 2, 1964, with the American destroyer USS *Maddox* supporting South Vietnamese forces engaging in covert actions against North Vietnamese targets in violation of the Geneva Accords. The *Maddox* came under attack from North Vietnamese torpedoes. The navy sent the USS *Turner Joy* to support the *Maddox*, and on August 4 the two ships reported being under attack. In adverse weather conditions, military personnel could not be certain that the radar was accurate; however, Johnson claimed that both ships had been attacked without provocation. Within days, the U.S. Congress enacted the Gulf of Tonkin Resolution; after minimal debate, it passed without opposition in the House of Representatives and with only two "nay" votes in the Senate. The resolution granted Johnson authority to repel and prevent further aggression. Johnson later used the resolution as a postdated declaration of war. Thus, many have since argued that America entered the war under false pretenses. See, for example, Herring *America's Longest War*; and Longley, "Congress and the Vietnam War."

The Watergate scandals uncovered President Richard Nixon's secret bombing campaign on Cambodia and his illegal wiretapping of National Security Council staff and journalists, ultimately resulting in his resignation.

3. See Appy, *American Reckoning*.

4. Recuperation signals recognizing the service and suffering experienced by participants of the war; its aim is to reestablish national cohesion. Reconciliation, however, stresses recognizing suffering between nations—the United States and Vietnam.

5. Kerry's complete testimony was published in the *Congressional Record*.

6. Fonda infamously visited American prisoners of war in 1972 in the northern Democratic Republic of Viet Nam's capital, Hanoi. For a discussion of the transformation of the actress into the mythic Hanoi Jane, see Lembcke, *Hanoi Jane*.

7. I would prefer to remove the "disorder" from PTSD and refer to it as PTS as a means of depatholigizing the term. The APA considered this and elected not to change the term in the 2013 DSM-5. I will use the proper term throughout.

8. For more about the Vietnam Syndrome, see Turner, *Echoes of Combat*; and Pease, "Post-National Spectacles."

9. These works include Ninh's *The Sorrow of War* (1993) and Duong's *Novel Without a Name* (1996), discussed in chapter 5.

10. In addition to Scruggs and Swerdlow, see Griswold, "The Vietnam Veterans Memorial and the Washington Mall"; Hagopian, *The Vietnam War in American Memory*; Hess, "Vietnam: Memorials of Misfortune"; Hixon, "Viet Nam and 'Vietnam' in American History and Memory"; and Ringnalda, *Fighting and Writing the Vietnam War*.

11. Short pieces promoting the Vietnam Women's Memorial appeared in nursing journals in the late 1980s; two such examples include Jezierski, "The Vietnam Women's Memorial Project," and Paul, "Wounded Healers." Mass publications included articles about the memorial's dedication in 1993; see, for example, Loose, "Vietnam Women's Memorial Dedicated before 25,000," the *Washington Post*'s account. Diane Carlson Evans, founder of the VWMP, has written about the history of the memorial in "Moving a Vision," available online at the Vietnam Women's Memorial website. However, scholarly examination of the memorial appears to be limited to Marling and Wetenhall, "Sexual Politics of Memory"; and Ringnalda, *Fighting and Writing the Vietnam War*.

12. See Berg and Rowe, *The Vietnam War and American Culture*; Walsh and Aulich, *Vietnam Images*; and Turner, *Echoes of Combat*.

CHAPTER ONE

1. See the introduction for a developed discussion of prosthetic memory.

2. See the introduction for a more thorough analysis of the origin and implications of the term "Vietnam Syndrome."

3. See also Griswold, "The Vietnam Veterans Memorial and the Washington Mall"; Hagopian, *The Vietnam War in American Memory*; Hass, *Carried to the Wall*; Hess, "Vietnam: Memorials of Misfortune"; Hixon, "Viet Nam and 'Vietnam' in American History and Memory"; and Ringnalda, *Fighting and Writing the Vietnam War*.

4. See Hass, *Carried to the Wall*, for an in-depth analysis of items deposited at the VVM.

5. By 1973 between four and ten million Americans were wearing bracelets engraved with the names of POWs and MIAs. Emotional ties with the POW/MIA named on the bracelet easily formed because anyone wearing the bracelet promised never to remove it until the POW/MIA was returned home or found to be dead. For a more detailed account of the origin of the bracelets, see Franklin, *M.I.A., or Mythmaking in America*.

6. See Vietnam Veterans Memorial Collection, "Unidentified Objects."

7. T. S. Eliot, in "Hamlet and His Problems," defines the objective correlative as follows: "the only way of expressing emotion in the form of art is by finding an 'objective correlative'; in other words, a set of objects, a situation, a chain of events which shall be the formula of that *particular* emotion; such that when the external facts, which must terminate in sensory experience, are given, the emotion is immediately evoked" (100).

8. For more about this amnesia, see Appy, *American Reckoning*.

9. The inscription on Panel 1 East reads: "IN HONOR OF THE MEN AND WOMEN OF THE ARMED FORCES OF THE UNITED STATES WHO SERVED IN THE VIETNAM WAR. THE NAMES OF THOSE WHO GAVE THEIR LIVES AND OF THOSE WHO REMAIN MISSING ARE INSCRIBED IN THE ORDER THEY WERE TAKEN FROM US." The epilogue on Panel 1 West reads: "OUR NATION HONORS THE COURAGE, SACRIFICE AND DEVOTION TO DUTY AND COUNTRY OF ITS VIETNAM VETERANS. THIS MEMORIAL WAS BUILT WITH PRIVATE CONTRIBUTIONS FROM THE AMERICAN PEOPLE. NOVEMBER 11, 1982."

10. For example, Lin noted that white, not black, is the Eastern color of mourning. See the film *Maya Lin: A Strong Clear Vision*, dir. Mock (1995).

11. Komunyakaa, "Facing It" 13.

CHAPTER TWO

1. See chapter 1 for a thorough discussion of the memorial, including the past presence and present absence phenomenon.

2. In *Dien Cai Dau*, (1988), the last line in the first edition of "Facing It" does not include final end punctuation. However, as Komunyakaa noted when I inquired, this was a typographical error and later published versions of the poem do include a final period.

3. After U.S. and South Vietnamese incursions into Cambodia turned the country into a war zone, the Khmer Rouge Communist revolution succeeded in 1975. The Khmer Rouge's concept of an agrarian utopia resulted in mass extermination, forced labor, the deaths of nearly two million Cambodians, and what has come to be known as the Cambodian Holocaust. See Herring, *America's Longest War*.

4. Kali, the Hindu "great mother" goddess, is associated with blackness and death. It is said that she carries away the spirits of slain warriors. Yet, Kali is also considered the goddess of creation. She represents the beginning and end of time, an appropriate choice considering the circle of life represented by the memorial's chronology. In the West, Kali is often appropriated as a symbol of wholeness and healing.

CHAPTER THREE

1. This chapter is a revised version of the following essay: "Aesthetic Limbo: Memory Making at the Vietnam Women's Memorial," *Thirty Years After: New Essays on Vietnam War Literature, Film, and Art*, ed. Mark Heberle (Newcastle upon Tyne, UK: Cambridge Scholars Publishing, 2009), 342–53.

2. Note 10 for the introduction lists other works that deal with the VVM debate.

3. See the introduction for more about the debate and media coverage.

4. For more about the Vietnam Syndrome and additional sources on the subject, see the introduction and note 8 for that section.

5. See Evans, "Moving a Vision," for detailed information about the founding and implementation of the Vietnam Women's Memorial Project.

6. Note 11 for the introduction lists other published writings about the VWM.

7. See Kulka et al., *Trauma and the Vietnam War Generation*.

8. While cultural examples abound in fictional narratives, especially films, Bonior, Champlin, and Kolly's *The Vietnam Veteran* historically investigates institutional failure to constructively reintegrate Vietnam veterans into American society, a neglect that encompasses American presidents from Lyndon Johnson through Ronald Reagan, veterans' organizations, Congress, and the Veterans Administration. It also examines the history of television, newspaper, and film coverage of the soldiers and veterans.

9. See, for example, Van Devanter, *Home Before Morning*; Walker, *A Piece of My Heart*; and Smith, *American Daughter Gone to War*.

10. The VWM is referred to as a "Circle of Healing" throughout Thomas, *Vietnam Women's Memorial*.

11. See chapter 1.

12. Some examples include Wilson, "Women Campaign for War Monument"; and Linda Kramer, "Women Veterans Seek Recognition."

13. See, for example, Carhart, "Insulting Vietnam Vets"; Forgey, "Women and the Wall Memorial Proposal"; and Will, "The Statue Sweepstakes."

14. Approved by Congress and President George W. Bush in 2007, the John Burnam Monument Foundation Inc., dedicated a sculptural memorial at Lackland Air Force Base, Texas in 2013.

15. See Viets, "A Bureaucrat To Pick A Bone With."

16. In *The Spitting Image*, Lembcke suggests that the image of the spat-upon veteran is a cultural myth wherein feminized "hippie" men or women are accused of spitting on veterans returned from the war (27–70).

17. For more on the GI movement against the war, see Lembcke, *The Spitting Image* 27–70.

18. See "Market Place" at http://www.vietnamwomensmemoriral.org.

19. See United States Cong., House, *Hearings on S. 2042*.

CHAPTER FOUR

1. The parade mentioned here seems to reference the 1985 parade held in New York City. See Appy, *American Reckoning*.

2. See image and discussion of the "love beads" poster in chapter 3.

3. Le Ly Hayslip founded the East Meets West Foundation in Quang Nam Province, Viet Nam, in 1988. The foundation builds educational and healthcare programs for Vietnamese children in addition to clean water and sanitation programs in an effort to heal the wounds of the war.

4. See chapter 2 for more on the Vietnam Women's Memorial.

5. The Viet Cong, or VC for short, is a disparaging term used to identify Vietnamese Communists in South Viet Nam.

6. Biedler, "The Last Huey," provides a closer examination of the last Huey as a primal scene of U.S. cultural history that repeatedly returns in film and literature about the war.

7. While the famous photograph taken by Hubert van Es was actually a helicopter atop a CIA building near the U.S. embassy in Saigon, the image has been replayed in cinematic and fictional accounts alike as the last Huey leaving the embassy. In the meantime, on the aircraft carriers in the South China Sea, a similar image of defeat and American waste was taking place, that of helicopters being pushed overboard to make room for more evacuees. See Gibson, *The Perfect War*; and *Last Days in Vietnam*, dir. Kennedy.

8. Stone seems to be referring to the controversial CIA Phoenix Program regarded by some as an "assassination program" wherein the CIA, U.S. Military Intelligence, and South Vietnamese military, police, and civilian officials, conducted an anti–Viet Cong campaign. The campaign consisted of infiltrating the peasant populations in search of Communist cadres in order to "neutralize" them. See Lawrence, *The Vietnam War* 132–33.

9. See Herring, *America's Longest War*; and Lawrence, *The Vietnam War*.

CHAPTER FIVE

1. See chapter 1 for more about material memory at the VVM.

2. See chapter 1 for more about the circular chronology at the VVM.

3. See Nora, "Between Memory and History" 7.

4. See the discussion of mediating female figures in chapter 4.

5. During the 1968 Tet Offensive, Communist soldiers coordinated preplanned surprise attacks during the lunar New Year ceasefire agreement on over a hundred cities, including Hué and Saigon, where they held the U.S. Embassy for several hours. At Hué, they stormed the Citadel, an ancient fortress. They controlled much of Hué for nearly a month, meanwhile conducting home searches and killing nearly three thousand Vietnamese. The battle for Hué lasted twenty-six days and is considered one of the bloodiest battles of the war. For a detailed account of the Tet Offensive and the battle for Hué, see Herring, *America's Longest War*.

6. See, for example, depictions of the Vietnamese in Moore, *The Green Berets*; *Rambo*, dir. Cosmatos; and *Missing in Action*, dir. Zito. For a historical survey, see Hunt, "Images of the Viet Cong."

7. See chapter 1 for a discussion of the names and material memory at the VVM.

8. See chapter 4 for a developed discussion of the helicopter as cultural icon.

9. While many scholars of the war address the exclusionary verisimilitude of experience phenomenon in the literary and cultural production of representing the American War in Viet Nam, a few include Bonn, "New Battles" 208; Mithers, "Missing in Action" 82; and Ringnalda, *Fighting and Writing the Vietnam War* x.

10. See chapter 1 for more about Eastern and Western memory at the VVM.

11. For more about the POW/MIA controversy and reclamation efforts, see Franklin, *M.I.A., or Mythmaking in America*; and Allen, *Until the Last Man Comes Home*.

12. For a detailed examination of the POW/MIA mythology, see Franklin, M.I.A., or Myth-making in America.

13. American works of reconciliation include, but are not limited to, those discussed elsewhere in preceding chapters: selections from the cycle of poetry about the Vietnam Veterans Memorial in chapter 2; and Frazier, I Married Vietnam, and Heaven and Earth, dir. Oliver Stone, in chapter 4.

CHAPTER SIX

1. A close version of the first half of this chapter appears as "Forgetting Viet Nam: We Were Soldiers," The Martial Imagination: Cultural Aspects of American Warfare, ed. Jimmy L. Bryan Jr. (TAMU Press, 2013) 201–18. It does not include the discussion of We Are Soldiers Still or prosthetic memories.

2. The Pleiku Campaign, what the Vietnamese call the Tay Nguyen Campaign, was a series of engagements between PAVN and American forces that occurred in October and November 1965 in the Ia Drang Valley of Viet Nam's Central Highlands.

3. For more on the cover-up of the battle at LZ Albany, see Moore and Galloway, We Are Soldiers Still 123–24.

4. The Viet Minh (Vietnamese League for Independence) was an anticolonial movement created in 1941 under the leadership of Ho Chi Minh.

5. Such characters include, but are not limited to: Jack Falen in Tracks (Henry Jaglom, 1977); Major Charles Rane in Rolling Thunder (dir. John Flynn, 1977); Colonel Kurtz in Apocalypse Now (dir. Francis Ford Coppola, 1979); John Rambo in First Blood (dir. Kotcheff, 1982); Wilkes in Uncommon Valor, (dir. Ted Kotcheff, 1983); Sergeant Barnes in Platoon (dir. Oliver Stone, 1986); and Ron Kovic in Born on the Fourth of July, dir. Oliver Stone, 1989).

6. For more about Custer, see Donovan, A Terrible Glory.

7. The divide between officers and draftees is only further exacerbated; however, I do not discuss draftees here because We Were Soldiers emphasizes that every American soldier in the battle voluntarily enlisted.

8. One of the provisions of the January 27, 1973, Paris Accords provided that Hanoi would return all American prisoners of war within sixty days. See Moss, Vietnam 399.

9. For more about claims of veteran mistreatment, see Bonior, Champlin, and Kolly, The Vietnam Veteran; and Lembcke, The Spitting Image.

10. In 1994, under the leadership of President Bill Clinton's administration, Congress lifted the trade embargo with Viet Nam, and in 1995 the Vietnamese reinstated the United States embassy in Ho Chi Minh City (formerly Saigon). Later that same year, Clinton extended formal diplomatic recognition to the Democratic Republic of Viet Nam.

11. See chapter 3 for a discussion of the "Jungle of Screaming Souls" in Bao Ninh's The Sorrow of War.

CHAPTER SEVEN

1. King Lapu Lapu of Mactan Island refused Magellan's demands that he be baptized. Thus the Battle of Mactan ensued, culminating in Magellan's death.

2. For a detailed examination of Philippine participation in the Iraq War, see Tyner, *Iraq, Terror, and the Philippines' Will to War*.

3. While it is most common to portray soldiers' friendly interactions with Vietnamese children, some films depict soldiers' impatience with or suspicion of the children.

4. The USO provides morale and recreational enrichment to the American military at home and abroad.

5. One of the provisions of the January 27, 1973, Paris Accords provided that Hanoi would return all American prisoners of war within sixty days. See Moss, *Vietnam*, 399.

6. As a conclusion to the French Indo-China War in Viet Nam, Cambodia, and Laos, the Geneva accords included a ceasefire and an interim division of Viet Nam in anticipation of a 1956 nationwide election. On Diem, see Miller, *Misalliance*.

7. For more on the symbiotic relationship between the military and Hollywood, see Suid, *Guts and Glory*; and Robb, *Operation Hollywood*.

8. Hagedorn's *Dream Jungle* follows Lina from childhood through adulthood. She works as a servant in Zamora's home and has a romantic relationship with American actor Moody.

9. For an overview of critical responses to *Apocalypse Now*, see Zuker, *Francis Ford Coppola*.

CHAPTER EIGHT

1. See Freeman, *Changing Identities*.

2. See Lam, *Perfume Dreams*.

3. See Pelaud, *This is All I Choose to Tell*.

4. Theorists such as Edward Said, Homi Bhabha, Gloria Anzaldua, Amitava Kumar, and Salman Rushdie, among many others, have written about these affective dimensions from literary, social, cultural, and historical perspectives.

5. See the introduction for a developed discussion of phantom limb syndrome, prosthesis, and prosthetic memory.

6. See the introduction and chapter 9 for discussions of the so-called Vietnam Syndrome and the New Vietnam Syndrome.

7. See Biedler, "The Last Huey," for a closer examination of the last Huey as a primal scene of U.S. cultural history that repeatedly returns in film and literature about the war (2–16). See also the discussion of the helicopter as symbol in chapter 4.

8. See note 7, chapter 4, for details about the helicopters being pushed overboard.

9. See chapter 1 for a discussion of material memory objects deposited at the Vietnam Veterans Memorial and their significance as markers of past presence and present absence.

10. See chapters 2 and 4 for examples of American veterans believing that a part of them died in the war.

11. The My Lai massacre during the American War in Viet Nam and the Haditha incident during the Iraq War resulted in American soldiers killing innocent civilians. For more about My Lai, see Lawrence, *The Vietnam War*. For more about Haditha, see "Rules of Engagement," a PBS documentary. "Hearts and Minds," more formally known as Pacification, is a political, economic and social strategy in war intended to garner popular support of civilians. It is not unique to the American War in Viet Nam but is often associated with the war. The phrase

"winning hearts and minds" is typically a derisive term for the hypocrisy or failure of such a strategy, particularly when combined with firepower and attrition.

12. See chapter 5 for a discussion of O'Brien's *The Things They Carried*.

13. For an exploration of the possibilities and limitations of cosmopolitan compassion in war literature, see Long, "Legacies Foretold."

14. See also Wang, "Politics of Return."

CHAPTER NINE

1. Cambodia shares a long, entangled history with Viet Nam because it was part of colonial French Indo-China, was at different times throughout the American War in Viet Nam neutral and not, and was subject to U.S. bombings, a civil war, and U.S. troop invasion in the early 1970s. Certainly, the American War in Viet Nam contributed to destabilizing Cambodia. The genocidal attacks by the Communist Khmer Rouge on Cambodia's civilians continues to symbolize yet another disaster associated with the American War in Viet Nam; however, Bush tried to reframe the "killing fields" of Cambodia as a result of American withdrawal from Viet Nam rather than as being rooted in the American military presence in Viet Nam. In 1978 the People's Army of Viet Nam invaded and occupied Cambodia in response to Khmer Rouge attacks. See Herring, *America's Longest War*; and Lawrence, *The Vietnam War*.

2. Moore, in "'Getting it Right.'" See chapter 6 for a developed discussion of this quotation and the film.

3. See Larsen and Collins, *Allied Participation in Vietnam*

WORKS CITED

Acton, Carol. "Diverting the Gaze: The Unseen Text in Women's War Writing." *College Literature* 32.2 (2004): 53–80.

Aguilar–San Juan, Karin, and Jessica Hagedorn. "A Conversation with Jessica Hagedorn." *Women's Review of Books* 21.6 (2004): 6.

Allen, Michael J. *Until the Last Man Comes Home: POWs, MIAs, and the Unending Vietnam War.* Chapel Hill: U of North Carolina P, 2009.

American Psychiatric Association. *Diagnostic and Statistical Manual of Mental Disorders.* 4th ed. Washington, DC: American Psychiatric Publishing, 1994.

Anderson, David L. *The Columbia Guide to the Vietnam War.* New York: Columbia UP, 2002.

Anderson, Doug. "The Wall." *Bamboo Bridge.* Amherst, MA: Amherst Writers & Artists, 1991. 31.

Apocalypse Now. Dir. Francis Ford Coppola. Zoetrope/United Artists, 1979.

Apocalypse Now Redux. Dir. Francis Ford Coppola. Zoetrope/Miramax, 2001.

Appy, Christian G. *American Reckoning: The Vietnam War and Our National Identity.* New York: Viking, 2015.

Australian Government. "Nominal Roll of Vietnam Veterans." Department of Veterans' Affairs website: http://www.vietnamroll.gov.au. 11 Jan. 2009. Accessed 2 Nov. 2009.

Bacevich, Andrew J. *Breach of Trust: How Americans Failed Their Soldiers and Their Country.* New York: Metropolitan Books, 2013.

Badsey, Stephen. "The Depiction of War Reporters in Hollywood Feature Films from the Vietnam War to the Present." *Film History* 14.3–4 (2002): 243–60.

Bankoff, Greg, and Kathleen Weekley. *Post-Colonial National Identity in the Philippines: Celebrating the Centennial of Independence.* Burlington, VT: Ashgate, 2002.

Ninh, Bao. *The Sorrow of War.* Trans. Phan Thanh Hao. Ed. Frank Palmos. New York: Pantheon, 1993.

Barry, Jan, Basil T. Paquet, and Larry Rottmann, eds. *Winning Hearts and Minds: War Poems by Vietnam Veterans.* Brooklyn, NY: First Casualty, 1972.

Basinger, Jeanine. *The World War II Combat Film: Anatomy of a Genre.* Middletown, CT: Wesleyan UP, 2003.

Berg, Rick, and John Carlos Rowe, *The Vietnam War and American Culture.* New York: Columbia UP, 1991.

Biedler, Philip. "The Last Huey." *Vietnam War and Postmodernity*. Ed. Michael Bibby. Amherst: U of Massachusetts P, 1999. 2–16.

Bleakney, Julia. *Revisiting Vietnam: Memoirs, Memorials, Museums*. Ed. William E. Cain. New York: Routledge, 1996.

Blight, David W. *Race and Reunion: The Civil War in American Memory*. Cambridge, MA: Belknap P/Harvard UP, 2001.

Bonior, David, Steven Champlin, and Timothy Kolly. *The Vietnam Veteran: A History of Neglect*. New York: Praeger, 1984.

Bonn, Maria S. "New Battles: Cultural Signification in Contemporary American Narrative." *The United States and Viet Nam from War to Peace: Papers from an Interdisciplinary Conference on Reconciliation*. Ed. Robert M. Slabey. Jefferson, NC: McFarland, 1996. 208–13.

Boose, Lynda. "Techno-Muscularity and the 'Boy Eternal' "From the Quagmire to the Gulf." *Cultures of United States Imperialism*. Ed. Amy Kaplan and Donald Pease. Durham, NC: Duke UP, 1993. 581–610.

Born on the Fourth of July. Dir. Oliver Stone. Universal Pictures, 1989.

The Boys in Company C. Dir. Sidney J. Furie. Columbia Pictures, 1978.

Bush, George Walker. Remarks. Veterans of Foreign Wars National Convention. Kansas City Conventions and Entertainment Center, Kansas City, MO. 22 Aug. 2007. Available online at *Presidential Rhetoric.com*: http://www.presidentialrhetoric.com /speeches/08.22.07.html. Accessed 7 Mar. 2016.

Calloway, Catherine. "'How to Tell a True War Story': Metafiction in *The Things They Carried*." *Critique* 36.4 (1995): 249–57.

Cao, Lan. *Monkey Bridge*. New York: Viking, 1997.

Carhart, Tom. "Insulting Vietnam Vets." *New York Times* 24 Oct. 1981.

Caruth, Cathy, ed. *Trauma: Explorations in Memory*. Baltimore: Johns Hopkins UP, 1995.

Chown, Jeffrey. *Hollywood Auteur: Francis Coppola*. New York: Praeger, 1988.

Coatney, Lou. Rev. of *We Were Soldiers*, dir. Randall Wallace. *American Historical Review* 108.1 (2003): 312–13.

"Complete Testimony of Lt. John Kerry to Senate Foreign Relations Committee." *Cong. Rec.* 22 April 1971: 179–210.

Coppola, Eleanor. *Notes on the Making of "Apocalypse Now."* New York: Limelight, 1979.

Cowie, Peter. *The Apocalypse Now Book*. 2000. Cambridge, MA: Da Capo, 2001.

Creed. Barbara. "From Here to Modernity: Feminism and Postmodernism." *A Postmodern Reader*. Ed. Joseph Natoli and Linda Hutcheon. Albany: State U of New York P, 1993. 398–418.

The Deer Hunter. Dir. Michael Cimino. Universal Pictures, 1978.

Demory, Pamela. "*Apocalypse Now Redux*: Heart of Darkness Moves into New Territory." *Literature Film Quarterly* 35.1 (2007): 342–49.

Donovan, James. *A Terrible Glory: Custer and the Little Bighorn—The Last Great Battle of the American West*. New York: Little, Brown, 2008.

Donovan, Josephine. "Toward a Women's Poetics." *Tulsa Studies in Women's Literature* 3.1–2 (1984): 99–110.

Dowell, Pat. Rev. of *Heaven and Earth*, dir. Oliver Stone. *Cineaste* 20.3 (1993): 56.

Duong, Thu Huong. *Novel Without a Name*. Trans. Phan Huy Duong and Nina McPherson. New York: Penguin, 1995.

———. *Paradise of the Blind*. Trans. Phan Huy Duong and Nina McPherson. New York: Penguin, 1993.

Ebert, Roger. Rev. of *Apocalypse Now Redux*, dir. Francis Ford Coppola. *Chicago Sun Times* 10 Aug. 2001. Web: http://www.rogerebert.com/reviews/apocalypse-now-redux-2001. Accessed 23 Oct. 2009.

———. "A Soldier's Story." *Chicago Sun-Times* 1 Mar. 2002, Weekend Plus: 29.

Ehrhart, William Daniel. "The Invasion of Grenada." *To Those Who Have Gone Home Tired*. New York: Thunder's Mouth, 1984. 12.

———. "Midnight at the Vietnam Veterans Memorial." *The Distance We Travel*. Easthampton, MA: Adastra, 1993. 21.

Eliot, T. S. "Hamlet and His Problems." *The Sacred Wood: Essays on Poetry and Criticism*. London: Methuen, 1920. 95–103.

———. "The Waste Land." *The Complete Poems and Plays: 1909–1950*. New York: Harcourt, 1952. 37–55.

Evans, Diane Carlson. "Moving a Vision: The Vietnam Women's Memorial." Vietnam Women's Memorial Foundation website. vietnamwomensmemorial.org/pdf/dcevans. 1993. Accessed 10 January 2008. PDF.

Feldman, Karen S. "The Shape of Mourning: Reading, Aesthetic Cognition, and the Vietnam Veterans Memorial." *Word & Image* 19.4 (2003): 296–304.

Fentress, James, and Chris Wickham. *Social Memory: New Perspectives on the Past*. Oxford, UK: Blackwell, 1992.

First Blood. Dir. Ted Kotcheff. Orion, 1982.

The Fog of War: Eleven Lessons from the Life of Robert S. McNamara. Dir. Errol Morris. Sony Pictures Classics, 2004.

Fontana, Alan, Linda Spoonster Schwartz, and Rosenheck Robert. "Posttraumatic Stress Disorder Among Female Vietnam Veterans: A Casual Model of Etiology." *American Journal of Public Health* 87.2 (1997): 169–75.

Forgey, Benjamin. "Women and the Wall Memorial Proposal: Honor Without Integrity." *Washington Post* 22 Oct. 1987: E11

Franklin, H. Bruce. *M.I.A., or Mythmaking in America*. Chicago: Lawrence Hill, 1992.

Frazier, Sandie. *I Married Vietnam*. New York: George Braziller, 1992.

Freeman, James M. *Changing Identities: Vietnamese Americans 1975–1995*. Boston: Allyn and Bacon, 1995.

Full Metal Jacket. Dir. Stanley Kubrick. Warner Bros., 1987.

Fussell, Paul. *The Great War and Modern Memory*. New York: Oxford UP, 1975.

"'Getting it Right': Behind the Scenes." *We Were Soldiers*. Dir. Randall Wallace. Paramount, 2002. DVD.

Gibson, James William *The Perfect War: Technowar in Vietnam*. New York: Atlantic Monthly P, 1986.

Going Back. Dir. Sidney Furie. GFT Entertainment, 2001.

Goodacre, Glenna. "Goodacre's Statement on the Women's Memorial." *Vietnam Women's Memorial: A Commemorative*. Ed. Julie Agnew Thomas. Paducah KY: Turner, 1996. 38–39.

Goodwin, Michael, and Naomi Wise. *On the Edge: The Life and Times of Francis Coppola*. New York: William Morrow, 1989.

Gotera, Vicente F. "'Depending on the Light': Yusef Komunyakaa's Dien Cai Dau." *America Rediscovered: Critical Essays on Literature and Film of the Vietnam War*. Ed. Owen Gilman and Lorrie Smith. New York: Garland, 1990. 282–300.

The Green Berets. Dir. John Wayne. Warner Bros., 1968.

Greenblatt, Stephen, Maya Lin, Andrew Barshay, and Stanley Saitowitz. *Grounds for Remembering: Monuments, Memorials, Texts*. Berkley: Doreen B. Townsend Center for the Humanities, 1995. 22–28.

Griswold, Charles L. "The Vietnam Veterans Memorial and the Washington Mall: Philosophical Thoughts on Political Iconography." *Critical Inquiry* 12 (Summer 1986): 687–719.

Grollmes, Eugene E. *At the Vietnam Veterans Memorial, Washington, D.C.: Between the Lines*. Washington, D.C.: Friends of the Vietnam Veterans Memorial, 1988.

Gustafsson, Mai Lan. "The Living and the Lost: War and Possession in Vietnam." *Anthropology of Consciousness* 18.2 (2007): 56–73.

Hagedorn, Jessica. "A Conversation with Jessica Hagedorn." Penguin Group website. us.penguingroup.com/static/rguides/us/dream_jungle. N.d. Accessed 13 Oct. 2009.

———. *Dream Jungle*. New York: Viking, 2003.

Hagopian, Patrick. *The Vietnam War in American Memory: Veterans, Memorials, and the Politics of Healing*. Amherst: U of Massachusetts P, 2009.

Halbwachs, Maurice. *On Collective Memory*. Ed. Lewis A Coser. Chicago: U of Chicago P, 1992.

Hall, Stuart. "Cultural Identity and Diaspora." *Colonial Discourse and Post-Colonial Theory: A Reader*. Ed. Patrick Williams and Chrisman. London: Harvester Wheatsheaf, 1994. 392–401.

Hallam, Elizabeth, and Jenny Hockey. *Death Memory and Material Culture*. Oxford, UK: Berg, 2001.

Hass, Kristin Ann. *Carried to the Wall*. Berkeley: U of California P, 1998.

Hayslip, Le Ly. "Heaven and Earth." *Oliver Stone's USA: Film, History, and Controversy*. Ed. Robert Brent Toplin. Lawrence: UP of Kansas, 2000. 178–87.

Heaney, Michael T., and Fabio Rojas. "The Partisan Dynamics of Contention: Demobilization of the Antiwar Movement in the United States, 2007–2009." *Mobilization: An International Journal* 16.1 (2011): 45–64.

Hearts of Darkness: A Filmmaker's Apocalypse. Dir. Fax Bahr and George Hickenlooper. Zoetrope, 1991.

Heaven and Earth. Dir. Oliver Stone. Warner Bros., 1993.

Heer, Jeet. "Remember When Vietnam War Movies Were Good?" *National Post* 15 Nov. 2002: PM7.

Heinemann, Larry. *Black Virgin Mountain: A Return to Vietnam*. New York: Doubleday, 2005.

Hellmann, John. *American Myth and the Legacy of Vietnam*. New York: Columbia UP, 1986.

Herr, Michael. *Dispatches*. New York: Knopf, 1977.

Herring, George C. *America's Longest War: The United States and Vietnam, 1950–1975*. 4th ed. Boston: McGraw-Hill, 2001.

Hersh, Seymour. "The Killing of Osama bin Laden." *London Review of Books*. 37.10. 21 May 2015. Web: http://www.lrb.co.uk/v37/n10/seymour-m-hersh/the-killing-of-osama -bin-laden. Accessed 10 Jan. 2016.

Hertz, Robert. "A Contribution to the Study of the Collective Representation of Death." *Death and the Right Hand*. Trans. Rodney Needham and Claudia Needham. Glencoe, IL: Free P, 1960. 27–86.

Herzog, Tobey C. "Managing the Elusive Veteran: Blank Page, Trip Wire, or Interstate Nomad." *The Unites States and Vietnam from War to Peace: Papers from an Interdisciplinary Conference on Reconciliation*. Ed. Robert M. Slabey. Jefferson, NC: McFarland, 1996. 113–22.

Hess, Elizabeth. "Vietnam: Memorials of Misfortune." *Unwinding the Vietnam War: From War into Peace*. Ed. Reese Williams. Seattle: Real Comet, 1987. 262–81.

Hirsch, Marianne. "Family Pictures: *Maus*, Mourning, and Post-Memory." *Discourse* 15 (1992–93): 3–29.

Hixon, Walter. "Viet Nam and 'Vietnam' in American History and Memory." *Four Decades On: Vietnam, the United States, and the Legacies of the Second Indochina War*. Ed. Scott Laderman and Edwin A. Martini. Durham, NC: Duke UP, 2013. 44–57.

Horner, Charles. "The Ghosts of Vietnam." *Commentary* 100.1 (1995): 50–52.

Houghtaling, David. Radio Interview with Yusef Komunyakaa. WCBU, Peoria, IL. 24 Feb. 1989.

Howell, Peter. "Hackneyed Look Back at Vietnam Struggle." *Toronto Star* 15 Nov. 2002: E05.

Hunt, David. "Images of the Viet Cong." *The United States and Viet Nam from War to Peace: Papers from an Interdisciplinary Conference on Reconciliation*. Ed. Robert M. Slabey. Jefferson, NC: McFarland, 1996. 51–63.

Hutcheon, Linda. "Postmodernism and Feminisms." *The Politics of Postmodernism: A Postmodern Reader*. Ed. Joseph Natoli and Linda Hutcheon. Albany: State U of New York P, 1993. 243–72.

Jarhead. Dir. Sam Mendes. Universal, 2005.

Jeffords, Susan. "Reproducing Fathers: Gender and the Vietnam War in American Culture." *Cultural Legacies of Vietnam: Uses of the Past in the Present*. Ed. Richard Morris and Peter Ehrenhaus. Norwood, NJ: Ablex, 1990. 124–41.

Jennings, La Vinia Delois. *Toni Morrison and the Idea of Africa*. Cambridge, UK: Cambridge UP, 2008.

Jezierski, Marlene. "Vietnam Women's Memorial Project: Donna Marie Boulay Highlights Women's Wartime Roles." *Journal of Emergency Nursing* 13:2 (1987): 122–24.

Kagan, Norman. *The Cinema of Oliver Stone*. New York: Continuum, 2000.

Kammen, Michael G. *Mystic Chords of Memory: The Transformation of Tradition in American Culture*. New York: Knopf, 1991.

Kaplan, Amy, and Donald Pease, eds. *Cultures of United States Imperialism*. Durham, NC: Duke UP, 1993.

Karlin, Wayne. *Wandering Souls: Journeys with the Dead and Living in Viet Nam*. New York, Nation Books, 2009.

Kirk, Donald. *Looted: The Philippines after the Bases*. New York: St. Martin's, 1998.

Komunyakaa, Yusef. *Blue Notes: Essays, Interviews, and Commentaries*. Ed. Clytus Radiclani. Ann Arbor: U of Michigan P, 2000.

———. "Facing It." *Dien Cai Dau*. Middletown, CT: Wesleyan UP, 1988.

Kramer, Linda. "Women Veterans Seek Recognition: Statue Proposed for Wall to Honor Those Who Served at the Real 'China Beach,'" *Portland Sunday Oregonian* 1 May 1988: B1.

Kulka, Richard A., et al. *Trauma and the Vietnam War Generation: Report of Findings from the National Vietnam Veterans' Readjustment Study*. New York: Brunner/Mazel, 1990).

Kwon, Heonik. *Ghosts of War in Vietnam*. Cambridge, UK: Cambridge UP, 2008.

Lam, Andrew. *Birds of Paradise Lost*. Red Hen P, 2013.

———. *East Eats West: Writing in Two Hemispheres*. Berkeley, CA: Heyday, 2010.

———. *Perfume Dreams: Reflections of the Vietnamese Diaspora*. Berkeley, CA: Heyday, 2005.

Lamb, David. *Vietnam, Now: A Reporter Returns*. New York: PublicAffairs, 2003.

Landsberg, Alison. *Prosthetic Memory: The Transformation of American Remembrance in the Age of Mass Culture*. New York: Columbia UP, 2004.

Larsen, Lt. Gen. Stanley Robert, and Brig. Gen. James Lawton Collins Jr. *Allied Participation in Vietnam*. Vietnam Studies Series. Washington, DC: Dept. of the Army/GPO, 1985. Available online at U.S. Army Center for Military History website: http://www.history .army.mil/books/Vietnam/allied/index.htm. 18 Dec. 2002. Accessed 28 Oct. 2009.

Last Days in Vietnam. Dir. Rory Kennedy. American Experience Films, PBS, 2014.

Lawrence, Mark Atwood. *The Vietnam War: A Concise International History*. Oxford, UK: Oxford UP, 2008.

Lembcke, Jerry. *Hanoi Jane: War, Sex, and Fantasies of Betrayal*. Amherst: U of Massachusetts P, 2010.

———. *The Spitting Image: Myth, Memory, and the Legacy of Vietnam*. New York: New York UP, 1998.

Lennon, John, and Malcolm Foley, *Dark Tourism: The Attraction of Death and Disaster*. London: Continuum, 2000.

Lin, Maya. *Boundaries*. New York: Simon and Schuster, 2000.

Lin, Maya, Andrew Barshay, Stephen Greenblatt, and Stanley Saitowitz. *Grounds for Remembering: Monuments, Memorials, Texts*. Berkeley, CA: Doreen B. Townsend Center for the Humanities, 1995. 8–14.

Long, Ngo Vinh. "Legacies Foretold: Excavating the Roots of Postwar Viet Nam." *Four Decades On: Vietnam, the United States, and the Legacies of the Second Indochina War*. Ed. Scott Laderman and Edwin A. Martini. Durham, NC: Duke UP, 2013. 16–43.

Longley, Kyle. "Congress and the Vietnam War." *The War that Never Ends: New Perspectives on the Vietnam War*. Ed. David L. Anderson and John Ernst. Lexington: UP of Kentucky, 2007. 289–310.

Loose, Cindy. "Vietnam Women's Memorial Dedicated before 25,000," *Washington Post* 12 Nov. 1993: 2.

Lowenstein, Adam. *Shocking Representation: Historical Trauma, National Cinema, and the Modern Horror Film*. New York: Columbia UP, 2005.

Machete Maidens Unleashed! Dir. Mark Hartley. Dark Sky Films, 2010.

Mailer, Norman. *Why Are We in Vietnam?* New York: Putnam, 1967.

Manhunt: The Hunt for bin Laden. Dir. Greg Barker. HBO, 2013.

Marling, Karal Ann, and John Wetenhall. "The Sexual Politics of Memory: The Vietnam Women's Memorial Project and 'The Wall.'" *Prospects: An Annual of American Cultural Studies* 14 (1989): 341–72.

Marvin, Thomas. "Komunyakaa's 'Facing It.'" *Explicator* 61.4 (2003): 242–45.

Maya Lin: A Strong Clear Vision. Dir. Frieda Lee Mock. American Film Foundation, 1995.

McCarthy, Todd. "Gibson Steps into the Duke's Combat Boots." *Variety* 25 Feb 2002: 69.

McLeod, Mark W., and Thi Dieu Nguyen. *Culture and Customs of Vietnam.* Westport CT: Greenwood, 2001.

Miller, Edward. *Misalliance: Ngo Dinh Diem, the United States, and the Fate of South Vietnam.* Cambridge, UK: Cambridge UP, 2013.

Mithers, Carol Lynn. "Missing in Action: Women Warriors in Vietnam." *The Vietnam War and American Culture.* Ed. John Carlos Rowe and Rick Berg. New York: Columbia UP, 1991. 75–91.

Moore, Harold G., and Joseph L. Galloway. *We Are Soldiers Still: A Journey Back to the Battlefields of Vietnam.* New York: HarperCollins, 2008.

———. *We Were Soldiers Once . . . and Young.* New York: Random House, 1992.

Moss, George Donelson. *Vietnam: An American Ordeal.* 4th ed. Upper Saddle River, NJ: Prentice Hall, 2002.

Murray, Aaron R., ed. *Vietnam War Battles and Leaders.* London: DK, 2004.

My Journey Home. PBS. WETA, Washington, DC, 2004.

Nadeau, Kathleen. *The History of the Philippines.* Westport, CT: Greenwood, 2008.

Nixon, Richard M. "Address to the Nation Announcing Conclusion of an Agreement on Ending the War and Restoring Peace in Vietnam." 23 January 1973. Available online at *The American Presidency Project.* http://www.presidency.ucsb.edu/ws/?pid=3808. Accessed 12 Mar. 2016.

Nora, Pierre. "Between Memory and History: Les Lieux de Mémoire." *Representations* 26 (1989): 7–24.

Norris, Margot. "Modernism and Vietnam: Francis Ford Coppola's *Apocalypse Now.*" *Modern Fiction Studies* 44.3 (1998): 730–66.

Obama, Barack. "Address to the Nation on the Way Forward in Afghanistan and Pakistan." United States Military Academy at West Point. Eisenhower Hall Theatre, West Point. 1 Dec. 2009. Available online at the White House website: http://www .whitehouse.gov/the-press-office/remarks-president-address-nation-way-forward -afghanistan-and-pakistan. Accessed 7 Mar. 2016.

———. "Osama bin Laden Dead." 2 May 2011. Available online at the White House website: https://www.whitehouse.gov/blog/2011/05/02/osama-bin-laden-dead. Accessed 12 Mar. 2016.

———. "Remarks by the President on a New Strategy for Afghanistan and Pakistan." 27 Mar. 2009. Available online at the White House website: https://www.whitehouse .gov/the-press-office/remarks-president-a-new-strategy-afghanistan-and-pakistan. Accessed 13 Mar. 2016.

————. "Remarks of President Barack Obama—Responsibly Ending the War in Iraq." Camp Lejeune, North Carolina. 27 Feb. 2009. Available online at the White House website: https://www.whitehouse.gov/the-press-office/remarks-president-barack -obama-ndash-responsibly-ending-war-iraq. Accessed 12 Mar. 2016.

————. "Remarks of President Barack Obama—State of the Union Address As Delivered." 13 January 2016. Available online at the White House website: https://www.white house.gov/the-press-office/2016/01/12/remarks-president-barack-obama-%E2%80%93 -prepared-delivery-state-union-address. Accessed 7 Mar. 2016.

————. "Statement by the President on the End of the Combat Mission in Afghanistan." 28 Dec. 2014. Available online at the White House website: https://www.white house.gov/the-press-office/2014/12/28/statement-president-end-combat-mission -afghanistan. Accessed 13 Mar. 2016.

O'Brien, Tim. *The Things They Carried*. New York: Broadway, 1998.

O'Neill, John E., and Jerome R. Corsi. *Unfit for Command: Swift Boat Veterans Speak out Against John Kerry*. Washington, D.C.: Regnery, 2004.

Palmer, Laura. *Shrapnel in the Heart: Letters and Remembrances from the Vietnam Veterans Memorial*. New York: Random House, 1987.

Paul, Elizabeth. "Wounded Healers: A Summary of the Vietnam Nurse Veteran Project." *Military Medicine* 150 (1985): 571–76.

Pease, Donald E. "Post-National Spectacles." *Cultures of United States Imperialism*. Ed. Amy Kaplan and Donald E. Pease. Durham: Duke UP, 1993. 557–80.

Pelaud, Isabelle Thuy. *This Is All I Choose to Tell: History and Hybridity in Vietnamese American Literature*. Philadelphia: Temple UP, 2011.

Piehler, Kurt G. *Remembering War the American Way*. Washington, DC: Smithsonian Institution P, 1995.

Pham, Andrew. *Catfish and Mandala: A Two-Wheeled Voyage through the Landscape and Memory of Vietnam*. New York: Farrar, Straus and Giroux, 1999.

Platoon. Dir. Oliver Stone. Orion, 1986.

"President George W. Bush Congratulates Obama on Bin Laden Killing." Foxnews.com. http://www.foxnews.com/us/2011/05/02/president-george-w-bush-congratulates -obama-bin-laden-killing. 2 May 2011. Accessed 26 April 2016.

Rambo: First Blood, Part II. Dir. George P. Cosmatos. TriStar, 1985.

Rescue Dawn. Dir. Werner Herzog. Metro-Goldwyn-Mayer, 2006.

Rickli, Christina. "Event 'Like a Movie'? Hollywood and 9/11." *COPAS* 10 (2009). Web: http://copas.uni-regensburg.de/article/view/114/138. Accessed 8 August 2009.

Ringnalda, Donald. *Fighting and Writing the Vietnam War*. Jackson: UP of Mississippi, 1994.

Rhee, Nissa. "Why US Veterans are Returning to Vietnam." *Christian Science Monitor* 10 Nov. 2013. Web: http://www.csmonitor.com/USA/Society/2013/1110/Why-US-veterans -are-returning-to-Vietnam. Accessed 18 Nov. 2015.

Robb, David L. *Operation Hollywood: How the Pentagon Shapes and Censors the Movies*. New York: Prometheus, 2004.

Rolling Thunder. Dir. John Flynn. American International Pictures, 1977.

"Rules of Engagement: What Really Happened at Haditha." Episode of *Frontline*. PBS. WGBH, Boston, 2008.

Saving Private Ryan. Dir. Steven Spielberg. DreamWorks, 1998.

Searle, William J. "Dissident Voices: The NVA Experience in Novels by Vietnamese." *War Literature and the Arts* 10.2 (1998): 224–38.

Schaller, Michael. Rev. of *We Were Soldiers,* dir. Randall Wallace. *Journal of American History* 89.3 (2002): 1173–74.

Schwenkel, Christina. *The American War in Contemporary Vietnam: Transnational Remembrance and Representation.* Bloomington: Indiana UP, 2009.

Scott, Grant F., "Meditations in Black: The Vietnam Veterans Memorial." *Journal of American Culture* 13 (1990): 37–40.

Scruggs, Jan C., and Joel L. Swerdlow. *To Heal a Nation: The Vietnam Veterans Memorial.* New York: Harper and Row, 1985.

Smith, Levi. "Window or Mirror: The Vietnam Veterans Memorial and the Ambiguity of Remembrance." *Symbolic Loss: The Ambiguity of Mourning and Memory at Century's End.* Ed. Peter Homans. Charlottesville: U of Virginia P, 2000. 105–25.

Smith, Winnie. *American Daughter Gone to War: On the Front Lines with an Army Nurse in Vietnam.* New York: Morrow, 1992.

Stein, Kevin. "Vietnam and the 'Voice Within': Public and Private History in Yusef Komunyakaa's Dien Cai Dau." *Massachusetts Review* 36.4 (1995): 541–62.

Steinman, Ron. *Women in Vietnam: The Oral History.* New York: TV Books, 2000.

Steptoe, Lamont B. "A Second Wall." *Mad Minute.* Camden, NJ: Whirlwind, 1990. 44–45.

Sturken, Marita. *Tangled Memories: The Vietnam War, the AIDS Epidemic, and the Politics of Remembering.* Berkeley: U of California P, 1997.

Suid, Lawrence L. *Guts and Glory: The Making of American Military Image in Film.* Lexington: UP of Kentucky, 2002.

Swofford, Anthony. *Jarhead: A Marine's Chronicle of the Persian Gulf War and Other Battles.* New York: Scribner, 2003.

Tal, Kalí. "The Mind at War: Images of Women in Vietnam Novels by Combat Veterans." *Contemporary Literature* 31.1 (1990): 76–96.

———. *Worlds of Hurt: Reading the Literature of Trauma.* Cambridge Studies in American Literature and Culture. Ed. Eric L. Sundquist. Cambridge, UK: Cambridge UP, 1996.

Tennyson, Alfred, Lord. "Charge of the Light Brigade." *Alfred, Lord Tennyson: Poems.* Ed. Mick Imlah. London: Faber, 2004. 73.

Tran, GB. *Vietnamerica: A Family's Journey.* New York: Villard, 2010.

Turner, Fred. *Echoes of Combat: The Vietnam War in American Memory.* New York: Anchor/ Doubleday, 1996.

Tyner, James A. *Iraq, Terror, and the Philippines' Will to War.* Lanham, MD: Rowman & Littlefield, 2005.

Uncommon Valor. Dir. Ted Kotcheff. Paramount, 1983.

United States. Cong., Senate. Subcommittee on Public Lands, National Parks and Forests of the Energy and National Resources. *Hearings on S. 2042 to Authorize the Vietnam Women's Memorial Project, INC., to construct a Statue at the Vietnam Veterans Memorial in Honor and Recognition of the Women of the United States who Served in the Vietnam Conflict.* 100th Cong. 2nd Sess. Washington: GPO, 1988.

Van Devanter, Lynda. *Home Before Morning: The Story of an Army Nurse in Vietnam.* New York: Beaufort, 1983.

Vietnam Veterans Memorial Collection. "Scope of Collection Statement." Draft. 15 July 2008. Museum Resource Center, National Parks Service, Landover, MD.

———. "Unidentified Objects." Museum Resource Center, National Parks Service, Landover, MD.

Viets, Elaine. "A Bureaucrat to Pick a Bone With: Official Links Canine Corps with Valor of Servicewomen." *Saint Louis Post-Dispatch* 26 Jan. 1988: 3D.

Vlastos, Stephen. "America's 'Enemy': The Absent Presence in Revisionist Vietnam War History." *The Vietnam War and American Culture.* Ed. John Carlos Rowe and Rick Berg. New York: Columbia UP, 1991. 52–74. Walker, Keith. *A Piece of My Heart: The Stories of 26 American Women Who Served in Vietnam.* Novato, CA: Presidio, 1985.

Walker, Keith. *A Piece of My Heart: The Stories of 26 American Women Who Served in Vietnam.* Novato, CA: Presidio, 1985

Walsh, Jeffery, and James Aulich. *Vietnam Images: War and Representation.* London: Macmillan, 1989.

Wang, Chih-ming. "Politics of Return: Homecoming Stories of the Vietnamese Diaspora." *Positions* 21.1 (2013): 161–87.

Weiner, Eric. "Mending Ties: The United States and Vietnam." National Public Radio. 21 June 2007. Web: http://www.npr.org/s.php?sId=11258262&m=1. Accessed 28 April 2007.

Westwell, Guy. *War Cinema: Hollywood on the Front Line.* London: Wallflower, 2006.

Wetta, Frank J., and Martin A. Bookli. "'Now a Major Motion Picture': War Films and Hollywood's New Patriotism." *Journal of Military History* 67.3 (2003): 861–82.

We Were Soldiers. Dir. Randall Wallace. Paramount, 2002.

Will, George F. "The Statue Sweepstakes." *Newsweek* 26 Aug. 1991: 61.

Wilson, Lillie. "Women Campaign for War Monument," *Syracuse Post-Standard* 18 July 1998: A5.

Woodward, Bob. *Obama's Wars.* New York: Simon & Schuster, 2010.

Young, James. *The Texture of Memory.* New Haven, CT.: Yale UP, 1993.

Zero Dark Thirty. Dir. Kathryn Bigelow. Columbia Pictures, 2012.

Zuker, Joel. *Francis Ford Coppola: A Guide to References and Resources.* Boston: G. K. Hall, 1984.

INDEX